Developing Skills for Human Interaction

Second Edition

Developing Skills for Human Interaction

Second Edition

Linda R. Heun
Northeast Missouri State University

Richard E. Heun
Northeast Missouri State University

Charles E. Merrill Publishing Company
A Bell & Howell Company
Columbus   Toronto   London   Sydney

Published by
Charles E. Merrill Publishing Company
A Bell and Howell Company
Columbus, Ohio 43216

This book was set in Helvetica.
The production editor was Lynn Stephenson Walcoff.
The cover was designed and prepared by Ron Starbuck Design.

Library of Congress Catalog Card Number: 77-90340

International Standard Book Number: 0-675-08396-6

Printed in the United States of America

1 2 3 4 5 6 7 8 9 10/ 85 84 83 82 80 79 78

Contents

Acknowledgments

We would like to most sincerely indicate our appreciation to numerous teachers, professors, and friends for their enthusiasm, creativity, and helpful improvements as they used these materials to develop their students' skills. Their experiences in developing competencies with thousands of students in diverse learning environments, including high schools, community colleges, colleges, universities, and non-academic settings greatly enhanced the scope of these materials and aided their adaptability to both individualized instruction and classroom learning. We especially thank the over 3000 Northeast Missouri State University students whose numerous suggestions and positive support sustained us through the seven years of development and refinement.

Several people's ideas and thoughts influenced the content of the materials. Outstanding among them were Chuck Petrie's ideas and materials which influenced Skill Areas Three and Four and Jack Brilhart's ideas and book which influenced Skill Area Four. Chuck Tucker's focus on important skills and usable objectives, Barb Bate's guidelines for nonsexist language, Bob Lapp's guidance on conflict management, and Bob Schnucker's model of tireless energy all greatly aided this revision. Other educators' thinking on individualized instruction, competency-based learning, and sequential skill hierarchies helped guide our approach to learning. We would like to especially thank Anita Taylor and Linn Ratcliff whose friendship, motivation, and insightful criticism were crucial to the development of materials.

The materials were excellently reviewed in detail by Jack Brilhart, Dick Johanneson, Bob Kemp, Anita Taylor, Al Weitzel. Their extensive time and thought enabled many improvements. Lynn Walcoff, Production Editor, provided considerable help and textual improvements. Bill Lochner, Speech Editor, coordinated, guided, and synthesized the entire process culminating in these materials for facilitating student learning of basic communication skills.

PHOTO CREDITS

1	Hank Young (left and right)
8	Larry Hamill
32	Tubbs and Baird
45	Tom Hutchinson
49	*Values in Education,* Merrill, 1978 (top)
	Editorial Photo Archives (bottom left)
	Hank Young (bottom right)
53	*Resource Teaching,* Merrill, 1978
61	Larry Hamill
77	*Values in Education,* Merrill, 1977
86	Larry Hamill (top left and right)
100	Larry Hamill
116	University of Southern California
119	Joan Bergstrom
129	Larry Hamill (top)
	Hank Young (bottom)
141	Larry Hamill
150	Weight Watchers Associates, Inc.
178	Hank Young (top)
	Larry Hamill (bottom left and right)
182	Hank Young
195	Larry Hamill
224	Larry Hamill
241	Hank Young
257	Larry Hamill
289	Larry Hamill
298	Larry Hamill
313	*Resource Teaching,* Merrill, 1978
335	Larry Hamill

To the Student

Hi! We think you're going to really like this book. For one reason, you'll be developing important communication skills which will help you grow into more meaningful relationships with your friends and others. We think you'll be excited at the visible improvements in your everyday communication as you progress through this course. One student came into our office and said, "My boyfriend (at another school) and I usually fight on the telephone. We talk for five or ten minutes, get angry, and hang up. Last night I used Gibb's communication behaviors to reduce defensiveness and they really worked! We talked for four hours! It was the first time we had ever really talked."

A second reason is that these materials were written for you as a unique individual. This is important. As we all know, each person learns differently, needs different amounts and kinds of learning materials, and needs practice to develop the same knowledge and skills. Because people learn differently, you will have the choice of learning the skills by using the Outlines, Learning Experiences, or Readings (*Cloze* readability measures imply that most students will be able to meaningfully read the Readings "independently"). Your professor may choose to supplement the available learning alternatives with additional learning aids for you. Finally, because this book is for you, your concerns (including what can be learned), what is important to learn, and what will be on the tests are right here in the book as stated in the Learning Objectives.

A third reason is that the material is organized for efficient learning. We have identified basic Skill Areas which reflect essential communication skills needed at every level and in various situations of communication. Skills are developed, not talked about. The first three Skill Areas deal with understanding communication and developing skills in listening and talking. Later Skill Areas enable you to apply those basic skills to accomplish other of your communication goals like being hired in employment interviews. Each Skill Area is subdivided into all of the parts and subparts necessary to do that skill. For example, improving your listening is based on such component skills as setting listening goals, choosing listening procedures to accomplish those goals, listening accurately and analytically, and communicating your reactions to what you've listened to. Within each chapter of a Skill Area, Learning Objectives are clearly stated to assist you to focus your learning on the important concepts, principles, and component skills. At the end of each Skill Area there is an application Skill Test which tests your competency to integrate all component parts of the skill into a real-life experience.

A fourth and extremely important reason is that our approach works. To make the book as useful to you as possible, the basic approach to the book focuses on you—choosing and attaining your communication goals. You will develop skills in the communication procedures necessary to attain your goals as well as skills in selecting and applying those procedures. In our experiences during the last seven years over 90 percent of the people in the course have developed competency in the first three Skill Areas and over half of those people have gone on to earn As in the course. Important skills really are improved and can be used to improve the quality of your life.

We hope your learning and communication experiences are good ones.

Linda Heun
Dick Heun

The Process
of Communication

Overview

Communication is the exciting process of human interaction. Every day we realize the personal and national need to communicate more accurately and more fully with others. And yet, this heightened awareness of the need for better communication is also bringing us face to face with our communication limitations.

First, we take for granted that "once it's said, it's understood." We have all heard, "But I distinctly told him to . . . ," or, "But she clearly said that she wanted me to . . . ." Our personal experiences will confirm how many "clearly stated" messages have been misunderstood and how many well-intended messages have led to misunderstandings.

Second, we are barraged with so much information that we have developed the ability to "tune out" unwanted messages. Sometimes we don't listen well enough to accurately understand another's thoughts or sensitively enough to understand another's feelings.

What happens when people communicate? What leads to the great potential for inaccurate and insensitive communication? Some experts suggest that misunderstandings are due to the inevitable basic differences among people. Others say that we are careless with our use of language or unaware of how listeners will think about our messages. Some suggest that we are not aware of the many nonverbal cues which would help us to understand how a message was meant. Most likely, these are only several of the reasons why there is so much ineffective communication. Because of these reasons and others it is safe to say that no one has attained his communication potential. We can all grow in this area. We can all improve our communication skills.

Skill Area One will assist you in learning basic communication concept areas, as a first step in improving your communication accuracy and sensitivity. Later skill areas will help you develop specific communication skills which incorporate these concept areas. This skill area is designed to assist you in gaining an overall understanding of the process of communication. Each of these chapters provides a background of vocabulary and basic component skills which will be used and further developed in later skill areas while developing integrated communication skills.

Learning was once described as a process of moving through the following four stages:

"Unconscious   →   *"Conscious*   →   *"Conscious*   →   *"Unconscious*
Uncompetent"   *Uncompetent"*   *Competent"*   *Competent"*

This sequence is particularly appropriate to learning communication skills. Very few of us have learned to communicate as effectively as we might. Yet because it is something we do daily and because we manage to communicate to other people well enough to satisfy our needs, we are largely unaware of our lack of skills. Therefore, a first step in learning is that of becoming aware of the limitations of our present skills and the vast potential of communicating effectively. We are then at the stage of the conscious uncompetent and ready to begin developing skills. The learning materials and activities in this course of study are designed to help you reach the level of the "conscious competent." Your own practice in your daily communication will move you to the level of the unconscious competent. This is not to suggest that communication ever becomes "unthinking." Instead, the awareness and planning which are crucial to effective communication will become a more natural part of your daily communication.

As described in the "To the Student" section, the concepts for each chapter can be learned through a variety of ways. Some people learn best by reading, some by listening, and some by experiencing. It may be helpful to first look at the Definitions to see if we are defining key terms in the same way you do. If you learn well by reading, the Outlines and Readings are two options. If you prefer structured material over concepts you know quite well already or if you learn well without examples, then the Outlines can be used. The Readings can be used if you prefer a more detailed description with examples. If neither works effectively alone, then a combination of the two methods, such as using the outlines for preview and review, or the Additional Learning Sources which follow each skill area could help. If you learn best by listening then you might choose between the class lectures or talking the concepts over with other people in the class. If you learn best by doing, then the Learning Experiences will help you.

Definitions

Behavior An observable action done by a person.

Communication The dynamic, unique process of calling up meaning by the use of symbols.

Communication Barrier Anything that inhibits or blocks accurate communication.

Communication Channel The means through which messages are sent and received between communicators. Available channels involve the human senses.

Communication Model A representation of the process of communication, showing the components and processes involved and their relationships.

Communication Situation The circumstances in which a given communication event takes place (e.g., the occasion, place, situation, relationships, and time in which communication occurs).

Connotative Meaning The feelings and attitudes associated with a symbol as decoded by people (affective meaning).

Decoding The process of attaching personal meanings to received symbols.

Denotative Meaning The object or idea called to mind when a person uses a symbol (cognitive meaning).

Encoding The process of translating personal meanings into symbols.

Feedback Messages The messages sent by the responding communicator to the originating communicator as a response to the original message.

Frame of Reference The unique interrelationship of a person's stored information, important needs, and perceptions of the situation for a given communicative situation.

Language Any system of symbols, used in a more or less uniform way by a group of people.

Meaning The entire set of denotative and connotative reactions called to mind by a symbol.

Message The communicated symbols which stand for the meaning intended by the communicator.

4

Noise	The distracting stimuli (external or internal) which can occur anywhere in the communication process.
Nonverbal Message	The process by which meanings are called up by nonword symbols.
Originating Communicator	The sender of the original message and the receiver of feedback messages.
Responding Communicator	The receiver of the original message and the responder to it by feedback messages.
Selective Perception	The ways our frame of reference influences what we "see."
Self-Concept	The complex set of interrelated attitudes one has toward oneself.
Self-fulfilling Prophecy	How we make the world what we want it to be by expecting certain meanings which might not be intended.
Symbol	Anything which is used to stand for or represent something else.
Thinking	The processing and analysis of decoded meanings.
Value	Strongly held attitudes which provide the basis for life choices.

Chapter 1

Relating Symbols
and Meanings

Objectives

Your learning should enable you to:

1. Define human communication.

2. Define symbol.

3. Define meaning and its two main kinds.

4. Describe the association processes of encoding and decoding in human communication.

5. Distinguish among symbols which have varying levels of abstractness.

6. Give your own connotative and denotative meanings for a symbol.

7. a. Choose examples of symbols for which you and specific other people would have different meanings.
   b. Explain the basis for the different meanings.

I. Human Communication
  A. Definition: the dynamic, unique process of calling up meaning by the use of symbols
    1. Dynamic refers to the impact of participants on each other
    2. Unique refers to changes in people and situations which make each experience different
  B. Levels of human communication
    1. Intrapersonal: communication within a person
    2. Interpersonal: communication between two or more people
    3. Public: communication between one person and a group of people
  C. Communication functions as a human survival skill
II. Symbols
  A. Definition: anything used to stand for or represent something else
  B. Symbols are vehicles for understanding, if meanings are shared
  C. Types of symbols
    1. Verbal: words whether written or spoken
       Example: "book"
    2. Nonverbal: nonword symbols
       Example: waving a hand as a greeting
  D. Attaching meaning to symbols
    1. Called decoding in communication ("out of" a code)
    2. Based on agreed-upon associations between meanings and symbols
III. Meanings
  A. Definition: the entire set of reactions that is called up in a person's mind when using a symbol
  B. Meanings are in people's minds, not the symbols
    1. We can't assume accurate meaning attaching
      a) more than one meaning for a symbol
      b) more than one symbol for a meaning
    2. Communicators use symbols which will call up intended meanings
  C. Types of meanings
    1. Denotative meanings
      a) Definition: the actual object or idea called to mind when a person uses a symbol
      b) Example: a denotative meaning for a "Police Officer" would be "someone hired to uphold the law"
      c) Number of denotative meanings for symbol
        (1) Concrete symbols: only one denotative meaning and referring to very specific objects or ideas
            Example: "margarine"
        (2) Abstract symbols: many denotative meanings and referring to qualities or general ideas
            Example: "love"
      d) Denotative meanings are usually found in dictionaries
      e) Very unlikely for two people to have exactly the same denotative meanings
    2. Connotative meanings
      a) Definition: the feelings and attitudes which are called to mind when a person uses a symbol
      b) Example: a connotative meaning for "Police Officer" could be "a kind, helpful person"

  c) Usually typified as favorable, neutral, or unfavorable
  d) Connotative meanings are based on past experience with the symbol
  e) Impossible for two people to have the exact same connotative meanings for a symbol
D. Attaching symbols to meanings
  1. Called encoding in communication ("into" a code)
  2. Associations between symbols and meanings learned through experience

Reading

Human Communication

Human communication can be defined as *the dynamic, unique process of calling up meaning by the use of symbols.* Basically, communication involves one or more people doing or saying something which "calls up" reactions in the minds of other people. Symbols such as words or gestures are the things that people use to communicate and meanings are the reactions that other people get from thinking about the symbols. In this study we will be concerned with developing the basic skills of communicating within one person (intrapersonal communication), between two or more people (interpersonal communication), and between one person and a group of people (public communication).

Skill Areas One through Three will help you develop your basic communication skills to a higher level. The remaining Skill Areas will enable the application of those basic skills in talking, listening, and nonverbal communication to a variety of applications including job interviews and problem solving.

Communication is defined by its result—calling up meaning in people. Communication happens when another person "gets the message" by attaching his or her meanings to the received symbols. We are saying that if the other person doesn't get the message, communication hasn't occurred. Therefore, both the symbol attaching and meaning attaching processes are integral necessities of the communication process and will be major concerns of this study. CB language (Citizens Band Radio) is an interesting example. Consider the following interaction:

"Breaker 23 . . . Old Shep you in there?"
  "Old Shep's on line."
"Hey, Old Shep, this is the Runner. What's your 20?"
  "Runner, old buddy, I'm 10–76 for home crossing the Chariton River bridge at Y-Town."
"10–4, Runner's on his way to your 44. I'm clear."
  "Old Shep's clear. KDL-1536 signing off."

If Old Shep and the Runner weren't attaching similar meanings for "your 20," "Y-Town," and other CB symbols, accurate communication wouldn't have happened.

The terms *dynamic* and *unique* are used to describe the communicative process. *Dynamic* is used to reflect the impact that the participants of a communicative experience have on each other as they each simultaneously send verbal and/or nonverbal messages. There is constant interplay as messages are initiated, adapted, and cancelled as each person considers new messages and responses to messages already sent. For example, if you are communicating with a friend and make a suggestion of what you would like to do on a date and see a frown on his or her face, you would be likely to make some change in your original proposal. *Unique* is used to reflect the changes which occur within people and the communication situations which make each experience different. Check out this uniqueness by watching a TV rerun. The show is the same but, because you have changed, your reactions will probably be different.

Communication as a Survival Skill

People in their natural state are less prepared for survival than the animals. However, people are distinguished from animals by more sophisticated brains and language. Human beings have often been defined as the "symbol-using" or "thinking" animals. These two learned characteristics enable people to survive. In fact, the most basic and most often-used human survival skill is communication. This chapter will consider the process of calling up meanings through symbols and how this process is used in human communication.

Symbols

People communicate by the use of languages. To communicate with *others,* whether from a foreign country or a "CBer," *you need to learn their language and the cultural codes for using it in order to attach the intended meanings to symbols.* The important key to using languages is the symbol. Languages are basically systems of symbols, and messages are composed of symbols.

A *symbol* is *anything used to stand for or represent something else.* A symbol becomes a vehicle for communication when those using the symbol know what meanings the symbol represents. Consider the development of slang symbols, such as "raggy" or "the pits." A person or a group of people start using a certain combination of letters to represent a certain meaning. Others pick up the use of that combination of sounds, and soon it "symbolizes" a common understanding for that group of people. Sometimes meanings change. For example, try asking your grandparents or other persons over sixty what their meanings are for the symbol "square."

We use many different things as symbols. *Words, whether written or spoken, are verbal symbols.* For example, your name stands for you. *Symbols also can be nonverbal, that is, nonword.* Gestures are used as nonword symbols. An example is the physical gesture a baseball umpire uses to indicate that a player did not touch second base before being tagged by a player on the other team. Often pictorial representations are used as symbols. For example, the highway department places a sign showing a curved road to represent an upcoming curve in the road. Symbols other than spoken or written words are called nonverbal (nonword) symbols.

Attaching Meanings to Symbols by Association

Symbols are useful vehicles for communication when they are used in a consistent way. For example, both you and your teacher know that the symbol "F" used on a grade report doesn't stand for "Fantastic." If the meaning for this symbol changed every school term, the symbol would be much less usable for accurate communication.

This relationship between things, symbols, and humans has been called the "triangle of meaning."[1] In figure 1 a dotted line is used to connect the object and the symbol to show that there is no necessary connection be-

FIGURE 1

tween the thing represented and the symbol used to refer to it. By common agreement the symbol is used to represent the object. By our encoding and decoding processes we make the association (shown by a solid line) between the object and the person. Words have meanings only when people create them. We determine that a certain symbol stands for or "means" a certain object or reference. For example, while we would call the object in figure 1 a "box," someone from France would refer to it as a "boite," a Spaniard as a "caja," and a Russian as a "koróbka."

Meanings

The *meaning* of a symbol is *the entire set of reactions that are called up in a person's mind when he or she uses that symbol.* Meanings are attached to symbols (decoding), and symbols are attached to meanings (encoding) by association. Association has been studied extensively by learning psychologists. The strength and nature of the association a person makes is influenced by the frequency of connection, the familiarity of the involved symbols and meanings, contextual words, similarity to other symbols and meanings, amount of time involved, closeness in time of the symbol and element, and other variables.

More than one meaning can be associated with a symbol or more than one symbol can be associated with a meaning. For each person some of these connections are stronger and some are less strong. This can be described as an association hierarchy. Figure 2 reflects two hierarchies.

---

1. C. K. Ogden and I. A. Richards, *The Meaning of Meaning* (London: Kegan, Paul, Trench, Trubner and Co., Ltd., 1923).

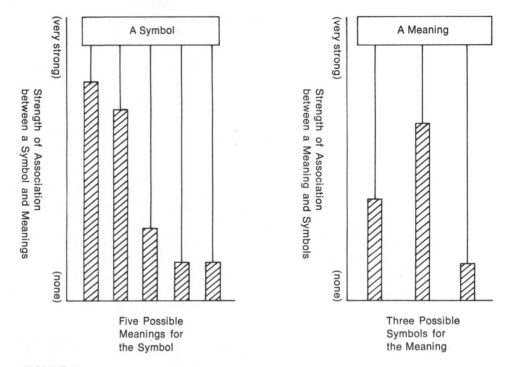

FIGURE 2

Figure 2 is a visual display of various strengths of association between a symbol and its five possible meanings and between a meaning and its three possible symbols. The number of associations and the strengths of associations could vary greatly for different people. The following Learning Experience will help visualize your personal procedures for attaching symbols and meanings.

Learning Experience

To test your hierarchy, write down the first ten words you associate with "ball." *Symbol: Ball*

The first words you wrote were probably those meanings you associated most strongly with the symbol "ball." Toward the bottom of the list the connections were probably weaker, and you may have taken longer to think of words.

Let's try it again with a meaning. Please write down the first ten symbols for the meaning. *Meaning:* "affection for people"

Variations of symbols also can call up meanings. If Archie Bunker describes the United States as being a "smelting pot" or talks of someone "committing insects in the family," most people can attach meanings to his symbols. *The meanings are attached in the mind of the receiver; they are not contained in the symbols that are sent.* When our goal is to communicate accurately, we must be concerned with choosing symbols which people will associate with the meanings we want them to call up. Meanings are in people, not in symbols.

There are two kinds of meanings which we have for a symbol—denotative and connotative. When you decode a symbol, you attach both kinds of meaning to it. Likewise, you have both denotative and connotative meanings in mind when you choose symbols to represent your meanings.

Denotative Meaning

The *denotative meaning* of a symbol is *the actual object or idea called to mind when a person receives a symbol*. When a CBer uses the symbol "your 20," the denotative meaning called to mind is "your location." You could discover its denotative meaning by looking in a CB manual or asking someone with a CB radio. When a symbol is used in a consistent way by a significant number of people, its denotative meaning can usually be found in a dictionary. In a sense, each person is like a dictionary of meanings to be connected with symbols. However, each person has different meanings. Consider the difference between your meanings for "a good date," "be in early," or "the ideal marriage partner," compared to your parents' meanings.

Some symbols have only one or a very small number of denotative meanings. They refer to very specific objects or ideas and are called *concrete symbols.* Examples of concrete symbols would be "margarine" or "the theory of relativity." They would call up very similar denotative meanings for people who knew the agreed-upon meanings. Other symbols can represent many meanings. They refer to qualities or general ideas and are called *abstract symbols.* Examples of abstract symbols would be "love" and "beauty." They have many meanings listed in the dictionary and would call up very different denotative meanings for people using them. Some words have only a few potential meanings. A relatively accurate meaning for such symbols could be called up by considering the context in which the symbol was used. For example, you could probably infer the appropriate denotative meaning to the symbol "ripped off" in these two contexts: "My wallet was ripped off when I stood in line at the movie," and "The bandage was ripped off with little concern for the pain it would cause."

It is very unlikely that any two people will ever have the exact same denotative meaning for a symbol. People who are very good friends or who use very concrete languages, like scientists and mathematicians, are examples of possible exceptions.

Select a newspaper article which relates to a current controversial issue. Underline examples of concrete and abstract symbols used. Note any abstract symbols which were used when concrete terms would have communicated more accurately. Can you infer why the abstract term was chosen?

List two communicative situations where the use of concrete terms is essential.

List two communication situations where abstract words are used for a specific purpose.

Learning Experience

Connotative Meaning

Connotative meanings are all *the feelings and attitudes which are called to mind when a person receives a symbol.* The connotative meanings which are called up will be based on the person's past experiences with that symbol. Such meanings are usually described in terms of their favorableness to that person. For example, symbols like "ice cream," "party," and "friend" have favorable connotations for many people because they are associated with favorable past experiences; while symbols like "poison," "pain," and "terror" have unfavorable connotations because of unfavorable past experiences. Because each of us has had very different experiences, our connotative meanings for symbols will be very different. In fact, we believe *no two people, no matter how similar they are, will ever have the exact same connotative meanings for a symbol.*

In summary, when a symbol is used, it may be associated with no denotative meaning (if the person does not know the symbol); one; few; or many denotative meanings. That symbol will also be associated in a person's mind with generally favorable, neutral, or unfavorable connotative meanings. You can better understand the many possible combinations of denotative and connotative meanings which are attached to symbols by filling out the chart in figure 3. Write a symbol in each box that represents the called-for combination of denotative and connotative meanings for "most Americans."

		Connotations		
		generally favorable	generally neutral	generally unfavorable
Denota-tions	none	(e.g., "Tweedles")		
	one		(e.g., "microscope")	
	few			(e.g., "rip off")
	many	(e.g., "love")		

FIGURE 3

You may not have recognized the word "Tweedles" in the above chart. "Tweedles" was invented as a potential name for a new corn chip product. Each year millions of dollars are spent on developing new names and acronyms for products, corporations, and the like. The following learning experience might help to give you the feeling of the word "invention."

Learning Experience   Choose a product (e.g., corn chips or cologne). Invent ten new symbols for the product.

Choose the one you prefer and decide what sex and age group would be most likely to buy it. You might ask a friend if he or she agrees with your choices.
Typical Buyer: Would he or she buy?

To better understand your own meanings for symbols and how they differ from other people's meanings, try the following learning experience.

For the following list of symbols, write the denotative and connotative meaning you connect with each word.

Learning Experience

	Denotative	*Connotative*
1. freak	_____	_____
	_____	_____
2. test	_____	_____
	_____	_____
3. honesty	_____	_____
	_____	_____
4. femininity	_____	_____
	_____	_____
5. grass	_____	_____
	_____	_____
6. bitch	_____	_____
	_____	_____

Select some specific older person (e.g., a teacher, a parent) and ask this person for denotative and connotative definitions for each of these terms. Jot these down beside your own.

Discuss any differences in yours and the other person's definitions. What led to the differences? How would these differences have influenced your communication with each other?

Attaching Symbols to Meanings by Association

We began this chapter by defining communication in terms of the end result of other people getting the message. In brief summary, we suggested that the process of human communication involves two essential subprocesses: meaning attaching (decoding) and symbol attaching (encoding). These associations between meanings and symbols are learned through experience. Through our childhood experiences we learned many of the denotative and connotative meanings which we now attach to the symbols we use. Because of the difference in the ways people experientially learned the meanings they associate with symbols, meanings for one symbol are very different for each person using it. The caterpillar in *Alice in Wonderland* was quite accurate when he asserted, "When I use a word, it means exactly what I want it to mean, nothing more, nothing less."

When your goal is to get your message across to another person, you may want to be a little less creative than the caterpillar in your choice of symbols. Others will be more likely to get your message if you choose symbols which will call up similar denotative and connotative meanings in the mind of the other person. You may find it helpful to use the Outline to review this chapter.

Chapter 2

Understanding Nonverbal Communication

Objectives

Your learning should enable you to:

1. Define nonverbal communication.

2. Identify five relationships between verbal and nonverbal communication.

3. Give examples of "miscues" and "missed cues" in the decoding of nonverbal communication.

4. Recognize principles concerning the following types of nonverbal communication:
    Gesture and body movement
    Facial expressions
    Vocal sounds
    Eye contact
    Physical appearance
    Environment
    Personal space
    Touch

5. Identify and decode nonverbal messages.

6. Select nonverbal symbols to communicate a meaning.

Outline

I. Nonverbal communication: the process by which meanings are called up by nonword symbols
    A. Nonverbal symbols are used in various relationships to verbal symbols
        1. Replace verbal message: example, a kiss instead of words
        2. Reinforce verbal message: example, saying something in a loud voice
        3. Contradict verbal message: example, smiling while saying, "I hate you!"
            a) In contradictions, the nonverbal message is most often believed
        4. Specify verbal mesage: example, pointing to something you're talking about
        5. Regulate the flow of verbal messages: example, using eye contact to encourage feedback
    B. Advantages of nonverbal communication
        1. Not enough verbal symbols to represent complex feelings
        2. More powerful in communicating emotion
        3. Less controllable, so more genuine
        4. Draws less attention
II. Decoding nonverbal symbols
    A. Most nonverbal symbols have different meanings in different cultures
    B. Meanings are integrated with other cues
        1. Cues related to the communication situation
        2. Cues related to other symbols received
        3. Cues related to sender's frame of reference
    C. Types of inaccurate decoding
        1. "Missed cues": nonverbal symbols which are not received
            a) Inexperience with a cue
            b) Temporary inattention
            c) Cue was weak and indistinct
            d) Other cues distracted attention
        2. "Miscues": misinterpretation of symbols received
            a) Cue was unintentional—a random movement
            b) Cue was unintentional, but indicated something about the person or the interaction
            c) Intentional message but misunderstood
III. Research results suggest common meanings for basic types of nonverbal communication
    A. Gesture and Body Movement
        1. Inferences based on general ease and naturalness with which people move and use their bodies:
            a) Being "sure of oneself" suggested by slower and more controlled movements
            b) Being "unsure of oneself" suggested by jerky, less controlled movements
        2. Specific body movements have accepted meaning *in our culture:*
            a) Hand waving—greeting; closure
            b) Shrug of shoulders—"I don't know"
            c) Hands on hips—anger or superiority
            d) Arms crossed in front of chest—firmness of stand or being closed
            e) Legs crossed toward a person—involvement with that person
            f) Legs crossed away from a person—exclusion from that person
            g) Leaning forward—involvement
            h) Leaning backward—noninvolvement
            i) Shaking of head—disagreement
            j) Nodding of head—agreement

B. Facial Expression
 1. Main way to communicate emotion
 2. Primary uses of facial expression
  a) Suggest personality characteristics
   (1) Structural features
   (2) Typical expressions
   (3) Characteristic reaction patterns
  b) Express emotion and interpersonal attitudes
   (1) Modified by cultural rules
  c) Interaction signals
 3. Basic facial expressions are the same for all humans
C. Vocal Sounds
 1. Vocal sounds are stereotyped
  a) Breathiness indicates femininity, youth, excitedness
  b) Throatiness indicates masculinity, maturity
  c) Monotone indicates disinterest, boredom
  d) Nasality indicates general undesirability
 2. Vocal sounds influence meaning of what is said
  a) Harshness, loudness, distinct punctuation associated with irritation or anger
  b) High pitched, irregularly spoken symbols associated with fear or general excitement
  c) Lower pitched, softly spoken symbols associated with sincerity, concern, often intimacy
  d) Variety in pitch, quality, volume, and rate more pleasant to listen to
 3. Vocal sounds are learned behaviors
D. Eye Contact
 1. Main meanings communicated
  a) Show liking
  b) Establish dominance
  c) Show threat
 2. Summary of research—when eye contact is used
  a) To encourage feedback
  b) To show communication channel is open
  c) To show need for involvement
  d) To reduce distance between people
  e) To produce anxiety
 3. Summary of research—when eye contact is avoided
  a) To hide feelings
  b) To increase distance if personal space invaded
  c) To avoid social contact
 4. Eye contact as regulator of communication
  a) Gazing at end of other's message for reinforcement
  b) Gazing during parts of own message to emphasize
  c) Gazing while speaking to be persuasive
  d) Gazing while asking questions about other to encourage response
E. Physical Appearance—usually the initial basis for our reactions to others.
 1. Body type is one of basic attributes people react to:
  a) Stereotypes reinforced by mass media
  b) Attempts to change body type (dieting, weight lifting) often reflect desire to influence others' perceptions
 2. Clothing influences personal assessment and communication.
  a) People attempt to influence others' assessment by choice of clothes:
   (1) Generally in terms of appropriateness to role
   (2) Specifically in terms of fashion

      3. Length of hair is often used to assess and influence communication:
         a) Own hair length is often used as standard
      4. Information communicated by physical appearance
         a) Feelings about oneself
         b) Group membership
         c) Age
         d) Sex
         e) Status
         f) Occupation
         g) Social role
         h) Personality characteristics
F. Environment in which people communicate
      1. Colors influence communication
         a) Warm colors (red, orange, yellow) encourage interaction, activity, and interpersonal communication
         b) Cool colors (blue, green, grey) encourage personal thought and quietness
      2. Comfort of environment influences communication
         a) Heat and humidity lead to irritable and unpleasant communicators
         b) Too much or too little comfort decreases involvement
         c) Pleasant sounds and smells lead to positive interpersonal reactions
      3. Spatial relations influence communication
         a) Communicates who is in charge and level of formality
         b) Superiority implied by higher elevation from, large distance away, or large object between people
G. Personal Space: a particular area of space around a person which the person feels is his or her own
      1. Possessiveness of personal space in most humans is strong
         a) Strength varies among individuals
         b) Strength depends on interpersonal relationship
      2. Distance between people suggests intimacy of relationship
         a) 2–3 feet is the distance for casual conversation
      3. Violation of personal space leads to defensive behavior
         a) Moving to reestablish comfortable distance
         b) Lack of eye contact
         c) Holding the body rigid
         d) Positioning the body away from the other person
         e) Leaning back
         f) Placing some barrier between oneself and the other person
H. Touch
      1. Restricted use among Americans
         a) Usually limited to intimate relationships
      2. Touching communicates feelings
         a) Putting arm around shoulder of saddened friend
         b) Gentle punching of shoulder in greeting friend
         c) Affectionate touching of friend
      3. Touching as interaction signal
         a) Shaking hands
         b) Physically directing someone
         c) Physically guiding someone

Did you know that *it is impossible not to communicate nonverbally?* You can choose not to talk to someone or write to them, but even your silence communicates something. You communicate by your body movement, the clothes you wear, the environment you function within, and your facial expressions.

Nonverbal communication is *the process by which meanings are called up by nonword symbols.* Nonverbal symbols include all those that are not words (verbal means word), either oral or written. Considering nonverbals in this way, nonverbal communication would also include tone of voice because it does not use words as symbols per se, but the way the words are said.

Nonverbal symbols can be used alone to call up meaning in others, such as when you wave good-bye to someone. Nonverbal cues are used most often with verbal symbols or other nonverbal symbols to reinforce a meaning, strengthen it, contradict other symbols, or to specify the way in which the other symbols are meant. For example, the phrase, "I did it," spoken with a quivering voice and with no eye contact would convey a very different meaning than those same words spoken in a firm voice with direct eye contact. Nonverbal symbols also function to regulate the flow of communication, such as giving cues to encourage the other person to continue or cues that the conversation should end.

Nonverbal symbols are mainly used in the area of communicating feelings. Through nonverbal communication we can communicate feelings that would be very difficult to do with words. Mehrabian cites an excellent example:

> Most of us have had accidents in social situations—a drink or a cup of coffee spilled, a vase or a lamp overturned. There are many possible reactions to such mishaps from companions and hostesses. But sometimes we've heard from good friends such reactions as "Clumsy!" "Slob!" said with a smile and in a tone of exasperated affection. The verbal message expresses the distress and dismay of the speaker; the smile and voice assure us that they are not personally mad at us. It would be difficult, if not impossible for most of us, to put across the complexities of that message in words alone, "I really don't like what you did; it hurts my feelings, but I still like you." Such a verbalization could sound phony, draws more attention to the situation, and few of us would probably try it.[1]

Generally speaking, nonverbal behavior has more impact on people than words in communicating feeling. Overall, the relative weighting is usually two to one. Research shows that where there is a contradiction between the two, the nonverbal message is the one most often believed.[2]

---

1. Albert Mehrabian, *Silent Messages* (Belmont, Calif.: Wadsworth Publishing Co., 1971), pp. 40–41.
2. Ibid., pp. 40–47.

Most of us are quite skillful in sending and receiving nonverbal symbols in some situations. However, there are many nonverbal symbol systems you may not have considered. Nonverbal communication is a very meaningful part of our relationships with other people because it serves purposes which verbal communication cannot. Several of the advantages are

1. In many areas of interpersonal relationships there are not enough verbal symbols to represent the complexity of feelings toward another person;
2. Nonverbal symbols are more powerful in communicating messages of emotion;
3. As nonverbal communication is less well controlled, it is likely to be more genuine; and
4. In some situations, such as the coffee-spilling example above, it would be disturbing to focus too much attention on some messages by making them too explicit.

In this chapter we will consider the basic types of nonverbal symbols systems and research results regarding the meaning of commonly used nonverbal symbols. In later skill areas you will become more skillful in using nonverbal symbols to better interpret the meaning of others (Skill Area Two) and to use nonverbal symbols more effectively when attempting to call up similar meaning in others (Skill Area Three).

The following are selected research findings regarding nonverbal symbols. You are encouraged to follow up on those areas you are most interested in by use of the suggested readings at the end of the skill area.

Attaching Meaning to Nonverbal Symbols

Nonverbal symbols are rather abstract. When attaching meaning to any nonverbal symbol, it is important to do so in light of the communication setting, other symbols being sent, and other information you have about the person(s) sending the message. Further, with certain exceptions, nonverbal symbols are culturally bound. Some nonverbal symbols have generally universal meaning. But do not assume, as is often done, that all nonverbal symbols mean the same to everyone. Arriving slightly early for an appointment in the United States would be considered appropriate, while in most South American countries it would connote naiveté and overeagerness. It would not be a wise business practice in South America. Discuss with a student from another country some of the meanings for common nonverbal symbols which were suggested in this reading. Would the meaning suggested be appropriate in that person's culture?

Before learning about specific nonverbal cues and their potential meanings, it is important to note two problems associated with the interpretation of nonverbal cues. Randall Harrison[3] calls these problems "missed

---

3. Randall P. Harrison, *Beyond Words* (Englewood Cliffs, N.J.: Prentice-Hall, Inc., 1974), pp. 18–21.

cues" and "miscues." He uses cues to refer to nonverbal behavior which could have meaning.

"Missed Cues" refer to those nonverbal cues which are not received. Given the many stimuli you respond to at a given time, understandably some cues are missed. Nonverbal cues usually are missed because (1) of a person's inexperience with a cue—not realizing it could have significance, (2) of a person's temporary inattention, (3) the cue itself was weak and indistinct, or finally, (4) although the cue itself was strong, there were other equally compelling cues fighting for one person's attention. An example of the latter might be people so highly attentive to their own needs and internal messages (e.g., being late) that they ignore or miss nonverbal cues sent by other persons. The reasons for missing cues themselves suggest remedies, and your increasing understanding of nonverbal cues is an important step in meaningful communication with yourself and others.

"MISSED CUES?"

"Miscues" refer to the misinterpretation of cues received. Basically Harrison suggests that we sometimes attach meaning to a meaningless cue or don't attach meaning to a meaningful cue. Miscuing is more likely with nonverbal cues than verbal because it is more difficult to determine if such a cue has meaning. For example, with nonverbal communication a particular cue might be (1) a random movement, (2) an unintentional movement, but indicating something about the person's state of mind or the interaction, or (3) an intentional message. Often we might "attend to" a particular cue but be unsure about how to interpret it.

Because of the major role of nonverbal cues in any human interaction experience, it becomes crucial to increase one's awareness and sensitiveness to interpreting nonverbal cues. As indicated earlier, such interpretation should always be done within the context of the situation, other symbols being sent, and with any previous knowledge about the person(s) sending the nonverbal message.

In this chapter we will consider the basic types of nonverbal symbol systems and research results regarding the meanings of commonly used nonverbal symbols. In later skill areas, you will work on nonverbal communication skills as they relate to listening (Skill Area Two), speaking (Skill Area Three), and applied communication skills used in interpersonal problem solving, interviewing, and attitude changing.

Gesture and Body Movement

This category of nonverbal cues is often referred to as "body language" and is currently receiving a great deal of attention in research circles and in popular literature. In addition to using body language to express feelings, conventional sign systems have been developed by occupational and other subgroups for use where direct verbal communication would be difficult. Examples of conventional sign systems would include sign language for the deaf and directional signals within the field of TV broadcasting.

People usually make inferences about other people based on the general ease and naturalness with which they move and use their bodies. We can all picture in our minds the movements associated with such characterizations as "stuck-up," "foxy," and "sexy." There are also movements associated with being sure of oneself (usually slower and more controlled) and those associated with being hesitant and unsure (usually jerky and less controlled).

Specific body movements also have meaning in our culture, such as hand waving as greeting or closure; shrug of shoulders to say "I don't know"; hands on hips to indicate anger or superiority; arms crossed in front of the chest indicating a strong opinion or being closed to others; legs crossed toward a person as indicating involvement; leaning backward as noninvolvement; shaking of head side to side to indicate disagreement or negation; nodding of head up and down to indicate agreement; body tension or jerky body movements to indicate uncomfortableness; wringing of the hands to indicate nervousness or tension.

Learning Experience

Sit in the student union or a restaurant for thirty minutes. Select three individuals as they come in. Watch them for ten minutes, jotting down symbols such as the way they walked, how they sit at the table, use of body in communicating. After the ten minute observation, make inferences about the individuals and their relationships with the people they are with. If possible, check out your inferences with the individuals you were observing. If this is not possible, try the experience again with someone you will be able to check your observation with. . . . What could people infer about you from watching your body movement? Write down some of your findings.

Facial Expression

The face is an extremely important area of nonverbal communication. Knapp suggests that facial expression *"is the primary site for communicating emotional states; it reflects interpersonal attitudes; it provides nonverbal feedback on the comments of others; and some say it is the primary source of information next to human speech."*[4]

---

4. Mark Knapp, "The Field of Nonverbal Communication: An Overview" (unpublished paper), 1971 [Italics provided by authors].

The main way in which people consciously control their facial features is by adopting certain expressions to suggest a feeling. The importance of facial expression in assessments of liking–disliking and dominance–submissiveness have been tested in various research settings. Mehrabian summarizes his review of the research in these two specific areas, comparing facial expression with verbal message and vocal emphasis in situations where the verbal and nonverbal messages were in conflict.

Total feeling = 7% verbal + 38% vocal + 55% facial[5]

This formula suggests that over one-half of our connotative meanings of feeling in message conflict situations are received from facial expression. To further emphasize the importance of facial expressions we need only consider the amount of information about what people are feeling that is lost when we talk to someone over the telephone.

Facial expression takes on increasing importance as a form of communication when we consider that it is one of the few "languages" which is generally universal. Generally speaking, *basic facial expressions—happiness, sadness, anger, fear, disgust, and surprise—are performed similarly all over the world.*[6] Of course, what makes people laugh and the *degree* to which they express the feeling indicated by laughter will vary among cultures.

Argyle suggests that facial expressions are used in three different ways: (1) to suggest personality characteristics by structural features, typical expressions and characteristic reaction patterns, (2) to express emotions and interpersonal attitudes (modified and controlled by cultural rules), and (3) as interaction signals such as eyebrow raising.[7]

Try turning to a TV program with the sound turned off. From the facial expressions, what kinds of feelings are being expressed? Infer what is happening in the situation and then turn up the sound to check your inferences.

Learning Experience

Vocal Sounds

As indicated in Mehrabian's equation for determining interpersonal assessment of feeling in message-conflict situations, vocal emphasis plays a major role. As with body types, people tend to stereotype various vocal patterns as related to certain personality types and to male or female characteristics. Although research does not indicate such associations to be valid, we often communicate as though they were.

In terms of general stereotypes, breathiness is usually associated with femininity, youth, excitedness; throatiness (deep voice) with masculinity, maturity; monotone with disinterest, boredom; and nasality with general undesirability.

---

5. Mehrabian, *Silent Messages,* p. 44.
6. Paul Ekman, "Universals and Cultural Differences in Facial Expression of Emotion," *Nebraska Symposium on Motivation,* ed., J. Cole (Lincoln, Neb.: University of Nebraska Press, 1972) [Italics provided by authors].
7. Michael Argyle, *Bodily Communication* (New York: International Universities Press, Inc., 1975), pp. 212–13.

In interpersonal interactions, harshness, loudness, and distinctly punctuated symbols are associated with irritation and anger. High pitched and irregularly spoken symbols are associated with fear or general excitement. Lower pitched and softly spoken symbols are associated with sincerity, concern, and often intimacy. Also, it is usually more pleasant to listen to someone who varies the pitch, quality, volume, and rate of speaking. A usual key to determining what the communicator thinks is important is the change in vocal emphasis he or she gives to that thought, usually accompanied by strategically placed pauses (another aspect of vocal emphasis).

Like our other symbols, vocal sounds are learned. Our dialects and the sound of our voices in normal conversation and in unusual situations were largely developed from modeling people early in our lives. Because these voice sounds were learned they can be changed if we choose. People on radio and TV work to develop more effective voice sounds.

Learning Experience

Listen to a professor lecture. How does the professor use vocal emphasis to identify main ideas? How is vocal emphasis used to communicate attitude toward the topic? Can you tell if that professor is enjoying himself/herself from his or her voice? You might try comparing how various professors use vocal emphasis. Does it make a difference in your understanding or enjoyment of the lecture?
Record some of your experiences.

Eye Contact

Eye contact is another aspect of body behavior which plays an important role in establishing relationships between people. The most significant messages communicated by eye contact are to show liking, to establish dominance, and to show threat. People usually use more eye contact while listening and look at the other person to get feedback while talking. The following are several research findings related to the use of eye contact and the absence of eye contact in communication.

When does eye contact occur?
1. When people want to encourage feedback concerning the reactions of others.
2. When we want to signal that the communication channel is open.
3. When we want to convey our need for affiliation, involvement, or inclusion. Individuals who have high affiliative needs tend to return glances more often.
4. Eye contact seems to increase when there is greater distance between two communicators. In such a case, eye contact reduces the psychological distance between communicators.
5. Eye contact is also used to produce anxiety in others. A gaze lasting longer than ten seconds is likely to make another person feel uncomfortable.

When is eye contact absent?
1. When people don't want to reveal something concerning their inner feelings, they may try to avoid eye contact.
2. Eye contact may also be lacking when the two parties are invading each other's personal space. Reducing eye contact will psychologically increase the distance.

3. When an individual wishes to avoid any social contact, his eye contact tends to be minimal.[8]

Argyle suggests the following additional ways in which eye contact functions to regulate communication.[9]

Symbol	*Effect*
gazing at the end of other's message	reinforcement; other will talk more
gazing during parts of one's own message	gives emphasis
gazes more while speaking	is more persuasive
gazes more while asking questions about other	other will talk more about self

Learning Experience

You might try this experiment on how people react to eye contact. Go to a classroom building and walk down a hallway. Choose a person walking toward you who is far down the hall. Look directly at her/his eyes until s/he walks past you. Repeat this with two other people. What nonverbal or verbal messages did the other people send in reacting to your sustained eye contact? What meaning did they think you were communicating (would this be different for the same versus opposite sex)? What meaning did their reactions communicate to you?

Physical Appearance

Physical appearance is usually the initial basis for our reactions to other people, probably because it is the first thing people notice. All of us have some relatively stable stereotypes, relating physical appearance to personality. In terms of the implications of physical stereotypes for communication, Eisenberg and Smith suggest that:

By acting as though body type really does make a difference, we change our communicative behavior in order to give reality to categories which may have little inherent value. In the same way, the possessors of particular body types come to learn from the reactions of others that they should be assertive or shy or domineering. . . . Weight-lifters, sunbathers, and dieters try to change their bodies in some sort of effort to control their physical appearance in order to control the reactions of others.[10]

The body you have and the image you succeed in presenting to others has an effect on your feelings toward yourself and on your behavior with others. Concern with physical appearance is more prominent in the United States than in many countries. It often becomes the major way a person determines his or her self-image. There is considerable emphasis in human

---

8. James McCroskey, Carl Larson, and Mark Knapp, *An Introduction to Interpersonal Communication* (Englewood Cliffs, N.J.: Prentice-Hall, Inc., 1971), pp. 112–13.

9. Argyle, *Bodily Communication*, p. 244.

10. Abne Eisenberg and Ralph Smith, Jr., *Nonverbal Communication* (Indianapolis: Bobbs-Merrill Co., Inc., 1971), p. 106.

liberation movements to free people of interpersonal evaluations based on physical factors over which they have little control.

Another aspect of physical appearance that influences self- and interpersonal assessments and communication is clothing. Very few individuals choose their clothing entirely in terms of what would be most functional. To varying degrees people are aware of and purchase clothes in terms of the impact those choices will have on others. This may range from a type of clothes which they would feel is appropriate for a particular role, to a need to be "in style" within that given role.

Length of hair is periodically a factor of concern in typing people and reacting to them. People tend to use their own hair length as a standard and be increasingly negative toward increasing deviations from that standard. By manipulating aspects of our physical appearance we are able to communicate messages about our feelings about ourselves, group membership, age and sex, status and occupation, social roles, and personality characteristics.

Learning Experience

Try this with another person in this course whom you have recently met, but do not *know*. Each person should make three inferences about the other's personality from only what can be seen. Compare your inferences. What aspects of "physical appearance" do most people use to make inferences about another person? Discuss with this person the impact of these kinds of inferences on your interaction with others. . . . Try this same experience with an older person (you may just want to have that person describe you). Write down some of your results.

Environment

We receive messages about people from the environment in which they function. Consider several of the offices you have been in recently—doctor's office, instructor's office, school official's, and so forth. What can you tell about the people who function there by being observant about the surroundings? Factors involved are the color choice, sounds present, physical comfort, smells, objects present, implied purpose of room, and potential for interaction allowed by spatial relations. Specifically, research has suggested that warm colors (red, orange, and yellow) tend to encourage interaction activity and interpersonal communication, while cool colors (blue, grey, and green) tend to encourage personal thought and quietness.[11] Spatial relations which keep a large desk (or some similar object) between you and the other person communicate a feeling of superiority and control.

Physical comfort is another environmental factor which influences human communication. Generally when the environment is hot and humid, people will have a greater tendency to be irritable and unpleasant to each other. There also appears to be a general continuum of comfort related to seating facilities which affects interaction. If the seating is too soft and comfort-

---

11. Don Fabun, "The Silent Languages," in *Communication Concepts and Processes,* ed. J. A. DeVito (Englewood Cliffs, N.J.: Prentice-Hall, Inc., 1971), p. 130.

able, overrelaxation detracts from involvement in communication, and if the seating is too hard and uncomfortable, personal awareness of discomfort will detract from communication involvement.

Spatial relationships, especially related to the positioning of seats, can discourage or facilitate communication. Such spatial relationships also can imply who may talk to whom and the level of the formality of the interaction. Compare the following research results with your own experiences.

—In a classroom with seats lined up in rows all facing in a single direction, the inference is that attention should be directed toward the front. It is also assumed that interaction between people sitting in the rows is not expected. Experimentation with various classroom seating arrangements has brought about suggestions for a horseshoe-type arrangement with the teacher at the opening. This arrangement highlights the focal opposition of the teacher but encourages interaction among students.

—At a typical rectangular conference table people sitting at some locations are more likely than others to talk. At such a table those "talkative" positions should be the seats at either end of the table and those in the middle of each side. To overcome this tendency, round tables with comfortable seating distances are becoming more common.

—Differences in elevation also are used to suggest focus and often status. Consider the elevated platform in some older classrooms and the raised pulpit in many churches.

Pleasant sounds and smells have been related to more positive reactions to people and events in an environment. We tend to be more open to others when we are in a familiar, pleasant environment.

Describe two classrooms (or instructor's offices) in which you function in a learning situation. Describe three nonverbal messages you receive in each situation from the environmental factors involved. Focus on nonverbal messages that relate to the kind of learning experience that is anticipated in this environment. For example, the kind of interaction anticipated between learner and instructor, or learner and learner. Specifically note how the colors present function as nonverbal messages.	**Learning Experience**

Personal Space

Personal space is a concept relating to a particular area of space around an individual which he or she feels is his or her own. It also refers to specific places which a person feels are his or her own, such as a chosen piece of furniture or a specific chair in a classroom. Research suggests that possessiveness regarding personal space is strongly felt in most humans (as with an animal's "territory"), and violation of that space will cause some type of protective behavior.

Before looking at specific implications of this concept for communication, it should be noted that both the need for and amount of personal space, as well as the general tendency to defend one's personal space, will vary with each individual in each setting. Two situational factors which influence a person's perception of needed personal space in a given situation are the role being assumed (e.g., boss, friend, lover) and the status associated with that role. For example, compare the typical office of a president of a corporation with those of immediate subordinates. The office of the president is usually larger, as is the desk.

The major implication of personal space for communication is the effect of the distance between people as they communicate. Generally speaking, there are basic distances which suggest intimate interaction, casual personal interaction, and we could extend this continuum to the more formal possible limits of large group communication (e.g., the lecture hall). Edward Hall in his insightful analysis of personal space suggests that a space of from two to three feet is a comfortable distance for most Americans involved in casual conversation. He further developed the following scale[12] for space, the vocal message, and the character of the communication involved.

1. Very close
   (3 inches to 6 inches)

   Soft whisper; top secret

2. Close
   (8 inches to 12 inches)

   Audible whisper; very confidential

3. Near
   (12 inches to 20 inches)

   Indoors, soft voice; outdoors, full voice, confidential

4. Neutral
   (20 inches to 36 inches)

   Soft voice; low volume, personal subject matter

5. Neutral
   (4½ feet to 5 feet)

   Full voice; information of nonpersonal matter

6. Public Distance
   (5 feet to 8 feet)

   Full voice with slight overloudness; public information for others to hear

7. Stretching the limits of distance

   20 feet to 24 feet indoors; up to 100 feet outdoors; hailing distance, departure

With a close friend, position yourselves at these various distances. Do Hall's categories and suggestions of intimacy involved correspond with your experience?

Consider how you and others you communicate with use space to suggest the amount of intimacy appropriate for a given communication event. Check the following examples of communication setting and the level of intimacy implied in the seating arrangements the next time you are in each setting.

—seating in a bus, train, car: When the maximum number of persons intended for any bus, train, or car seat is filled, the physical personal space between people is minimal, usually less than twelve inches apart. When placed next to a stranger in this kind of transportation, many people will not say anything. Their silent withdrawal communicates "Leave me alone." This minimal space between strangers would be an example of an invasion of personal space.

—seating in a library: When the maximum number of people is seated at the typical library table, appropriate communication would again be intimate. The

---

12. Edward Hall, *The Silent Language* (New York: Fawcett, Inc., 1959), pp. 163–64.

space allowed invades most individuals' personal space, and conversation, except among intimates, would be minimal.

—seating in a classroom with rows of seats: This close seating arrangement in most classes leads to minimal communication among students with the exception of those who know each other well.

—seating in an office: Seating arrangements are often used to suggest and maintain status and perceived roles. Also, it is generally true that people of more status have a greater amount of personal space at their disposal.[13]

An excellent way to maintain distance is the practice of placing a desk between those communicating. This practice is most often used when the intended communication atmosphere is that of impersonalness, business-like, etc. The amount of space left in a waiting room can also imply whether interaction is appropriate.

When someone perceives that his or her personal space has been invaded, an attempt will be made to reestablish a comfortable distance for that situation. If the invasion of personal space involves someone else taking over a place you consider to be your own (e.g., a seat in a classroom), depending on the individual, you may request the person to move or find another place. If a person is in a particular place and someone moves in too close, the first reaction is to move back, if possible. Interesting experiments show that it is possible to edge another person quite a distance while standing and talking by gradually and continually moving in on his or her personal space. If it is physically impossible to actually increase the physical space, such techniques as lack of eye contact, holding the body rigid, body positioning away from the other person, leaning back, or placing some barrier between you and the other person are frequently used to create the illusion of comfortable physical space. How many of these techniques have you used in a crowded elevator, bus, or when someone is trying to sell you an unwanted item?

Try this experience carefully. Go into the library and look for a table at which there is only one person studying. Take the seat immediately beside the person. Begin working but be very conscious of the person's reaction to you. Try this several different times and note the varying reactions to this imposition on someone's personal space. How do the individuals cope with the situation? (You'll probably want to explain to the individuals what you were attempting to learn after several minutes.)

Learning Experience

Touch

Touch as nonverbal communication is perhaps the most restricted form of communication for many Americans. Outside of intimate relationships, our use of touching to communicate personal meaning is governed by many social rules. What are some of the social rules you are aware of that you feel restrict your touching of other people?

---

13. Mehrabian, *Silent Messages*, p. 34.

Examples of more commonly used touching behaviors in close relationships include putting an arm around the shoulder of a friend who is experiencing sadness, a gentle punching of the shoulder in greeting a friend, and the many examples of affectionate touching associated with intimacy. Touching is also used as an interaction signal to indicate greetings and farewell (e.g., shaking hands); physically directing someone toward an object of interest; and physically guiding someone who is ill, blind, or elderly.

The current interest in sensitivity training stems in part from a concern that most people in our culture are not very free in their body language and ability to use the sense of touch to communicate. There are social limitations, often associated with severe "penalties," as to whom we can touch and where we can touch them. Certain implications are associated with touching people of the opposite sex and of the same sex. Most of us would be quite uncomfortable if someone we did not know well grasped our hand when talking to us or gave us a hug. Our discomfort would likely be stronger in the case of someone of the same sex doing such touching behavior. In our culture we would be apt to attach sexual connotations to the touching of someone of the opposite sex. This inhibition toward touching is not true of all cultures. Arabs, for example, use touch frequently in communication with colleagues or strangers.[14]

When we consider how comforting and meaningful touching can be, it is unfortunate to limit the use of this mode of communication to so few situations.

14. Eisenberg and Smith, *Nonverbal Communication*, p. 87.

Chapter 3

Understanding Frames of Reference

Objectives

Your learning should enable you to:

1. Define frame of reference.

2. Name the components of a person's frame of reference.

3. Define self-concept.

4. Describe the processes of selective attention, selective processing, and selective remembering in human communication.

5. Within a personally experienced communicative situation, describe your own frame of reference.

6. Define Jack Gibb's supportive and defensive communication behaviors.

7. In a given situation, recognize the use of Gibb's communication behaviors.

8. For your personally experienced communicative situation in number 5 above, select communication behaviors which would facilitate sharing and minimize distortion of meanings.

Outline

I. Frame of reference
  A. Definition: the unique interrelationship of a person's stored information, important needs, and perceptions of a communication situation
  B. Components of a frame of reference
    1. Stored information: all past experiences which have become part of a person
      a) Attitudes: combinations of thoughts and feelings about ourselves, others, things, and ideas that lead us to act in certain ways
      b) Values: strongly held attitudes that provide the basis for our life choices
    2. Important needs: the things which most immediately concern us at a given time
      a) Physical needs
      b) Problems and responsibilities
    3. Perceptions of the situation: how you see the immediate communicative situation
      a) What you think others expect
      b) What you expect of yourself
II. Selective Perception: the ways the frame of reference influences what people "see"
  A. Specific influences
    1. Selective attention: focusing on certain stimuli based on our frame of reference (we screen out some kinds of stimuli)
    2. Selective processing: the unique way we think about decoded meanings based on our frame of reference
    3. Selective retention: remembering only parts of what we decode and think about (we usually retain what is understandable and important to us)
  B. Resulting distortion of meanings
    1. "Self-fulfilling prophecy": we make the world what we want it to be by expecting certain meanings which might not be intended
III. Understanding one's own frame of reference
  A. Values most difficult to clarify
    1. Criteria for identifying values
      a) Must be prized and cherished
      b) Must be publicly affirmed
      c) Must be chosen from alternatives
      d) Must be chosen after considering consequences
      e) Must be chosen freely
      f) Must be apparent in one's actions
      g) Must be acted upon consistently
    2. Various activities can be used to clarify your values.
  B. Self-concept: the complex set of attitudes we have about ourselves
    1. Most influential part of the frame of reference
    2. Developed by comparing self to others and accepting opinions of others
      a) Others' reactions to you are based on their frame of reference
      b) Developed at a time when you were not able to determine appropriateness of opinions
    3. Influences messages we send on all levels of communication
IV. Sharing the frame of reference
  A. Varying levels of shared information in relationships
  B. More shared information leads to more accurate communication
  C. Amount and content of sharing depend on relationship, situation, and feelings about self

V. Establishing a communication climate to facilitate sharing
   A. More trust leads to more sharing
   B. Communication climates influence trust and openness
   C. Gibb's communication behaviors which *increase* openness—supportive climates
      1. Description: nonjudgmental statements or questions
         Example: "I feel good when you compliment me."
      2. Problem Orientation: to communicate a desire to work *with* someone
         Example: "Let's see if we can find a solution."
      3. Spontaneity: to be direct and honest about your motives and meanings
         Example: "I'd like you to go to the store with me because I need a ride and you have a car."
      4. Empathy: to show understanding and respect for another person
         Example: "I think I understand how difficult this is for you."
      5. Equality: to communicate respect for the equal human worth of another person
         Example: "We'll work well together on this."
      6. Provisionalism: to use appropriate qualifications in your statements suggesting openness to change
         Example: "Based on what I've read in *Newsweek,* his data is inaccurate."
   D. Gibb's communication behaviors which *decrease* openness—defensive climates
      1. Evaluation: to make a judgment about something
         Example: "That was a dumb thing to do."
      2. Control: direct attempts to make another person do what you want him or her to
         Example: "If you don't give that back, I'll call the police."
      3. Strategy: to be dishonest with someone; indirect attempts to make another person do what you want the person to do
         Example: "I'd love to go to the movie with you if I don't have to go home. I'll let you know Thursday." (You're really waiting for a more preferred person to call; if s/he doesn't, you'll go.)
      4. Neutrality: to treat another person with indifference
         a) Example: "I'm really too busy to listen to you."
         b) Most often communicated nonverbally
      5. Superiority: to communicate that you're better than the other person as a human being
         Example: "You'd better let me do that. I'll do it right."
      6. Certainty: to appear to know all the answers and be unwilling to change your mind
         Example: "Obviously the man was guilty."
   E. Guidelines for using Gibb's behaviors
      1. Important consideration is how the other person will perceive behavior, not how you intended it; meanings attached to behaviors by the other person are influenced by their level of defensiveness
      2. Behaviors function together and can partially neutralize each other
         Example: behaviors of equality and empathy can reduce defensive reactions to evaluation

Reading

Where is she coming from?

"Mom is right, of course—*as she sees it.*" And in this perhaps humorous self-deception lies a basic aspect of human experience: we never fully come into direct contact with reality. Everything we experience is influenced by our own internal filters—our frame of reference.[1]

The question, "Where is she coming from?" asked in the context of human communication recognizes the very different meanings which each of us attach to the experiences we have. In chapter 1 we stated that because of these differences, *no two people would attach exactly the same meanings to a symbol or experience.* Because these differences represent such a challenge to accurate communication, we're going to look more specifically at the nature of these differences and the way they influence our communication.

Frame of Reference

Just like the people in the cartoon above, we all have within us a unique storehouse of meanings which we attach to the situations we experience. This storehouse has been called our frame of reference for a given situation. More specifically our *frame of reference* can be defined as *the unique interrelationship of a person's stored information, important needs, and perceptions of the situation for a given communicative experience.* This frame of reference works as a screening system to selectively determine what we pay attention to, how we think about what we experience, and what we remember from that experience.

1. William V. Haney, "Perception and Communication" in *Basic Readings in Interpersonal Communication,* ed. Kim Giffin and Bobby R. Patton (New York: Harper and Row, 1971).

Components of the Frame of Reference

For any given situation the components of a person's frame of reference include the following:

$$\begin{array}{l}\text{Relevant} \\ \text{Stored} \\ \text{Information}\end{array} + \begin{array}{l}\text{Important} \\ \text{Needs}\end{array} + \begin{array}{l}\text{Perceptions} \\ \text{of the} \\ \text{Situation}\end{array} = \begin{array}{l}\text{Frame of} \\ \text{Reference}\end{array}$$

Stored information refers to all of our past experiences which have now become part of us. Some of those experiences have been recorded on the brain with little conscious effort on our part. Others have been carefully processed and consciously stored for later use. These experiences take the form of attitudes and values. *Attitudes* are *combinations of thoughts and feelings about ourselves, others, things, and ideas that lead us to act in certain ways.* For example, your stored information about some people may lead you to feel that they will try to take advantage of you and, therefore, you avoid them. *Values* are *very strongly held attitudes which provide the basis for our life choices.* For example, you may have the value of being out of debt. Our different life experiences have led to each of us storing different information and developing different attitudes and values. As we have new experiences and gather more information, our attitudes and values change.

To better understand how your frame of reference has changed, fill in the following chart by writing two words below which reflect your attitudes toward the "thing" represented by the symbol on the left.

Learning Experience

	Three Years Ago	Today
School		
Your Parents		
Yourself		

Cite examples for each symbol on the left of how the change in your farme of reference has influenced your communication.

Important needs refers to the things that most immediately concern us at a given time. This would include physical needs, such as the desire for food or drink, as well as specific problems or responsibilities you are facing. Sometimes the important needs which are "on our minds" are so strong that it is difficult to focus on anything else. Consider the last two times you interacted with someone you know quite well. Try to remember what your important needs were in each of those situations. Perhaps you were antici-pating an upcoming exam or having a bad cold. How did your different important needs in each situation influence your communication with that person? What are your important needs right now? How are they influencing your processing of our messages?

Your perceptions of the situation refer to how you see the immediate communicative situation. These perceptions would include how you think others expect you to behave in that situation; for example, how or what you should say, what your relationship to other communicators is, and the consequences for inappropriate behavior. It also includes how you see yourself in that situation.

Learning Experience

Consider each of the following situations in terms of expectations you believe others have of you and those you have of yourself in that situation. Briefly describe how your communication differs in each situation.

Situation	Others expect of me	I expect of me	My communication
Talking with a close friend			
Talking with a police officer after being stopped for speeding			
Explaining to a teacher why an assignment is late			

These three components interact to become your frame of reference for any situation. Because each of these components changes over time, your frame of reference, even for a very similar situation, is never the same. Imagine the frustration that people might experience if they felt they "knew you," but in a particular situation you reacted very differently than they expected you to. This is a common experience when visiting with an old friend you haven't seen for several years. Comments like, "I couldn't believe you. You were always such a clown at the office," might suggest his or her surprise.

Selective Perception

Selective perception refers to the ways our frame of reference influences what we pay attention to (selective attention); how we think about symbols (selective processing); and what we remember about situations (selective retention).

First, *your frame of reference influences what you will pay attention to.* In any situation there are millions of potential stimuli on which you could focus your attention. For example, when walking across campus between classes there are many environmental stimuli, other-people stimuli, and self-awareness stimuli. It is your frame of reference that will determine what you notice and what you won't notice. In much the way a colorblind person does not see some colors, your frame of reference leads you to have blindspots for certain kinds of stimuli. When you are listening to someone, your frame of reference will influence what you hear in his or her message.

Second, *your frame of reference will lead you to selectively process the stimuli you receive.* The different kinds of thinking about messages which people do lead to different levels of understanding and different attitudes and values. Even *if two people were involved in the same situation, the meaning of that situation would be very different for both of them.*

Finally, *your frame of reference will lead to selective retention of information* which is decoded and thought about. If something was understandable and important to you, you will likely remember it. Information that is not personally meaningful will not be efficiently stored in your memory and could not be easily called up.

These three implications of selective perception have often worked to the frustration of attorneys as they attempt to learn from different witnesses what happened at the scene of a crime. They also help us to maintain a rather consistent and personally acceptable view of our world. If our storage of information becomes outdated, if our important needs become overpowering, or if we misperceive the communication situation, our frame of reference can lead to distortions of the meanings we attach. Such distortions can lead to what has been called the *self-fulfilling prophecy.* That is, based on my frame of reference, I will expect certain meanings even when you didn't intend those meanings. We almost literally make the world fit our expectations of it. We need to continually be aware of our own selective perceptions and their potential influence on accurate communication.

SELF-FULFILLING PROPHECY?

Such unavoidable differences in people's expectations often lead to mis-communication and recurring conflict. Both are inevitable aspects of human communication. Sometimes miscommunication is only a minor irritant, while other times it can lead to more serious conflict. Such conflict is potentially productive, as it encourages us to consider the appropriateness of our own frame of reference and to better understand others' frames of reference. Without such conflict the potential for growth and change would be lessened. Unmanaged conflict, however, is not a pleasant way to grow.

One of the ways that conflict can be managed productively is by understanding where people are "coming from"; that is, what their frame of reference is and what resulting goals and expectations they have. Without that understanding, accurate communication is not possible.

Understanding Your Own Frame of Reference

Accurate communication assumes some shared perceptions regarding the participants' frames of reference. An important beginning to that process of sharing involves each person understanding his or her own frame of reference. Such understanding involves stating the components of your frame of reference for specific, important communicative situations. This is an extremely valuable experience to have and one that can be repeated to maintain a realistic and up-to-date frame of reference. However, one of the most influential parts of the frame of reference is often the one we are least able to state. We are referring to the values which influence our life choices. It is difficult for most people to clearly state their values because they have been developed gradually, through the influence of important others in our lives. Values are introduced at an early age, and few people spend time carefully thinking through the basis for their life choices. You may even be in the process of questioning some of the values you accepted earlier in your life. If you want to understand yourself better, develop relationships with other people, and determine what you value strongly enough to speak out about in public, a valuable place to start is by clarifying your own values.

Values Clarification

The clarification of personal values is a lifelong goal. We would like to share several procedures that we and others have found to be valuable for getting at your own values or developing new ones. Having a procedure for looking at values is an important skill which provides a foundation for more meaningful communication.

You have already been in important situations where you have asked yourself what you really value. Perhaps one of the following has come up for you: "School doesn't seem important to me. Why not drop out and educate myself?" or "Should we live together before marriage to see if we really love each other?" or "What occupation should I choose so I don't end up hating my job later in life?" or "Why do I feel guilty at the end of a day because I haven't accomplished what I wanted to do?'' Such decisions are difficult to make, as they all depend on what you value most highly.

Earlier we said that values were those strongly held attitudes which form the basis for life choices. It has been suggested that for something to be a fully developed value it must meet the following criteria:

Prizing one's values,
1. it must be prized and cherished
2. it must be publicly affirmed, when appropriate
Choosing one's values,
3. it must be chosen from alternatives
4. it must be chosen after considering consequences
5. it must be chosen freely
Acting on one's values,
6. it must be apparent in one's actions
7. It must be acted upon consistently and with a pattern[2]

These are pretty high standards. If one of the criteria is not true for one of the things you believe strongly, it may be that it is a developing value, one that has not yet become a fully developed basis for action.

Below is a series of three experiences in values clarification[3] which may help you to discover some of "where you come from." You can do these by yourself or with others. If you find these valuable, you may want to follow up with several of the sources listed in the Bibliography for more experiences in values clarification.

In each of the experiences below, we suggest you complete each part of the experience step by step, without reading the total description of the experience first.

VALUES CLARIFICATION EXPERIENCE 1

"Things I Love to Do"

Sometimes we get the feeling that we're going through life not really being able to do the things we'd like to do. On a piece of paper, write down 20 things you really love to do. They might be big things or small things. Go ahead and make your list. It may turn out to be a little longer or shorter than 20 items. When you are finished, code each item on the left-hand margin of your list as follows:

1. Place a dollar sign ($) beside any item that costs more than $3.00 each time it is done.
2. Place the letter A by those things you prefer to do alone; a P by those things you prefer to do with other people.
3. Place an NF by those items you wouldn't have listed five years ago. Place an F by those items you won't be likely to list five years from now.
4. Place a PL by those which require planning to do.

---

2. Louis Raths, Merrill Harmin, and Sidney Simon, *Values and Teaching* (Columbus, Ohio: Charles E. Merrill, 1966).
3. These experiences were adapted from Sidney Simon, Leland Howe, and Howard Kirschenbaum, *Values Clarification* (New York: Hart Publishing Co., Inc., 1972).

5. Number from 1–5 those items which you most love to do. The most loved would be 1.
6. Letter from A–E those items which you have spent the most time at during the last week. The most time spent on would have an A by it.
7. Write when you last did each of the items.
8. Place the letter R by any of the items which involves an element of risk. It might be physical, emotional, or intellectual risk.
9. Put an I next to any which involve intimacy.
10. Place an IQ next to any item which you think you would love more if you were smarter.
11. Place the letter U next to any item which you think others would judge unconventional.

After completing your coding, consider what values are suggested by that coding. Make a list of those potential values. How do you feel about your list? Check to see how many of the seven criteria, listed earlier, they meet. Share as much of this as you like with another person.

VALUES CLARIFICATION EXPERIENCE 2

Sometimes it is quite surprising to see how we actually spend our time and money. We have found the following experience valuable in visualizing on a very personal level how we are "spending" ourselves. Draw a large circle on a piece of paper. Start by dividing your circle into four quarters using dotted lines. Each slice represents six hours and the total circle represents a day of your life. Estimate the amount of time you spend on the activities which make up your day and write those activities in an appropriately sized wedge of your circle. Make as many subdivisions as necessary to show the ways in which you spend your typical week day. Actually write the approximate number of hours into each wedge, checking to see that your total is 24 hours. When you are satisfied with your circle, you might consider the following:

your satisfaction with the relative size of your wedges
your satisfaction with the activities which make up your day
the values suggested by your activities and their part of your day
what your ideal day's circle would look like
what you can realistically do to change to more closely approximately your ideal day

Now draw another circle. Above it write the typical amount of money you have available to you each week. Follow the same procedure as you did above to approximate the percentage of that total you spend on different things. Make as many divisions as necessary to show the ways you typically spend money during a week. Actually write approximate amounts of money in each wedge and check to see that the total equals the amount you wrote on the top of the circle.

When you are satisfied that you have represented your spending as accurately as you can, consider the same areas listed above as they relate to spending money.

VALUES CLARIFICATION EXPERIENCE 3

We all have attitudes toward issues that face us personally and that face our school, community, and nation. Some are more strongly felt than others. The following experience helps to visualize how closely our personally felt attitudes come to being values that guide our life choices.

On a piece of paper, make the following categories and seven lines down the left side:

Issue	My Attitude	1	2	3	4	5	6	7
1.								
2.								
3.								
4.								
5.								
6.								
7.								

Going down the left column, write seven important issues for you now. They may all be personal, all be public, or some combination of the two. Your list may include such issues as religion, intimate relationships, a specific school issue, or the energy crisis. After writing your seven issues, briefly state your attitude about each issue in the second column. Make these attitude statements as specific as you can. After completing your attitude statements, ask yourself the following seven questions for each of your written attitudes. For those that you can answer "yes" to, place a check under the appropriate number beside it. If you don't answer "yes," leave that box blank.

1. Are you *proud* of your attitude?
2. Have you *publicly affirmed* your attitude?
3. Have you chosen your attitude from *alternatives?*
4. Have you chosen your attitude after thoughtful consideration of the *pros* and *cons* and *consequences?*
5. Have you chosen your attitude *freely?*
6. Have you *acted on or done anything* about the issue based on your attitude?
7. Have you acted with repetition or *consistency* on the issue, based on your attitude?

After completing your checklist take a look at it in terms of how closely your attitudes come to being full values. You might want to save your checklist and refer to it again at a later time. It will be helpful to note changes in the content of your attitudes and in the quality and degree of your process of valuing.

We might note here that, in doing these values clarification experiences, you may have identified attitudes which might become the basis for messages you would like to share with others. In Skill Area Three you'll be working on skills in developing messages which help another person understand an attitude or value you hold.

Self-Concept

One of the most important implications of the attitudes and values that you hold is how you apply them to the perceptions you have about yourself. Many of the messages you communicate intrapersonally reflect your perceptions of yourself. *Self-concept* can be defined as *the complex set of attitudes we have about ourselves.* Your self-concept is the most influential part of your frame of reference and, thus, is a major determiner of your goals and expectations for any communicative situation.

We usually develop our self-concept as a process of comparing ourselves to others (I am tall, I am fat, I am smart, and so on) and by accepting the opinions of others who are important to us ("You're such a helpful person"; "You're such a quiet person"; "Isn't she cute when she . . ."). It is very challenging to sort out the messages we and others send in order to develop a realistic self-concept. As you try to sort out messages about yourself, two observations might be helpful. First, *others' reactions to you are based on their frames of reference.* They are actually saying more about themselves and what they value than about you. We are not suggesting that you disregard others' comments about you, but that you consider "where they're coming from" and try to determine the appropriateness of their values and attitudes for you. For example, someone may comment, "You're selfish," when you choose not to let them borrow something of yours. First of all, it would be helpful to recode his or her statement into "this person thinks I'm selfish" to clarify that this is an opinion not necessarily accurate. Then determine what attitude or value that person might hold that would lead to such a statement. He/she might feel that "good people are those who share everything with others." If this attitude is one that you feel is appropriate for you, you might wish to reconsider your behavior. If not, it explains how that person made the assessment of you. However, it would not be an appropriate feeling to accept as part of your self-concept.

The other observation is that *many of your perceptions of yourself were developed at a time when you were not in the best position to determine the appropriateness of the message.* It is very difficult to think back and determine where and how you developed a certain perception of yourself. Because of this you may have inappropriate feelings about yourself, your abilities, and your acceptability to others.

These feelings about yourself do exist, however, and they have a strong influence on your intrapersonal, interpersonal, and public messages—both the ones you send and the ones you receive. Consider students who think of themselves as "shy people who don't express themselves well," and an instructor on the first day of class asks for volunteers to lead discussion groups. These people would probably not volunteer and, if assigned to that task, may use various compensating behaviors depending on the strength of their self-perceptions.

Learning Experience

Write down five adjectives *you* would use at this point in your life to describe yourself. Beside each adjective, briefly describe how you came to see yourself in this way (e.g., comparing yourself to others, what others said about you, and so forth). For each adjective list one way in which it would influence your interacting with a person of the opposite sex whom you had just met. Do you feel the influences you inferred would be positive?

Sharing Our Frame of Reference

We mentioned earlier that one of the reasons for miscommunication and inability to manage conflicts was not understanding your own frame of reference. By now you have taken a major step in developing skills in that area. This is an important factor in meaningful intrapersonal communication. When you move to the levels of interpersonal communication it becomes important to understand the frame of reference of those you are interacting with as well as your own. *The less people know about each other, the easier it is to distort meanings attached to each others' symbols.* However, if you can decode and think about other people's messages in terms of their frame of reference, meanings become more understandable and, if not acceptable, at least discussable. You are then able to communicate meaningfully in spite of the uniqueness of the ways in which each of you perceive the world.

Figure 4, the Johari window,[4] is used to visualize the areas of knowns and unknowns about another person which could exist in an interpersonal communicative situation.

How much you choose to disclose about yourself will likely depend upon the other person, the situation, and your own feelings about yourself and the development of the relationship. However, the openness and meaningfulness of a personal relationship is usually directly related to the degree to which the individuals involved know each other's frames of reference.

In a close relationship the Johari window would perhaps look more like figure 5.

---

4. Reprinted from *Groups Processes: An Introduction to Group Dynamics* by Joseph Luft by permission of Mayfield Publishing Company (formerly National Press Books). Copyright © 1963, 1970 by Joseph Luft.

	Known to self	Not known to self
Known to Others	1 Free to self and others	2 Blind to self, seen by others
Not Known to Others	3 Hidden Area: self hidden from others	4 Unknown self

FIGURE 4

In a more public communicative situation you may feel less of a need to reveal very personal information. However, revealing relevant parts of your frame of reference in public communicative situations can establish a basic credibility which is an important part of having others accept your ideas.

Working toward more self-understanding and more openness with significant others is a vital step to improving the effectiveness of your communication. We realize that it is one thing, however, to talk about what you are willing to share to make communication more meaningful, and quite another thing to consider what the other person might be willing to share. A barrier to the mutual sharing of perceptions is often the trust relationship between those involved.

1	2
3	4

FIGURE 5

Defensiveness and Openness in Human Communication

In a comfortable, open climate, people are more able to disclose their frames of reference and understand another's point of view. Even if there are real differences between people (age, status, point of view, experiences, and so forth) under conditions of openness, people are more capable of dealing with those differences maturely, without feeling personally threatened.

When trust does not occur between those involved in a communication situation, *the individuals often are more concerned with defending them-*

selves rather than understanding and interacting with the other person. Usually a new relationship begins with communication probes which are meant to determine the level of trust and openness which is possible in this relationship. The probes usually are made without much conscious intent and take the form of openers such as "What's your major?" "Did you have psychology class with _____?" "Do you know _____?" These questions are not just for the purpose of information (and are perhaps not at all for that purpose), but are attempts to establish rapport and are actually saying, "What are you like? Can I trust you?"

We have all been in communication situations where we feel on edge with the person with whom we are interacting. We also have all been on the other side of that relationship (but have not so readily recognized the discomfort). For example, we intend to help, be friendly, establish a contact, and are not quite sure why we are turning off the other person . . . why the other person is defensive, irritable. Many of these responses we have to others and others have to us are based on the kind of overall communication behaviors we use in our interaction with them.

Jack Gibb has done extensive research regarding communication behaviors which tend to create defensiveness and those which tend to reduce it and to create trust and lead to openness. After an eight-year study of recordings of interpersonal discussions, Gibb identified six communication behaviors as leading to defensiveness and six opposite communication behaviors as reducing defensiveness and leading to a supportive, trusting relationship.[5] As you consider each set of opposites think of your own communication behavior and that of others. Which climates are you usually involved in when you interact with others? Which climates are more typically used by people you really feel comfortable with?

Characteristics of Defensive and Supportive Communication Climates and Verbal Indicators

Communication Behaviors Leading to Defensiveness

1. *Evaluation*—to make a judgment about something; to blame or praise based on one's values; to make moral assessments of another; to question standards, values, and motives of another. Use of words like "good," "bad," "right," "wrong." **Example:** "That was a dumb thing to do."

2. *Control*—direct attempts to make other people do what you want them to; to attempt to change an attitude or the behavior of others

Communication Behaviors Leading to Supportiveness

1. *Description*—nonjudgmental; to ask questions which are perceived as genuine requests for information; to present feelings, perceptions, or processes which do not ask or imply that the receiver change behavior or attitude. **Example:** "I feel good when you compliment me."

2. *Problem Orientation*—to communicate a desire to work with someone; to define a problem and seek a solution; to imply that you have

---

5. Jack Gibb, "Defensive Communication," *Journal of Communication* 11 (1964): 141–48.

Characteristics of Defensive and Supportive Communication Climates and Verbal Indicators

Communication Behaviors Leading to Defensiveness	*Communication Behaviors Leading to Supportiveness*
—to try to restrict others' fields of activity or choices (implied in attempts to change others is that they are now inadequate). Use of words like "should," "ought to," and "need to." **Example:** "If you don't give that back, I'll call the police."	no preconceived solution, attitude, or method to impose; to allow others to set their own goals, make their own decisions, and evaluate their own progress or to share with you in doing so. **Example:** "Let's see if we can find a solution."
3. *Strategy*—to be dishonest with someone; indirect attempts to manipulate others; to use tricks to involve another. **Example:** "I'd love to go to the movie with you if I don't have to go home." (knowing you're waiting for a better offer).	3. *Spontaneity*—to be direct and honest about your motives and meanings; to communicate that you have no hidden motives directed toward that person. **Example:** "I'd like you to go to the store with me because I need a ride and you have a car."
4. *Neutrality*—to express a lack of concern for others; to communicate a detached, "indifferent" attitude. **Example:** "I'm really too busy to listen to you."	4. *Empathy*—to express understanding others; to identify with problems, share feelings, and accept emotions at face value. **Example:** "I think I understand how difficult this is for you."
5. *Superiority*—to communicate the attitude that you are better than the other person as a human being; to raise feelings of inadequacy in the other. Use of self-references and comparative terms. **Example:** "You'd better let me do it. I'll do it right."	5. *Equality*—to communicate respect for the equal human worth of another person; to attach little importance to differences in talent, ability, worth, appearance, status, and power. Use of plural pronouns (e.g., "we"). **Example:** "We'll work well together on this."
6. *Certainty*—to appear dogmatic; to seem to already know all the answers and be unwilling to change; needing to win an argument rather than solve a problem; seeing your own ideas as "truths" to be defended. Use of symbols like "obviously," "certainly." **Example:** "Obviously the man was guilty."	6. *Provisionalism*—to use appropriate qualifiers in your statements suggesting openness to change; to be willing to reconsider your own behavior, attitudes, and ideas; to investigate issues rather than take sides. Use of tentative language (e.g., "it seems like," "as far as I know"). **Example:** "Based on what I've read in *Newsweek,* his data is inaccurate."

Add other examples of each behavior from your own experiences.

As was indicated in chapter 2, nonverbal messages have a greater effect when communicating feelings than verbal messages. Also, when there is a difference in verbal and nonverbal messages, nonverbal messages are the ones that are believed. Sometimes people do not intend to communicate in ways that create defensiveness, but they do so anyway. By observing their nonverbals and by observing the nonverbals of the receivers of the communication, we can tell when feelings of defensiveness are happening. *Defensiveness-producing communication behaviors will often result in hostility* indicated by hands on hips, leaning forward, accentuated vocal emphasis, use of pauses, changed personal distance, extended eye contact or will result in the reactions described in chart 1. Because *defensive-climate-reducing communication often is characterized by empathic involvement and equality,* the nonverbals of both people will probably be very similar.

CHART 1.   *Nonverbal symbols which increase and decrease defensiveness and the responding communicator's nonverbal reactions*

Sender	Receiver	Sender and Receiver
Certainty	*(Uncertainty)*	*Provisionalism*
direct eye contact crossed arms hands on hips	lack of eye contact turning body away leaning back jerky body movements wringing hands body tension	nodding head head tilted to side eye contact
Superiority	*(Inferiority)*	*Equality*
long eye contact hands on hips large desk in office formal setting higher elevation	lack of eye contact hanging head silence wringing hands body tension	warm colors slower body movements leaning forward eye contact informal setting same elevation
Evaluation	*(Devaluation)*	*Description*
long eye contact pointing hands on hips shaking head shaking index finger	increasing personal distance body tension jerky body movements leaning back wringing hands	slower body movements leaning forward eye contact
Neutrality	*(Unconcerned)*	*Empathy*
legs crossed away monotone voice	lack of eye contact leaning back	pleasant background sounds

CHART 1—*continued*

Sender	Receiver	Sender and Receiver
staring somewhere else	legs crossed away	decreasing personal distance
cool colors	wringing hands	eye contact
leaning back	body tension	warm colors
body distance of 4½ to 5 feet		legs crossed toward
		nodding head
		personal distance of 20–36 inches
Control	*(Manipulated)*	*Problem Orientation*
sitting in focal seat	lack of eye contact	decreasing personal distance
hands on hips	turning body away	legs crossed toward
shaking head	wringing hands	leaning forward
long eye contact	body tension	eye contact
firm voice		
Strategy	*(Manipulated)*	*Spontaneity*
shaking head	leaning back	leaning forward
long eye contact	lack of eye contact	legs crossed toward
	turning body away	eye contact
	wringing hands	animated natural gestures
	body tension	

Nonverbal cues become increasingly important as we consider the number of "games people play" with each other. Although it is occasionally the case that a person may send insincere verbal cues, it is much more difficult to control one's nonverbal behavior—especially to do so consistently over a period of time. For example, people may be displaying a lack of concern by the comments they are making, such as "Oh, who cares what he thinks anyway!" At the same time they may be revealing body tension and wringing of hands, suggesting that perhaps they really do care about the reaction of the third person being discussed.

Several considerations modify the typical reactions to the twelve communication behaviors described by Gibb. First, *people's reactions are based on how they perceive the other's communication behaviors.* Constant attention to verbal and nonverbal feedback provides an indication of how that other person is perceiving one's communication behaviors. Building from the discussion of nonverbals in chapter 2, it would be possible that the words one is saying would be supportive, but one's nonverbal tone of voice, body positioning, use of space, eye contact, etc., would increase defensiveness. For example, if a person says, "I'm really interested in your opinion," but disinterest is communicated nonverbally by a lack of eye contact and by turning away from the other person, then defensiveness is likely to increase.

A second qualification is that while the types of communicative behavior generally lead to the kind of reactions indicated, the particular reaction can be significantly influenced by the communication setting and the nature of the people's interpersonal relationship.

Finally, the *communicative behaviors can function together and partially neutralize the effect of each other.* For example, there may be situations where evaluation is given, but the receiver considers the communicator an equal and feels cared about and understood. In such a situation the negative effect of the evaluation can be somewhat neutralized.

Learning Experience

Consider the following communication situation, in light of communication behaviors and barriers:

A father is talking to his son about the son's poor mid-semester college grades. He charges, "You've blown it again; I never had less than a 3.0 when I was in college." Crossing his arms over his chest, he says in a firm voice, "Until your grades come up, you will leave your car at home."

Note any examples of supportive communication behaviors? How about defensive communication behaviors?

Did you note the following: "You've blown it again" (evaluation); "I never had less than a 3.0" (superiority); "You will leave your car at home" (control). There are also nonverbal indications of the father's certainty that he has the correct approach (e.g., crossing arms over chest and talking in a firm voice.) How much different the interaction might have been if the father's message had sounded more like this:

"Looks like your grades are lower than you anticipated they'd be (description). I understand how you must feel (empathy). I felt uncomfortable, too, when I saw them. What do you think might be a workable approach to doing something about it? Maybe I could help (problem orientation)."

What a change! We think you, too, will gain great benefits and be somewhat surprised if you try to be consciously aware of the climate which you use verbally and nonverbally when you interact with others.

It is often challenging to develop a supportive climate for communication, especially in a potentially hostile situation. However, the development of this skill may be the most important step in improving your communication with others.

An important part of developing a supportive climate is being willing to describe and express your own feelings at a given time, but not expressing those feelings as though you were implying fault with the other person. Consider the difference between the following expressions of feeling:

"You make me angry when you shout at me!"
   and
"I feel angry when you shout at me."

The first evaluates—places blame on the other person. The second describes your own feelings and leaves open the possibility that your anger is an inappropriate response.

Learning Experience

Write down (on a piece of paper) an area of disagreement you have with someone you live with. Write a short dialogue which you might say to that person describing how you feel about yourself, him/her, and your interaction related to this area of disagreement. Write this as you might say it in an argument with this person.

Identify in the written dialogue examples of statements which (using Gibb's communication behaviors) would be likely to encourage defensiveness. After identifying all defensiveness-producing statements, substitute alternative statements which would be examples of behaviors Gibb suggests would reduce defensiveness.

At the next appropriate opportunity, communicate your defensiveness-reducing dialogue to the person involved. Compare his/her reaction to previous reactions during arguments over this area.

Discuss the alternative approaches with the person and try to interact on this issue using only trust-producing communication behaviors. Write down some of your conclusions.

Developing supportive communication climates is an important skill in both interpersonal and public communicative situations. It is a major factor in facilitating the sharing of perceptions which lead to more accurate communication of meanings and resulting management of conflict situations.

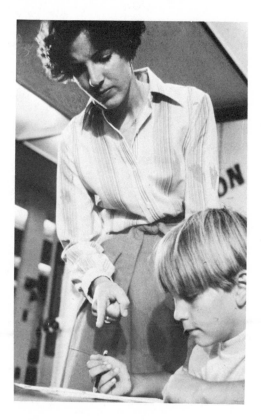

Chapter 4

Representing Communication in a Model

Objectives

Your learning should enable you to:

1. Define communication situation.
2. Define communication barrier.
3. Draw a model of communication.
4. Explain how communication situations could influence communication.
5. Describe an example of a personally experienced communication barrier. Identify it, correct it, and develop a personal recommendation to avoid it in the future.

I. A Model of Human Communication
   A. Models are attempts to visualize the components and processes involved and how they're related
   B. Sequential model does not reflect dynamism of communication
      1. Messages are continually sent and received by all communicators
      2. Steps of the process are often bypassed
      3. Internal steps constantly adjusted by new messages received
   C. Sequential model useful for understanding basic process and relationships among components
   D. Figure 6 represents one model of communication

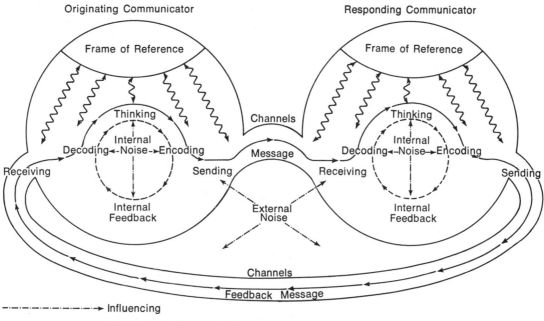

FIGURE 6.   *A model of the communication process*

II. Components and Processes in communication model
   A. The originating communicator: the sender of the original message and the receiver of feedback messages
   B. The responding communicator: the receiver of the original message, and the responder to it by feedback messages
   C. Encoding: the process of translating personal meanings into symbols
   D. Channel: the means through which stimuli are sent and received between communicators; available channels are the five human senses: sight, sound, smell, taste, touch

   E. Receiving: the physical process of message reception

   F. Decoding: the process of attaching personal meanings to received symbols; may involve recoding: tranlating the decoded meanings into a more usable form

   G. Thinking: further processing of the decoded message; varies with the thinking style of the communicator: structural, comparative, or relational

   H. Remembering: the process by which information is retrieved from the frame of reference (continual process which influences each step)

   I. Sending: the physical process of message expression

   J. Message: the encoded symbols which stand for the meaning intended by the communicator; four potential messages in communication
      1. Intended message: what the sender wanted to communicate
      2. Actual message: what the sender actually communicated; all the symbols sent
      3. Received message: what the receiver actually received after selective attention
      4. Interpreted message: the meanings which the receiver attached to the message

   K. Feedback message: the symbols sent by the responding communicator to the originating communicator as a response to the original message sent; it enables originating communicator to make corrections in original message

   L. Frame of Reference: the unique interrelationship of a person's stored information, important needs, and perceptions of the situation for a given communicative situation

   M. Noise: any distracting stimuli, occurring anywhere in the process of communication
      1. External noise: happening outside a person
      2. Internal noise: happening within a person

III. Relationships of components and processes
   A. Receiving results in symbols
   B. Decoding results in meanings
   C. Thinking results in ideas, feelings, reactions to messages
   D. Encoding results in symbols
   E. Sending results in messages

IV. Communication situation: the entire circumstances in which communication takes place
   A. Influence on communication
      1. Who may talk to whom
      2. What may be discussed
      3. Level of formality
      4. Time limits on communication
      5. Comfortableness of participants
   B. Aspects of communication situation
      1. Initial relationship between communicators
      2. Sounds present
      3. Physical furnishings
      4. Time of day
      5. Organizational context

V. Adaptation of model
   A. Intrapersonal communication visualized as communication within a person; originating communicator and responding communicator could visualize two roles which one person has
   B. Public communication would have one originating communicator with many responding communicators (greatly increases the number of channels involved)

VI. Communication Barriers: anything which inhibits or blocks accurate communication
   A. Barriers identified by number in model of communication (figure 7)
   B. Originating and Responding communicator viewed as one communicator
      1) and 6) Potential barriers associated with the communicator's encoding a personal meaning into message symbols appropriate for sending

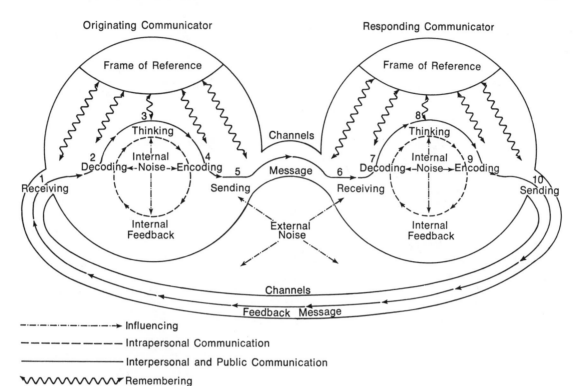

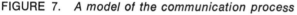

FIGURE 7. *A model of the communication process*

        a) Not thinking through intended meaning
        b) Disregard for other's frame of reference
        c) Sending inappropriate amount of symbols
        d) Lack of experience with symbol system
        e) Disregard for communication situation
        f) Inappropriate choice of symbols
        g) Inappropriate channel
        h) Internal noise
        i) External noise
2) and 6) Potential barriers associated with physical process of sending messages
        a) Inaccurately produced message
           (1) Faulty mechanisms
           (2) Carelessness
        b) Disregard of nonverbal messages
        c) Internal noise
        d) External noise
3) and 8) Potential barriers associated with physical process of receiving messages
        a) Inaccurately received messages
           (1) Faulty mechanisms
           (2) Carelessness
        b) Internal noise
        c) External noise
4) and 9) Potential barriers associated with decoding messages
        a) Lack of experience with symbol system

      b) Disregard of cues associated with intended meanings

      c) Attaching meaning to meaningless cues

      d) Internal noise

      e) External noise

5) and 10) Potential barriers associated with the process of thinking about decoded meanings

      a) Not choosing appropriate pattern of thinking

      b) Skipping this step inappropriately

      c) Faulty processing of meaning due to selective processing

      d) Distortion of self-concept

      e) Internal noise

      f) External noise

We have been talking about *human communication* as *the dynamic, unique process of calling up meaning by the use of symbols.* You've considered the basic encoding and decoding processes by which symbols are attached to meanings and meanings are attached to received verbal and nonverbal symbols. Further, you've considered the complexity which individual perceptions add to these processes. The uniqueness of communication makes it a challenging study. However, even though people, situations, and meanings change, there are certain components that are always involved in human communication. We have found that if we understand the components that are always present, we are better able to understand and deal with specific communicative interchanges in our everyday lives.

To understand a complex process, such as human communication, it helps to represent it in visual form. Let's try to put together what we've been saying about human communication into a representative model of that process. That model can then be a helpful reference as you develop skills which use the process in meaningful communicative interactions. Many models have been used to describe communication. They attempt to represent the common components and processes in a diagram, which visualizes what happens when people communicate. You might stop reading at this point and build your own model which represents how you see the processes we've talked about. As you work include any additional components and processes you want to. You might start with a pencil and paper model and then move to building a three-dimensional model which will allow more freedom in representing the dynamic nature of communication.

After completing your model, you may share it with others involved in this study and develop a group model. Your instructor may also share with you other models which have been developed to represent human communication. Compare the differences in what was included and how the relationships among components and processes were visualized.

A Model of Communication

Figure 8 represents a model of communication which has been useful to us in our growing understanding of this complex process. We had difficulty, as you probably did, trying to represent on a flat sheet of paper the many components and processes which occur. Such a representation seems to suggest that everything is neat and orderly with each step happening sequentially. However, we know that messages are continually sent and received; that often steps of the process, such as thinking, are bypassed; and that internal steps are constantly adjusted by new messages received. Nevertheless, we have found value in representing sequentially a basic process and, through the explanation which follows and our use of the

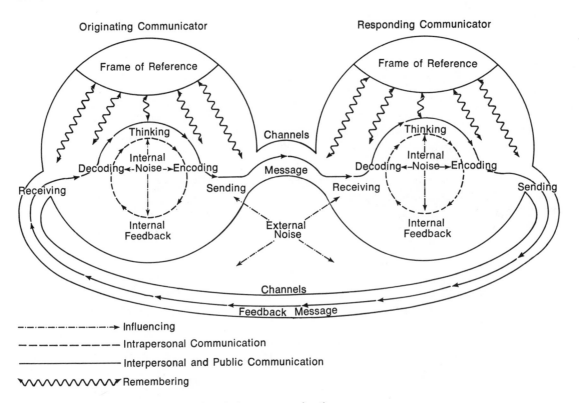

FIGURE 8. *A model of the communication process*

model in later skill areas, suggest the dynamic and unique way in which it functions in everyday communication.

Communication Components and Processes

There are at least thirteen components and/or processes involved in all human communication. The following explanation of these components and processes is done in terms of communication between two individuals. However, the same components and processes are involved if the model represents a person talking intrapersonally or interpersonally. We'll then consider adaptations of the model for intrapersonal and public communication.

The originating communicator.   The sender of the original message and the receiver of feedback. This more encompassing term is used rather than "sender" or "speaker" because, as is indicated in the definition, this person (or group of persons) is also a receiver and listener. The originator receives feedback from others and receives his or her own messages internally, e.g., you hear yourself speak.

The responding communicator.   The receiver of the original message and the responder to it. Similar to the originating communicator, this more encompassing term is used rather than "receiver" or "listener" because this person is also a sender and speaker. The responding communicator sends feedback messages as a response to the messages received. The responding communicator is named to describe the response role. This role is determined by the chronological occurrence of someone else initiating the communication. Actually as indicated earlier, people are simultaneously assuming the roles of originating and responding communicators.

Encoding. The process of translating personal meanings into symbols. Often this step occurs quite rapidly when you are using well-known symbols or do not have much at stake. Otherwise, the process becomes more conscious and time-consuming. For example, you would likely encode messages while casually talking with a friend much more quickly than in explaining to your boss your reasons for not arriving at work on time.

Channel. The means through which stimuli are sent and received between communicators. The available channels correspond to the human senses. "Speech" primarily travels between people through the senses of sound and sight.

Receiving. The physical process of message reception. Any of the receiving senses can be used. For example, using the eyes to see a hand motion or the ears to hear sounds.

Decoding. The process of attaching personal meanings to received symbols. The ability to denotatively attach an appropriate meaning to a symbol is dependent upon what you remember from your frame of reference. For example, if you have not stored necessary information for understanding the French language, you will not be able to attach meaning to

French phrases. In some situations there may be a second step here which has been called "recoding." Essentially recoding involves translating the decoded meanings into a more usable form. This sometimes happens in listening to people with dialects or from a foreign country. Many people, because of being unsure of the metric system, recode Celsius temperatures into Fahrenheit temperatures.

Thinking.   After the received message is decoded, further processing usually occurs. Such further processing is influenced by the individual's frame of reference and may take many forms, depending on the nature of the communicative situation and the thinking style of the communicator. Typical forms of thinking include structural thinking (e.g., an instant liking), comparative thinking (e.g., using similarities and differences), and relational thinking (e.g., using examples).

Remembering.   The process by which information is retrieved from the frame of reference. The better developed a person's skills in remembering, the more information he or she will be able to use in communicating intrapersonally and interpersonally. The remembering process is a continual one which influences each "step" of the communication process.

Sending.   The physical process of message expression. Any of the five senses can be used. For example, using the muscles to wave a hand or using the diaphragm, vocal cords, and lips to pronounce a word, applying perfume before a date, serving highly seasoned food to someone you know likes it, or shaking hands when you meet a business acquaintance.

Message.   The encoded symbols which stand for the meaning intended by the communicator. Actually, at least four messages potentially exist in interpersonal communications, more if more than two people are involved. The *intended message* is what the originating communicator wanted to communicate. The *actual message* is the totality of the communicated symbols which were actually sent. The actual message is always more than the intended message and the received message. The *received message* is what the responding communicator actually received. He or she may not have been sensitive to all potential cues and as a result of selective attention may only receive part of the actual message. Finally, the *interpreted message* which is screened by the responding communicator's frame of reference leads to a necessarily different message than the intended or the actual. These fundamental differences provide the basis for many misunderstandings in communication.

Feedback Messages.   The messages sent by the responding communicator to the originating communicator as a response to the original message sent. These responses become communication when received by the originating communicator and thus serve as a basis for correction of a given message by the originating communicator. Feedback messages are actually no different from messages which the originating communicator sends.

"Feedback" is used to denote that this message functions as a reaction which is "fed back" to the originating communicator.

Draw three doodles of similar complexity on a piece of paper. Have another person take a blank piece of paper and pencil. Do not let this person see your doodle. Sit with your back to this person and carefully give oral instructions to this person so that s/he can reproduce one of your doodles on the sheet of paper. The other person may not give you feedback in any way. After completion, compare the doodles. Now face each other. Repeat the same process with another doodle with the difference that the other person may now send feedback to you through all nonverbal (nonword) channels. Again, repeat the process with your last doodle with the difference that the other person may send feedback through any of the channels. Compare each of the reproductions of the doodle with the original. How were the three experiences different? in quality of reproduction? in both of your feelings toward it? Talk about this experience in terms of the "corrective function of feedback." Talk about your real-life interaction with other people in terms of these three kinds of experiences and the "corrective function of feedback." Write down some conclusions as a result of this experience.

Learning Experience

Frame of reference. The unique interrelationship of a person's stored information, important needs, and perceptions of the situation for a given communicative experience. Each person involved in communication has a personal frame of reference through which interactions are filtered. The frame of reference is functioning in a given communicative experience in terms of personal assumptions, expectations, and goals.

Noise. Any distracting stimuli, occurring anywhere in the process of communication. The communicative process is affected by both *external noise,* happening outside of the persons involved in a communicative experience (e.g., traffic noises, background music) and *internal noise,* those distractions occurring within persons involved in a communicative experience (e.g., thinking about something unrelated to the exchange, overconcern with something *about* another communicator rather than what that person is attempting to communicate).

We receive messages with our eyes every minute they're open. Often in doing so, we're less aware of other senses. Consider your communication today or yesterday.
Write two examples of external noise you experienced.

Write two examples of internal noise you experienced.

Learning Experience

These thirteen elements are involved in any communicative experience. They interact and affect each other. Chart 2 might help to indicate some of the relationships within a communicator.

CHART 2

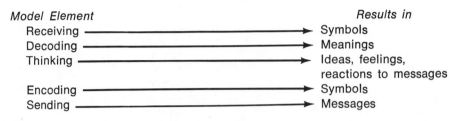

Model Element   *Results in*
   Receiving ———————————————————→ Symbols
   Decoding ————————————————————→ Meanings
   Thinking —————————————————————→ Ideas, feelings,
                                                     reactions to messages
   Encoding ————————————————————→ Symbols
   Sending —————————————————————→ Messages

Using these elements, the process of communication can be described verbally.

The originating communicator, motivated by the meanings from some decoded external or internal stimulus and influenced by his or her own frame of reference, encodes a message to communicate some meaning to another person or persons. The person selects a channel(s) to communicate those symbols and sends it. The symbol(s) and channel(s) may be subconsciously selected. Some or all of these symbols are received by the responding communicator and will be decoded and thought about in terms of his or her frame of reference, and some meanings will be attached. Some form of feedback will be sent to the originating communicator through a chosen channel after the responding communicator translates his or her response into a message. If the feedback is received, the originating communicator may use it to send further messages and the process will continue. During the interchange, noise, usually both internal and external distractors, will minimize the likelihood that the interpreted message is similar to the intended message.

When examining a specific communication event by the use of a communication model, we can describe either the overall interaction or a specific interaction as in stopping a film to look at a single frame.

Using the Model

Let us now consider a very simple example of a specific interaction and follow it through each step of the communication model.

Don (the originating communicator) walks past a movie theater and sees an advertisement for a movie. Don is receiving verbal and pictorial stimuli. Don decodes the stimuli, thus attaching meanings both denotatively (what the stimuli represent) and connotatively (how he feels about them). Through remembering information from his frame of reference, his past experiences of attending movies lead Don to the translation of the code—that it is an advertisement for an upcoming movie. Don's past pleasurable experiences at movies (e.g., in terms of the movie and companionship of people he was with) and his attitudes about this specific movie from newspaper reviews and friends' opinions lead to the association of positive connotative meanings. Because these stimuli are very familiar to Don, the process seems automatic to him. Don thinks about these decoded meanings and based on memory associations makes a decision that asking Donna to go with him

to this movie would be pleasurable. Don, through this complex interaction with his frame of reference and the personal meanings attached while decoding the stimuli, is motivated to encode a message which hopefully will result in Donna's accompanying him to the movie. In his mind he considers options of how he will phrase the message ("Hey, babe, let's see this great show," "I know it's late but . . . ," etc.). He also considers the appropriate channel for sending the message (e.g., phone, letter, direct contact). After completing his encoding decisions, Don calls Donna, the responding communicator. She receives the message by the medium of telephone and her sense of hearing. During the process of sending and receiving, a friend enters Don's house and asks to borrow a book, creating a brief distracting stimulus (external noise). Donna misses many potential message cues because the interaction is not face-to-face. Influenced by information remembered from her frame of reference, Donna decodes the message, attaching meanings to the received symbols. Because she is familiar with the symbol system and the specific symbols Don has chosen, she attaches denotative meanings quite similar to those which Don intended. Because of a past pleasant experience with Don and positive attitudes toward the movie, she attaches positive connotative meanings to the messages received. Her con-

cern over where her roommate is causes some internal distraction (internal noise). Donna processes the decoded meanings and thinks about them, and because she has a highly developed comparative thinking skill, she compares going to the movie with Don with her other options for activity this evening.

She is then motivated to encode a message which communicates to Don that she would like to go to the movie with him. She will consider how she will phrase her message and what tone of voice she will use. Since the telephone medium has already been chosen, she will use it. She then sends the encoded feedback message which is received through the phone by Don. This received feedback message becomes another stimulus for Don and the process will likely run through several "loops" of the model before it is terminated.

By using the basic concepts suggested by a model of communication, we can better consider the intricacies of specific communicative experiences. The uniqueness of a communicative experience can be understood by considering the situation in which it occurred.

Consider, by yourself or in a discussion with others, the complexities of a communicative interchange between the U.S. Secretary of State and the Arabian Ambassador as leaders in two powerful, but different, governments. These very different frames of reference would lead to very different values, expectations, and goals for a given interaction. Write down several of your observations about the elements of communication functioning in an interaction between the Secretary and Arabia's Ambassador.

Communication Situation

The communication situation refers to the entire circumstances in which communication takes place. This includes the initial relationship between the communicators, sounds present, other people not directly involved, time, lighting, colors, odors, physical furnishings, and perhaps an organizational context in which the communication occurs. The communication situation can influence who may talk to whom, what may be discussed, the level of formality, comfortableness of participants, and time limits placed on interaction.

We all use the implications of the situation in our interactions with others. You learned quite early when was the best time and place to ask your parents for a favor. If you want to have a serious discussion with someone, you know that some times and places seem to make it easier to talk. Finally, you send some messages privately to friends which you wouldn't send if strangers were present.

Therefore, different meanings may be associated with a message depending on the setting in which it is communicated. The awareness and sensitivity to this variable alone could improve the accuracy and effectiveness of human interaction. Consider how differently you would react if someone asked you, "Is college as exciting as you thought it would be?" (1) after a difficult exam, (2) when you first got up in the morning, (3) just after meeting an interesting new person, or (4) just after an exciting discussion. Also consider how differently you would react if the question were asked by (1) a close friend, (2) your father, or (3) a teacher.

"WHAT TIMING!"

Intrapersonal Communication

As visualized by the dashed lines in figure 8, intrapersonal communication occurs within a person as you "talk" and listen to yourself. By visualizing this internal process as such, its continual role in our communication with others is suggested. The entire model could also be useful for viewing intrapersonal communication by labeling the originating communicator and responding communicator as two different roles which are part of your life. For example, you might represent the originating communicator as "my role in a love relationship with _____," and the responding communicator as "my role as student at _____ school." Communication within yourself from each of these two perspectives could be considered.

Sometimes it is difficult to be aware of the messages we send to ourselves. Increased attention is being paid to helping individuals develop skills in decoding their own intrapersonal messages through procedures such as biofeedback.

Public Communication

When we use the term *public communication* we are referring to one person sending messages to a number of responding communicators who are in direct visual and aural contact with that person. Thus, there is an increased number of channels and messages involved. The originating communicator will be sending a message and receiving nonverbal feedback messages from each of the responding communicators. Skill Area Three will help you develop skills in becoming an originating communicator in both public and interpersonal communicative situations.

Communication Barriers

A *communication barrier* can be defined as *anything which inhibits or blocks accurate communication.* Trying to isolate or categorize the many reasons why people fail to communicate accurately is a difficult challenge.

We will use our model to focus on potential areas of misunderstanding and identify the basic places in the communication process where barriers are likely. From this perspective we will be better able to look back at any given communication event or plan for future communication and focus on potential areas of misunderstanding. An essential concept is that *communication barriers can happen in or between any component in the communication process.*

Figure 9 visualizes what happens when people communicate. Numbers 1–10 indicate the key points where barriers are most likely to occur. A discussion of the main barriers follows. You probably will be able to add to those indicated here based on your own model and experiences.

We will start with the communicator's encoding of the message. Because all people use the same components in communication, we will consider the

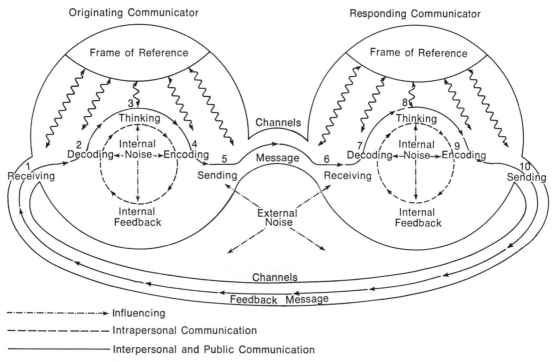

Influencing

---------- Intrapersonal Communication

_____ Interpersonal and Public Communication

WWWWWWW Remembering

FIGURE 9. *A model of the communication process*

originating communicator and the responding communicator together as a "communicator."

1) and 6) POTENTIAL BARRIERS ASSOCIATED WITH THE COMMUNICATOR'S ENCODING A PERSONAL MEANING INTO MESSAGE SYMBOLS APPROPRIATE FOR SENDING:

   a. *Not fully thinking through a personal meaning.* Perhaps from lack of experience, contrary attitudes or not taking the time to clarify personal values, this person's meaning is not clear in her or his own mind.

   b. *Disregard for the frame of reference, role or status of the person, or persons, to whom the message is being sent.* For example, not recognizing the difference between greeting a close friend and greeting the president of a university, not taking into consideration that the other person is uncomfortable in the communication situation, or not recognizing that the other person has no experience or knowledge in the area the communicator is talking about.

   c. *Sending too much or too little information in one message.* The appropriate amount would be dependent upon the idea being talked about, the person you are interacting with, and the demands of the particular situation.

   d. *Lack of experience with the symbol system.* Consider trying to use a language other than your own or joining a new group and being unsure of the in-group meanings.

  e. *Disregard for the situation in which communication is taking place.* Not adapting to special sending and receiving behaviors necessary for a given situation, such as criticizing someone's education at his or her graduation or not choosing a place appropriate to the type of of interaction for that event.

  f. *Careless or calculated choice of inappropriate symbols.* The use of abstract symbols where concrete would be more accurate would be an example. Oversimplification, generalization, and exaggeration are other examples.

  g. *Inappropriate channel chosen or too few channels chosen.* An example might be explaining a math problem over the telephone.

  h. *Internal noise* such as thinking about other things or feeling uncomfortable in the situation. (Note: this type of barrier would influence any of the processes.)

  i. *External noise* such as environmental stimuli which distract the responding communicator's attention such as a favorite song or unpleasant air conditioner noises. (Note: this type of barrier could influence any of the processes.)

2) and 7) POTENTIAL BARRIERS ASSOCIATED WITH THE PHYSICAL PROCESS OF THE COMMUNICATOR SENDING A MESSAGE.

  a. *Inaccurately produced message due to faulty message-sending mechanisms.* This potential barrier would include individuals with speech or physical impediments or one using an unfamiliar symbol system in which the sounds are difficult to pronounce.

  b. *Inadequately produced message due to careless message sending.* This barrier would include talking too fast to be understood, talking too softly or too loudly depending on the listener and the situation. Sometimes in talking with people from other countries who have trouble understanding English, we talk louder as if they had a hearing problem instead of slower to allow them additional time for translation.

  c. *Disregard of nonverbal messages being sent* with verbal messages so that there is contradiction or confusion among messages. For example, saying "I'm very comfortable here" and sitting with a tensed body posture.

  d. *Internal noise*

  e. *External noise*

3) and 8) POTENTIAL BARRIERS ASSOCIATED WITH THE PHYSICAL PROCESS OF THE COMMUNICATOR RECEIVING A MESSAGE.

  a. *Inaccurately received messages due to faulty message-receiving mechanisms.* These potential barriers would include someone being deaf or hard of hearing, blind or having some sight problems which would screen out certain nonverbal and nonoral messages. Messages could also be missed due to poor skill development in sending or receiving skills through that sense.

    b. *Inaccurately received message due to careless receiving behaviors or selective perception.* These barriers would include not listening carefully, looking away, or ignoring nonverbal clues which give additional cues to the meaning intended. The absence of carefully chosen listening procedures is a typical example.
    c. *Internal noise*
    d. *External noise*

4) and 9) POTENTIAL BARRIERS ASSOCIATED WITH THE PROCESS OF THE COMMUNICATOR DECODING THE MESSAGE RECEIVED.
    a. *Lack of experience with the symbol system used by the originating communicator.* Examples would include foreign languages and technical terms used by a stereo components salesperson.
    b. *Disregard of cues associated with the meaning intended.* Examples would include not being aware of nonverbal communication or not remembering to relate a previous idea due to selective attention.
    c. *Attaching meaning to meaningless or unrelated cues.* An example would be focusing on a person's physical appearance or hair style.

5) and 10) POTENTIAL BARRIERS ASSOCIATED WITH THE PROCESS OF THE COMMUNICATOR THINKING ABOUT THE MEANINGS ATTACHED TO THE MESSAGE SYMBOLS.
    a. *Not choosing an appropriate pattern of thinking for processing input.* For example, applying a rule when making relationships would be more appropriate or the reverse (as in stopping to contemplate a message such as "Duck!"). Another example is people not using criteria in making important choices.
    b. *Skipping this "step."* Many times individuals react to decoded meanings without the benefit of further consideration. Such snap decisions are often less meaningful than reactions preceded by more careful thinking.
    c. *Faulty interpretation of meanings,* perhaps due to conflicting or very favorable attitudes within the frame of reference due to selective processing. A communicator is not then using all the available information and cues to further process the decoded meanings.
    d. *Self-attitudes which could distort, filter, or prevent the intended message from being understood.* This is often called the "self-fulfilling prophecy."
    e. *Internal noise*
    f. *External noise*

What additional barriers would you add based on the model you developed? How would you overcome each of the barriers?

Additional Learning Sources

Argyle, Michael. *Bodily Communication.* New York: International Universities Press, Inc., 1975.

Austin-Lett, Genelle, and Sprague, Jan. *Talk to Yourself.* Boston: Houghton Mifflin, 1976.

Borden, George, and Stone, John. *Human Communication, The Process of Relating.* Menlo Park, Calif.: Cummings Publishing Co., 1976.

Bourne, Lyle E., Jr. *Human Conceptual Behavior.* Boston: Allyn and Bacon, Inc., 1966.

DeVito, Joseph. *The Interpersonal Communication Book.* New York: Harper and Row, 1976.

Eisenberg, Abne, and Smith, Ralph, Jr. *Nonverbal Communication.* Indianapolis: Bobbs-Merrill Co., Inc., 1971.

Haney, William V. "Perception and Communication" in *Basic Readings in Interpersonal Communication.* Kim Giffin and Bobby R. Patton, eds. New York: Harper and Row, 1971.

Harrison, Randall P. *Beyond Words.* Englewood Cliffs, N.J.: Prentice-Hall, Inc., 1974.

Heun, Linda. "Speech Rating as Self-Evaluative Behavior: Insight and the Influence of Others." Unpublished Ph.D. dissertation, Department of Speech, Southern Illinois University, 1969.

Higbee, Kenneth. *Your Memory, How it Works and How to Improve It.* Englewood Cliffs, N.J.: Prentice-Hall, Inc., 1977.

Johnson, David W. *Reaching Out.* Englewood Cliffs, N.J.: Prentice-Hall, Inc., 1972.

Koneya, Mele, and Barbour, Alton. *Louder Than Words: Nonverbal Communication.* Columbus, Ohio: Charles E. Merrill, 1976.

McCroskey, James; Larson, Carl; and Knapp, Mark. *An Introduction to Interpersonal Communication.* Englewood Cliffs, N.J.: Prentice-Hall, Inc., 1971.

Mehrabian, Albert. *Silent Messages.* Belmont, Calif.: Wadsworth Publishing Co., 1971.

Schnucker, Robert; Heun, Linda; Heun, Richard. *Learning to Learn Better.* Kirksville, Mo.: Learning Instruction Facilitators, 1977.

Simon, Sidney; Howe, Leland; and Kirschenbaum, Howard. *Values Clarification.* New York: Hart Publishing Co., 1972.

Speer, David, ed. *Nonverbal Communication.* Beverly Hills, Calif.: Sage Publications, Inc., 1972.

Stewart, John. *Bridges Not Walls.* Reading, Mass.: Addison-Wesley Publishing Co., 1973.

Taylor, Anita; Rosegrant, Teresa; Meyer, Arthur; and Samples, B. Thomas. *Communicating.* Englewood Cliffs, N.J.: Prentice-Hall, Inc., 1977.

Wilmot, William. *Dyadic Communication, A Transactional Perspective.* Reading, Mass.: Addison-Wesley Publishing Co., 1975.

Skill Test

This skill test will give you the opportunity to check your communication knowledge and skills in a personal interaction. You and your instructor might want to select a situation which will be the best test for you. We suggest that you might interact with a person quite different from yourself or someone whom you don't know. You will start and maintain an interaction with your chosen person, learning about his or her frame of reference as it relates to the area you choose to talk about. Since a meaningful goal for this skill test is to begin knowing another person, we suggest that you do not tell this person you are doing this for an assignment.

Before your conversation, complete the following precommunication form. When you select a topic on which to interact, keep in mind the likely situation you will choose for the experience (especially if this will be your first interaction with this person). Your instructor may want to talk about your preparation with you before the conversation.

After your conversation, complete the postcommunication form and share it with your instructor.

Skill Test Precommunication Form

Complete this form on other sheets of paper.

1. State your predetermined topic.
2. List three things you will want to discover about the other person's frame of reference in relationship to this topic.
3. List three things you will likely share about your own frame of reference in relation to this topic.
4. State one of your values (or partially developed values) which will likely be reflected in your messages.
5. List two nonverbals which you predict will be present if the other person feels comfortable interacting with you.
6. List two nonverbals which you predict will be present if the other person feels uncomfortable talking with you.
7. List two of Gibb's communication climates which you'll use to establish a sharing relationship.
8. List two potential communication barriers you might experience during your conversation.
9. For each barrier listed, suggest how you might overcome that barrier during the conversation.

Skill Test Postcommunication Form

Complete this form on other sheets of paper.

1. List three or more parts of the other person's frame of reference, related to the topic discussed, which you discovered during the conversation.
2. List three or more parts of your frame of reference, related to the topic discussed, which you revealed during the conversation.
3. List two examples of how the other person's frame of reference influenced his or her communication in this situation.
4. List two examples of how your frame of reference influenced your communication in this situation.
5. Describe one barrier that happened within you during the conversation.
6. Describe one barrier that you infer happened within the other person during the conversation.
7. List two actual nonverbal messages you received which you interpreted as communicating that the person was (or wasn't) comfortable interacting with you.
8. Describe in two or more sentences the degree of accuracy of communication attained in your understanding of each other regarding this topic. (Comment on the degree of similarity of your frames of reference, similarity of symbols used, and the use of feedback for corrective purposes by both of you.)

Skills for the Responding Communicator

Overview

You have come a long way toward understanding the communication process, as well as yourself and others as communicators. This skill area will focus on improving your skills as a responding communicator.

The person on the right in the model of communication (page 55) is called the responding communicator. This person receives message symbols, decodes them, calls up meanings, and processes those meanings. This is often called listening. Then he or she encodes and sends responses which we call feedback messages. This is often described as responding.

Skill Area Two deals with some of the most challenging of communication skills, yet ones which are most taken for granted—listening and responding to messages. The role of the responding communicator is often mistakenly perceived as a more passive role. Yet, it is a difficult, complex, and very active role.

Research reveals that we spend on the average at least 45 percent of our daily communication in listening activities, and that 85 percent of what an individual knows is learned by listening. Yet studies of freshmen in several colleges and universities reveal that they listen at about 25 percent efficiency (i.e., they understand and remember for a short period of time only 25 percent of what they hear).

We have all been in the frustrating situation where not understanding or misremembering directions has led us to do poorly on a test, go out of our way, or lose money. Just as frustrating are the interaction situations when someone insists, "You really didn't hear what I said," or "That's not what I meant at all." Many such misunderstandings stem from poor listening.

Listening is a complex set of skills. Effective listening enables you to paraphrase the originating communicator's message in such a way that the person would accept your paraphrase as an indication that you understood the meanings as intended, both denotative and connotative. Such listening requires attention, interpretation, thought, and imagination because as we all know, "People don't always say exactly what they mean or mean exactly what they say." In order to accurately and sensitively understand what the originating communication means, the listener must pay attention not only to the words, but also to the nonverbal cues and the situation in which the interaction is occurring.

Your overall objective for this skill area is to become a better listener and responder as you communicate with others. The following chapters will assist you in developing skills in a four-step process which will maximize the likelihood that you can accomplish effective listening. These four steps are: (1) specific goal setting and choosing listening procedures; (2) accurate message receiving and decoding; (3) analytical message processing; and (4) purposeful feedback sending. (The physical skills of hearing have not been included as an objective to be learned. If you have problems in this area, please talk with your instructor.)

To translate these understandings into skills, we strongly recommend that you begin applying your understandings each day as you are in the role of a responding communicator. Improved listening skills will pay off for you. After completing this skill area 80 percent of one class scored 100 percent on a commercial listening test.

Definitions

Analysis	The appraisal of a message by the use of criteria.
Communication	The unique, dynamic process of calling up meaning by the use of symbols.
Communication Channel	The means through which messages are sent and received between communicators. Available channels correspond to the human senses.
Criterion (plural: Criteria)	A standard by which something can be assessed. For example, cars might be compared by their miles per gallon.
Decoding	The process of attaching personal meanings to received symbols.
Encoding	The process of translating personal meanings into symbols.
Fact	A statement which can be made only after direct sense experience and is therefore limited to statements about past or present events.
Feedback	The messages sent by the responding communicator to the originating communicator as a response to the original message.
Feedback Goal	What the listener wants the sender to understand about the listener's reactions to the sender's message.
Frame of Reference	The unique interrelationship of a person's stored information, immediate needs, and perception of the situation for a given communicative experience.
Inference	A statement which is a guess, sometimes reasoned, which goes beyond observation.
Listening Goal	What the responding communicator wants to accomplish during a listening experience.
Listening Procedures	The specific behaviors which the responding communicator will do to achieve a personal listening goal.
Meaning	The entire set of denotative and connotative reactions called to mind by a symbol.
Message	The communicated symbols which represent the meaning intended by the communicator.

Metacommunication   Additional symbols which help an individual decode the original message; they are verbal and/or nonverbal symbols and occur before, during, and after the original symbols.

Nonverbal Communication   The process of calling up meaning by nonword symbols.

Receiving   The physical process of message reception. Any of the senses can be used.

Sending   The physical process of message transmission. Any of the senses can be used.

Value   A strongly held attitude which meets the criteria of being prized, carefully chosen, and a consistent basis for action.

Chapter 5

Choosing Listening Goals and Procedures

Objectives

For a listening situation, your learning should enable you to:

1. Set a personally meaningful listening goal.
2. Explain how your listening goal is appropriate for you.
3. State two specific influences that your frame of reference could have on your listening in this situation.
4. Choose three listening procedures which will enable you to accomplish your listening goal for this situation.
5. Explain how each chosen procedure will enable you to accomplish your stated goal.

Outline

I. Types of Listening Situations: distinguished by various levels of listener involvement
  A. Hearing
    1. Example: background noise
    2. Minimum personal involvement
      a) Minimum conscious decoding
      b) Minimum imprint on memory
  B. Listening for Pleasure
    1. Example: listening to music
    2. More conscious receiving and decoding; decoding is largely classification
    3. Limited goal setting
    4. Focus of attention based on listener's frame of reference
  C. Listening for Content
    1. Example: listening to travel directions
    2. High involvement in decoding and remembering (Note taking may be used to aid memory)
    3. Listener has specific listening goal
  D. Listening for Analysis
    1. Example: listening to a salesperson
    2. High involvement in decoding and thinking
    3. Listener has specific listening goal

II. Goal Setting
  A. Listening Goal: the specific result which a responding communicator intends to accomplish in a listening situation
    1. Example: "I want to learn the reasons behind Joe's decision to quit his job."
    2. Maximizes the personal productivity of the experience
    3. Based on important personal needs
    4. Basis for maintaining and refocusing attention
    5. Adjusted during listening as messages change
    6. Used to determine listening success
  B. Guidelines for setting listening goals
    1. How listener wants to be able to use the message
    2. How listener will be expected to use the message

III. Listening Procedures: specific behaviors which lead to accomplishing listening goals
  A. Suggested basic procedures
    1. Before the listening situation
      a) Set listening goals
      b) Be physically prepared
      c) Review content area
      d) Remind yourself of the personal value the listening could have
      e) Review your frame of reference related to topic
      f) Review Originating Communicator's frame of reference
    2. During the listening situation
      a) Demonstrate interest
      b) Concentrate and refocus attention
      c) Search for intended meanings
      d) Avoid evaluation
      e) Review and preview main ideas

      f) Use mnemonic devices to remember key ideas
      g) Ask questions when you don't understand
      h) Take notes
      i) Tape record the message
      j) Use the difference between talking and decoding speed
      k) Decode nonverbals
      l) Consider situation and its influence
   3. After the listening situation
      a) Review notes
      b) Use criteria
B. Determining appropriate procedures
   1. List all procedures necessary to accomplish goal
   2. Eliminate inappropriate procedures
      a) Those impossible to use in situation
      b) Those uncomfortable for other person
   3. Reduce list to smallest number possible to attain goal

Reading

Types of Listening Situations

Each day you experience varying types of situations which imply the use of listening behaviors. Let's consider the following continuum of types of listening situations: hearing, listening for pleasure; listening for content; and listening involving analysis. The continuum varies from minimal involvement to maximum involvement.

Hearing is a behavior that goes little beyond your being in the range of some oral stimulus (receiving sounds). There is little personal involvement in this type of listening. You may not even be aware of the incoming sound unless it is called to your attention. Background music and environmental sounds are often in the realm of "hearing." Input which arrives on this level has minimal imprint on one's memory, and there is minimal conscious decoding. If you get tired of someone's verbal message, you may "tune them out" by reducing your participation in the communication to that of "hearing." This is an example of selective attention and often happens in families.

Listening for pleasure goes beyond that of hearing in terms of personal involvement. There is more conscious reception of the input and some decoding, largely on the classification level (noting differences or changes). Musical ballads are perhaps the first example that occurs to most people. However, many times verbal messages can be received at this level. For example, when listening to poetry or a message from someone who has a pleasing voice and the material is sent in a pleasurable rhythm, we often focus more on the medium rather than the message. The major focus of attention in a situation where the listening is for pleasure will depend on the frame of reference of the person involved.

When *listening for content,* involvement in the process of communication greatly increases. Decoding and thinking become consciously controlled, and there are usually attempts to maximize understanding. An example of listening for content would be listening to someone giving you directions to get to his house. When listening for content a person has a specific listening goal in mind. In the above example your listening goal would be to understand how to get to the person's house. If a person doesn't have highly developed skills in listening and remembering, s/he should concentrate on decoding and take written notes for later use.

Listening for analysis leads to even more involvement by the responding communicator. Participation goes beyond accurate receiving and retention to the critical assessment of what is received. An example of listening for analysis would be listening to a salesperson trying to sell you a new car.

Keep a record of each listening experience in which you are involved for a three-hour period during the day. Specify the times and what you did during

Learning Experience

the listening period. Classify the listening experience as: (1) hearing, (2) listening for pleasure, (3) listening for content, or (4) listening for analysis, or a combination.

As you reconsider the listening experience logged and the type(s) of listening you used, where might you more appropriately have used a different type? Were there any experiences where you shifted to a different type during the interaction?

Goal Setting

To maximize the productiveness of any listening situation, research and experience indicate that the first step should be goal setting. A *listening goal* is *a specification of what the responding communicator wants to get out of the situation.* Specific listening goals are usually motivated by important needs. You might want to remember portions of the message's content such as its purpose, main ideas, facts, inferences, or value judgments. Or you may want to analyze the message's inferences or implied values. By specifying a goal such as these prior to the experience, it is more likely that the goal will be accomplished.

You are able to focus on a given stimulus for only brief periods at a time. Thus, receiving a message is a continual process of focusing and refocusing your attention. Your listening goal becomes the basis for your selective attention as you listen.

In the give-and-take of most communicative interchanges you may need to adjust your listening goal as the interchange develops. For example, what may have started to be a casual conversation, with a general listening goal of getting ideas on what to do on a Saturday night, might develop into a serious discussion about participating in activities which involve potential health hazards. Thus, you might wish to change your listening goal to something such as "to discover the values on which the other person bases his or her choices."

In any given experience there are many stimuli on which you could focus as you redirect your attention. Having a specified goal increases the chances that your redirection will be toward stimuli that will lead to a productive outcome.

Beyond the more obvious values of goal setting is the advantage of having a meaningful basis for evaluating and reviewing a given experience. That is being able to assess, "How well did I achieve my goal of . . . ?" instead of reacting to an experience in terms of a good-bad or evaluative assessment. You can react by comparing the actual experience outcome with the goals you set for that experience as a receiving communicator.

To identify what specific listening goals would be appropriate for a specific input situation, consider the following two questions: (1) How would you personally like to be able to use the input from the situation? (2) How will you be expected (by others) to use the input from that situation?

Select two of the listening situations you recorded earlier in your listening log. Write a *very specific* goal for each situation. Briefly write your reason(s) for setting each stated goal.

Listening Procedures

Once specific listening goals have been chosen, the next concern is to determine behaviors which will most likely help you achieve the goals you have set. We call these behaviors listening procedures. Many of the listening procedures go beyond receiving behaviors to related decoding, thinking, and encoding behaviors. The procedures are divided into *before, during,* and *after,* based on when you would use them in attaining your listening goals.

Before the listening experience:

1. *Set listening goal(s).*
   The more specific the goal(s), the more you will find yourself focusing and refocusing to get your desired meanings.
2. *Be physically prepared.*
   Listening takes considerable energy. Most often we know ahead of time when higher level listening situations will occur (classes, appointments, meetings, etc.). If possible, be rested physically and open mentally for the experience.
3. *Review the content area to be dealt with.*
   Think through what you remember about it. For class lectures it will be helpful to review previous notes.
4. *Determine the personal value the interchange could have for you.*
   Sometimes you may feel you have to stretch to do this, such as with required classes, but seeing personal value provides excellent motivation for maintaining the energy needed to accomplish your goals.

Learning
Experience List three listening situations you will participate in later today or tomorrow. For each, list at least one personal benefit for you in that situation.

Just before participating in that experience, recall the specific potential benefit for you. Note any differences in your ability to concentrate and your accomplishment of your listening goals.

5. *Review your frame of reference related to the topic.*
   As discussed in chapter 3, each of us screen all incoming messages through our frames of reference. By reviewing your stored information, important needs, and perception of the situation, you can minimize distortion of the sender's message. This procedure can also help you select other listening procedures. For example, if you discover you know very little about the sender's credibility, you would review that part of your frame of reference.

6. *Review the originating communicator's frame of reference.*
By reviewing the sender's frame of reference you will be more likely to attach the intended denotative and connotative meaning to the symbols they use. It could also alert you to goals and expectations which could influence the intended meaning.

During the listening experience:

7. *Demonstrate interest.*
This will help to keep you alert and give the originating communicator full opportunity to express the intended meaning.
8. *Concentrate and refocus attention.*
As indicated earlier, listening is a process of continually refocusing attention rather than unbroken concentration. Internal messages as well as other external stimuli will compete for your attention. If you predict that concentration will be challenging, you might also use the procedure of note taking.
9. *Search for intended meanings.*
Based on the sender's frame of reference and message cues, consider which of the possible denotative and connotative meanings for abstract symbols are most likely.
10. *Avoid evaluation.*
Try to understand the message as the sender intended. Avoid arguing. This is often a difficult behavior to practice. It is especially difficult when you are opposed to the idea which the person is talking about, or the person uses communicative behaviors which tend to create defensiveness. Your evaluation and feedback, however, will be more appropriate and effective if you can be relatively sure that you listened openly enough to understand the person's point of view before you react to it.

11. *Review and preview main ideas.*

Reviewing main ideas is another way to use the difference between listening and speaking speed and help you keep the overall view of the message in mind. If the originating communicator gave an overview of the message at the beginning, you will be able to preview the next main point mentally after reviewing earlier points. This process is especially valuable if note taking is inappropriate.

12. *Use mnemonic devices to remember key ideas.*

A mnemonic device is a combination of letters, each of which is the first letter of a group of words you are trying to remember. For example, if a person communicated that his or her main objection to taking your advice about jogging were the **c**ost, personal **a**bility, and the **t**ime involved, you might develop the mnemonic C A T to remember the main ideas. In that way you would be more able to allow the other person to develop a full idea without interrupting and yet be ready to discuss each of the ideas when he or she is finished.

13. *Ask questions when you don't understand.*

Be sure your timing on this does not interfere with the sender's development of thought. In a more formal situation it might be more appropriate to write down your question or use a mnemonic device to ask it later.

14. *Take notes.*

William Brooks makes the following suggestions[1] for taking effective notes:

    a. Decide whether or not you need to take notes. Take into consideration your goal, your own concentration and retention abilities, whether the information will be used immediately or at some later date.

    b. Decide what type of notes you should take—key-word outline, phrase outline, or complete outline. The key-word outline permits maximum attention to the sender.

    c. Identify the organizational pattern of the message and let your notes reflect it. Sometimes the sender will have no actual pattern, but it is better to take notes which reflect the sender's meaning and then organize in your own style if necessary at a later time.

    d. Keep your notes brief so that they are notes.

    e. Keep your notes clear. Avoid doodling and other random marks which can become noise at a later time.

Learning Experience

Do this with a friend who will share with you a listening experience in which it would be appropriate to take notes, such as a class meeting. Agree to both take notes in the form of a key-word outline, trying to get the meaning of the sender and following the note taking suggestions above. After the listening experience, compare your outlines. As you were both trying to get at the

---

1. William Brooks, *Speech Communication* (Dubuque, Iowa: Wm. C. Brown Inc., 1974), pp. 112–13.

meaning of the sender, your outlines should be very similar. Discuss and note any differences in the outlines. Decide what led to the differences.

15. *Tape record the message.*
    This procedure is appropriate if a complete record of the inter-action is important and it would not be otherwise detrimental to the interaction. This would only be used in more formal situations.
16. *Use the difference between talking and decoding speed.*
    Message decoding can be done at approximately 400 words per minute, while most people speak approximately 150 words per minute. This gives a great deal of time to review, process, and preview ideas.
17. *Decode nonverbals.*
    The nonverbal behaviors of the originating communicator will pro-vide additional meanings. Of special concern are nonverbals in-dicating involvement, sincerity, and stress of what's most important. You might review chapter 2 on nonverbal communication.
18. *Consider situation and its influences.*
    Consider the influence of the situation on the sender and yourself. Does it (including status and roles of the participants) limit either's open involvement in the interaction?

After the listening experience:

19. *Review ideas and/or notes.*
    This procedure is more helpful if done soon after the listening ex-perience, especially if no notes were taken. If this was the case, you might want to write a few summary notes immediately after. If you did make notes, look over them for points which need clarification.
20. *Use criteria as the basis for assessment.*
    We are actually previewing material from chapter 7 here. We did so to reinforce that assessment comes only after making sure the message was accurately decoded. In chapter 7 you will develop skills in using criteria to assess messages.

Determining Appropriate Listening Procedures

The procedures listed in this reading would not all be valuable for all listening (receiving) situations. For example, to tape record a conversation where a friend is describing a personal problem would be inappropriate. Figure 10 may help in selecting helpful listening procedures. A crucial skill is the ability to select appropriate procedures for specific situations. To determine which procedures are appropriate, consider the following.

1. List all procedures necessary to accomplishing your determined goal.

		Hearing	Pleasure	Content	Analysis
Before:	1. Set listening goals			✓	✓
	2. Be physically prepared		✓	✓	✓
	3. Review content area			✓	✓
	4. Determine the personal value			✓	✓
	5. Review your frame of reference related to topic			✓	✓
	6. Review originating communicator's frame of reference		✓	✓	✓
During:	7. Demonstrate interest			✓	✓
	8. Concentrate and refocus attention		✓	✓	✓
	9. Search for intended meanings		✓	✓	✓
	10. Avoid evaluation		✓	✓	✓
	11. Review and preview main ideas			✓	✓
	12. Use mnemonic devices			✓	✓
	13. Ask questions when you don't understand			✓	✓
	14. Take notes			✓	✓
	15. Tape record		✓	✓	✓
	16. Use difference between talking and decoding speed			✓	✓
	17. Decode nonverbals			✓	✓
	18. Consider situation and its influence			✓	✓
After:	19. Review notes			✓	✓
	20. Use criteria			✓	✓

FIGURE 10

2. Eliminate those procedures that would:
   a. be impossible to use in the situation;
   b. make the other person(s) involved uncomfortable (harming long-range interaction goals).
3. Reduce the list of procedures to the smallest possible number that would still enable you to accomplish your listening goals. Until good listening habits are fairly well established, it will take concerted effort on your part to carefully think through each situation in terms of appropriate goals and procedures. Also, many of the listening–receiving situations you are in happen without your having advance preparation time. However, as skills in goal and procedure setting improve, you will be able to use the difference in speaking and thinking speed to quickly assess situations and make decisions early

in an interaction. The minutes you spend doing so may save time, money, and even the relationship itself.

An example of listening that we all face is the life insurance salesperson. Specific listening goals you might set for the interaction include: (1) to determine if I really need life insurance; (2) to determine how much I need; and (3) to determine what type of policy best meets my needs and financial situation. What other goals might you include?

Listening for content and analysis will enable us to attain these goals. Note in figure 10 that all twenty of the listening procedures could be used for situations involving content and analysis. Try using the three steps listed above to determine the most helpful listening procedures for each goal you set. We might choose listening procedures 1, 3, 4, and 11 to attain our first goal and 1, 3, 6, 9, 10, 13, and 20 to attain the third goal. Which ones would you use?

Chapter 6

Listening Accurately

Objectives

Your learning should enable you to, for a brief message, use appropriate listening procedures (except note taking) to allow you to accomplish the following listening goals:

1. Write the viewed communicator's stated overall goal for the message.
2. List the viewed communicator's main points made in the message.
3. Accurately answer questions about the content of the communicator's message.
4. Accurately answer questions about messages sent nonverbally by the communicator.

Outline

I. Accurate listening: process of decoding the verbal message, the nonverbal messages and integrating them
   A. Goal of understanding a received message as the sender intended it
   B. Active participatory role of responding communicator
II. Recognizing message goals
   A. Position of goal in message
      1. To gain understanding: goal directly indicated early in message
      2. To attain attitude or behavior change: goal indirectly indicated near end of message
   B. Situation and contextual cues reveal message goals
   C. Nonverbal cues indicate message goals
      1. Pausing after goal is mentioned
      2. Change in volume and rate of speaking
      3. More direct eye contact
      4. Change in body position
III. Identifying main points of a message: points which sender considers important
   A. Verbal indicators
      1. Direct reference by transitions
      2. Repetition
      3. Positioning of point early or late in message
   B. Nonverbal indicators
      1. Change in loudness of speech
      2. Change in rate of message sending (usually slowing down)
      3. Pauses before and after the point
      4. Change in body position
IV. Metacommunication: additional messages which serve to clarify the main meaning intended by a communicator
   A. Both verbal and nonverbal messages function as metacommunication
   B. Metacommunication occurs along with, prior to, and following the main message
   C. Types of meanings communicated by metacommunication:
      1. Why people said what they did
      2. How people feel about themselves
      3. How people feel about the person they're talking to
      4. How strongly the person feels the message
   D. Nonverbal metacommunication
      1. Role of nonverbal cues
         a) Repetition of verbal message
         b) Substitute for verbal message
         c) Complement the verbal message
         d) Emphasize the verbal message
         e) Contradict the verbal message
      2. Nonverbal cues as regulators of communication
         a) Eye contact: waiting for other person to react
         b) Pausing: waiting for other to react
         c) Raising of eyebrows: encouraging other to react or explain
         d) Head nod: encouraging communicator to continue
         e) Placing feet flat on floor, leaning forward, placing hands on thighs, starting another project—indicating that the person is ready to conclude the interchange

V. Listening to yourself
    A. Learn more about yourself
        1. Physical self-awareness
        2. Mental self-awareness
    B. Improve accurate listening by recognizing influence of own frame of reference

Reading

We use the term *accurate* in reference to listening to emphasize the goal of accurately decoding and processing what we listen to. When the goal is to interpret the meaning as intended by the originating communicator, you will be decoding, thinking, and integrating information from the many cues received from the sender. *To listen accurately you will need to decode the verbal and nonverbal messages and integrate them.* Fundamental to meaningful interchange with others are the goal setting and listening procedure skills involved in accurately trying to understand a message as the other person means it.

Throughout each listening experience, it is important to remember that *a message reflects both denotative and connotative meaning.* Accurate understanding necessitates sensitivity to both. Some messages are predominantly expressive of feelings and are not intended for literal translation. For example, if someone were to exclaim after a frustrating attempt to complete a carpentry job, "I'm all thumbs," and you decoded that message in terms of its denotative content alone, you would miss much of the meaning.

Recognizing Message Goals

When setting goals for a specific listening experience (as discussed in chapter 5), it is wise to take into consideration the goal of the sender. Your listening will be aided by discovering early in the exchange what the sender's goal for his or her message sending is. In situations where the sender's goal is to share information, it is indicated early in the message and is often announced before the message in more formal situations. For example, speakers' topics are usually announced prior to the event, and classroom lectures are usually scheduled so that you know the topic to be covered. This greatly facilitates your own goal setting as a listener. In interpersonal situations where information is to be shared, there also is usually direct reference to the topic involved very early in the message. This reference to a goal usually occurs immediately after introductory comments or informal greeting. Something like the following is common:

"Hi, Joe. Did you hear about the sale at the bookstore?"

or

"I have a problem that I need help with."

or

"Good morning. My name is _____. I'd like to tell you about our new magazine subscription offer."

The goal, therefore, in information-giving situations usually is stated directly and done at the beginning of the message. Listen for that goal and plan your own listening goals accordingly.

In situations where the sender's goal is attitude change in the responding communicator, the goal may be less obvious. There is often a lead-in (a "pitch") before the actual goal of the message (to sell a car, to get you to help on a project, and so forth) is mentioned. In these situations, however, you have contextual cues which will help you to infer the goal of the communicator. The situation of a person with a carrying case stopping at someone's home or room and beginning the message with, "Could I take a moment of your time . . . ? What a lovely home you have . . ." might indicate a salesperson.

In messages to entertain or in casual interaction there may be no specific initial goal other than enjoying the interchange or getting to know another person. However, a specific goal often develops later and your sensitivity to such an emerging goal will assist you in adapting your listening procedures.

Nonverbal cues also will help to indicate the goal of the sender. The following are some likely nonverbal cues.

1. Pauses often occur after a communication goal is mentioned;
2. A change in volume;
3. A change in the rate of speaking;
4. More direct eye contact; and
5. A change in body position, such as shifting of body weight or recrossing of legs from one side to another.

Identifying Main Points of a Message

As the sender gets into his or her message, listen for those parts of the message which the sender considers important or vital. There are usually verbal and nonverbal indicators that a point is being made which is important to the sender.

Verbal indicators that an important point is being made include:

1. *Direct reference* to the point by transitions: "First . . . ," "the second thing involved is . . . ," "another important point is . . . ," "now get this," "and finally . . ." are examples;
2. *Repetition*—if a sender repeats something several times, you can infer that he or she considers it an important main point; and

3. *Position in the message*—communicators usually highlight important points by placing them at the very beginning or the very end of a message. In highly organized messages the main ideas may be previewed at the beginning or reviewed at the end.

Nonverbal indicators that an important point is being made are similar to those for indicating a goal:

1. Change in loudness of speech;
2. Change in speed (usually slowing down);
3. Pauses before and after the point;
4. A change in body position; and
5. Maintaining eye contact for a slightly longer period of time just before making the point.

Although such verbal and nonverbal indicators suggested above will take on a more consistent and parallel form in more organized and formal communication, most people quite naturally provide signposts that they are changing focus even in casual conversation. For example, a friend might begin a conversation saying, "Hey, let me tell you what happened yesterday," (Goal) and go through a chronological order with internal transitions such as "and then . . . ," "After he did that, I . . . ," "Then he brought up . . . ."

As you identify each main point the sender is making, you can use the difference in speaking and listening speed to review main points as new ones are added—perhaps even to form some mnemonic device to help you remember the points. This will help you in remembering and effectively responding to the full meaning.

Do this learning experience with a friend who will share two similar listening situations with you in which it would be appropriate to take notes.

During the first experience ask your friend to take careful notes in the form of a phrase outline. During the experience, you listen carefully reviewing and previewing main points. You are not to take notes. Each time you see and/or hear indicators of a main point, review the main points already given and add the new point.

As soon as the listening experience is over, write down the main points as you remember them. Compare your recalled main points with your friend's notes. Discuss any differences.

Reverse the roles and try the experience again. Continue the experiences until the remembered main points match those in the notes.

Learning Experience

Metacommunication

Already in this reading we have been using the concept of *metacommunication.* Literally the term means "about communication." It is used to refer to *additional messages which serve to clarify the main message,* or meaning, intended by a communicator. Both verbal and nonverbal symbols can function as metacommunication. For example, I might say, "I didn't get any sleep last night," and further add (as metacommunication to clarify my comment), "I wanted to let you know why I was a bit touchy this morning" while slumping my body and yawning. These three additional messages communicate additional meaning. Metacommunication functions as a further message about the main message sent. It can convey indications about (1) why people said what they did; (2) how people feel toward themselves; (3) how people feel toward you; and/or (4) how strongly they feel about the message.[1]

Another example of metacommunication might be a man saying, "and that's how I feel about it," and folding his arms across his chest. This behavior would be nonverbal metacommunication which gives additional firmness to the message and lets you know more about how strongly the sender means the message.

Being aware of all message and message-related cues greatly enhances the likelihood of understanding the full meaning. In interpersonal situations this skill is crucial if you wish to interact meaningfully with others. People indicate needs, desires, intentions, and many other vital things indirectly through metacommunication. Your sensitivity to this level of communication will aid greatly in your understanding of people and in making a meaningful response.

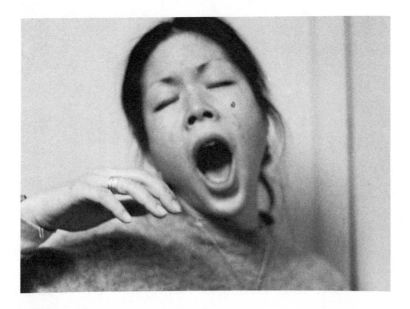

Nonverbal messages most often function as metacommunication rather than functioning as an independent message. They interrelate with verbal messages in the following ways:

1. As repetition of the verbal message—an index finger pointing to the door might accompany the message, "Leave the room";

1. Virginia Satir, "Communication: A Verbal and Nonverbal Process of Making Requests of the Receiver," in *Messages,* ed. Jean Civikly (New York: Random House, Inc., 1974), pp. 14–15.

2. To substitute for a verbal message—this is often done when it would be considered inappropriate to "come right out and say it" or if it's more comfortable for the sender to indicate his message in that way. For example, a person indicates his general mood by the way he moves his body, the level of body activity, and the rate of speech. This example is typical of the situation where the message may not be consciously sent;
3. To complement the verbal message—to clarify by adding an additional cue;
4. To emphasize the verbal message; and
5. To contradict the verbal message—this may be done intentionally to add a "double-meaning" to the message as in irony or be an unintentional indicator of more true feelings than the ones verbalized.[2]

The next time you are communicating in a small group, choose one group member to observe. Note a specific verbal message sent by that person. (Write it down if you can do so inconspicuously). Then, watch for (and write down, if possible) any nonverbal or verbal cues which accompany or follow the message which further explain what the person meant. Consider how you might have interpreted the message without such metacommunication.

Try this again with another person taking the course. Observe the same person and compare observations.

Learning Experience

Nonverbal messages also serve as regulators during interpersonal interaction. Eye contact can indicate that we are waiting for the other person to react. Pausing and raising of the eyebrows indicate the same thing. A head nod is often used to encourage the other person to continue. Signals which usually indicate that a person is ready to conclude the interchange include nonverbals, such as change in body position, placing hands on thighs with thumbs inside of legs (usually accompanied by verbal indications such as "well . . ."), leaning forward, placing of feet flat on floor, or starting another project.

As we have indicated, accurate listening requires noting things *not said* as well as those which *are said*. Reviewing your listening goals and what you know about the subject often will highlight the unstated messages. It is the total awareness and interpretation of all cues which give indication of the sender's meaning. The goal is to be able to paraphrase the originating communicator's message in such a way that he or she would accept your paraphrase as an indication that you accurately understood the intended meanings—connotative and denotative.

With a friend, select a subject for discussion which has personal meaning for both of you. The rules for this interchange are that each statement made by either of you must be *paraphrased* by the other to demonstrate that he or she has heard and *understood* what was intended. Before you continue the discussion, the originator of the statement must be satisfied that the paraphrase

Learning Experience

---

2. P. Ekman and W. Friesen, "The Repertoire of Nonverbal Behavior: Categories, Origins, Usage, and Coding," *Semiotica* 1 (1969): 49–98.

expressed what was intended. In paraphrasing, do not repeat the words used by the originator. Write down two of your conclusions about the experience.

Listening to Yourself

Another very important skill as a listener is that of listening to yourself. Basically this means being open to your own messages, both internal and external. Awareness of our physical sensations is being encouraged through attention to biofeedback and of our mental sensations through such experiences as consciousness raising. Not only is listening to yourself a valuable skill for personal growth, but it is a vital part of effective listening to others' messages. As we become more sensitive to our own frames of reference and their influence on our decoding and thinking, we will be much more likely to get at another person's intended meaning.

Accurate Listening in Action

In actual communicative situations prepare yourself for accurate listening by setting specific listening goals and choosing listening procedures that will help you to attain those goals. Accurate listening skills are then used to decode the meanings as intended by the originating communicator. These skills include listening for the goal of the communicator, noting the main points important to that person, noting nonverbal cues and their relationship to the verbal message, and finally interrelating all cues as the communication progresses. By the use of these skills your meanings should be very close to those intended by the sender and will be the basis for your feedback messages.

The skills of accurately listening to yourself and others are developed by extensive practice. In early stages of skill development, it will take concerted effort. Active listening never becomes an inactive process, but the skills will become more a part of you and be more natural as you work on them.

Learning Experience

Listen to a television talk show, like "The Tonight Show." Take notes if you prefer. Write out what you've retained. Also tape record the show. Compare the product of your listening and the tape. Try to understand differences based on selective attention, processing, and remembering. Write down three of your conclusions.

This would be a valuable experience to share with another person. Analyze the difference between your listening records. Write down three of your conclusions.

Chapter 7

Listening Analytically

Objectives

For a specific message, your learning should enable you to:

1. Infer values that are likely to be a part of the sender's frame of reference.
2. Compare the sender's values with your own.
3. Differentiate between facts and inferences used in the message.
4. Determine the acceptability of the facts and inferences in the message.
5. Choose appropriate criteria for analyzing the message.
6. Explain your choice of criteria for analyzing the message.
7. Use your criteria to analyze the message.

Outline

I. Definition of analytical listening: analyzing evidence or ideas presented in a message and making critical judgments about the validity, quality, and importance of the message.

II. Identifying the values which influence a person's message
   A. Values are strongly held attitudes which meet the criteria of being prized, carefully chosen, and a consistent basis for action.
      1. Example: "friendship"
      2. Values typically are abstract, unclarified, and unstated
   B. How values influence messages
      1. Value statements are clarifications of values.
         a) Example: for the situation of "borrowing," a value statement which clarifies the value of "friendship" might be "friends share their things with each other"
         b) Value statements are rarely stated in messages
      2. Value judgments are evaluations based on value statements
         a) Example: for the value statement of "friends share," a value judgment might be "Jean is stingy" if she, as a friend, doesn't share
         b) Value judgments are the form in which values appear in most messages
   C. Importance of determining values which underlie the value judgments in messages
      1. To better understand reasons behind a judgment
      2. To decide if the judgment is acceptable or applicable to you
   D. Technique for discovering underlying values
      1. Ask, "What would that person have to believe to say (or do) what he or she did?"
      2. Review the sender's frame of reference

III. Distinguishing fact from inference
   A. Statements of fact are made after direct sense experience and limited to statements about past or present
      1. Example: "It is raining"
      2. Statements of fact can be verified by one of the senses
      3. Statements of fact are influenced by the frame of reference of the observer
         a) Most acceptable facts are supported by a number of people
         b) Most acceptable facts are supported by observers skilled in the sense used to collect data (experts)
   B. Statements of inference are guesses, sometimes reasoned, which go beyond observation
      1. Examples: "It will rain tomorrow" or "There is a 40 percent chance of rain tomorrow morning"
      2. Statements of inference have an element of chance
      3. Acceptability of statements of inference varies
         a) Most acceptable inferences are based on appropriate facts and reasoning
         b) Most acceptable inferences are supported by a number of experts in that field

IV. Analysis through the use of criteria
   A. Definition: concrete statements of standards for analysis
   B. General criteria which apply to most messages
      1. Is the source qualified to make the judgment he or she is making?
      2. What are the source's motivations in sending the message?
      3. Are the judgments in the message supported by evidence?
      4. Is the information used in the message up-to-date?
      5. Does the message contain limited or false reasoning?
      6. Does the sender use propaganda devices to gain acceptance of a message?
      7. What importance does the message have for me?

Analytical listening is that *listening* in which you, as a responding communicator, attempt *to assess the evidence or ideas presented in a message and to make critical judgments about the validity, quality, importance, and other relevant aspects of that message.* It goes beyond receiving, decoding, and retaining information to analysis of the original message.

Analytical listening is an important part of most human interaction. Each of us is faced with making choices and decisions which will meaningfully affect our lives or those of other people. We are constantly receiving messages which try to influence our decisions. People's suggestions (and commands) to help us make decisions are based on their inferences and value judgments which are based on their facts, experiences, and values. Since it is impossible in our complex world to experience directly all that will influence our life choices, we are dependent on others for advice and assistance. We cannot afford, however, to accept uncritically all that we receive. Everyone does not have our best interests in mind, and even those who do cannot necessarily prescribe what is best for us. Sometimes what others tell us with the best of intentions is not appropriate for us. It is our critical functioning that makes us able to direct our own lives as free adults.

Analytical functioning also extends to the level of intrapersonal communication. As mentioned earlier, there is great value in learning to listen effectively to yourself. Potential for self-growth and self-understanding accelerates as one analyzes intrapersonal messages.

Identifying Values

A value can be defined as *a strongly held attitude which meets the criteria of being prized, carefully chosen, and a consistent basis for action.* Because values are so deeply personal, many times they exist in an unstated, unclarified, and abstract condition. Through self-understanding we can state and clarify our values. These clarifications are called *value statements.* From them, we make judgments of how we see our own actions and the actions of others. This three-step application of values is visualized in figure 11.

FIGURE 11

As indicated in figure 11, there could be more than one value statement for each value and many value judgments could be made from each value statement. For example, your participation in the values clarification experiences in chapter 3 may have identified for you a personal value of "friendship." The symbol "friendship" is quite abstract. Somewhere between that abstract value and your resulting actions and messages is a clearer statement of what "friendship" means within your frame of reference. Within your frame of reference for "borrowing," your value of "friendship" could be translated into the value statement of "friends share their things with each other," and to the value judgment that "Jean is really being stingy" if you consider Jean a friend and she isn't willing to share something with you.

The main characteristic of a value judgment is an evaluation based on what a person believes to be good or bad. These evaluations are usually expressed in terms of "should" or "should not," "do" or "do not," or "good" or "bad." Figure 12 visualizes a number of values, value statements, and value judgments.

Values	Value Statements	Value Judgments
Money	"The customer is always right."	Keep the customer satisfied.
Time	"Time is money."	Don't waste a minute.
Initiative	"The longest journey is begun with a single step."	Don't put off till tomorrow what you can do today.
Ecology	"Waste not, want not."	Recycle everything.
Friendship	"Friends are worth their weight in gold."	Never turn your back on a friend.

FIGURE 12

As a listener, inferring the values and value statements which lead to a judgment in a message will enable you to (1) better understand the reasons behind a judgment and (2) decide if the judgment is acceptable or applicable for you.

A helpful means of discovering values is to ask yourself the question, "What would that person have to believe to say (or do) what s/he did?" Considering what you know about that person's frame of reference will also be helpful in inferring values and value statements. If the person has a value statement that is acceptable to you, you might wish to accept the advice or judgment. On the other hand, if the other person is coming from a value you disagree with, you would be more likely to reject the advice.

For example, an older person asks you in a surprised way, "Are you questioning my recommendation?" To get to the value judgment, let's translate the question into a "should" judgment. He or she is indirectly expressing the value judgment that you shouldn't question the recommendation. To infer the value statement, let's ask the question, "What would that person have to believe to say what he or she did?" The answer might be "Older people know more" or "Experience is the best teacher." In other words, the person values experience. If you know something about that person's frame of reference, you will be better able to determine if that is a likely inference. If you can accept that value statement, then the judgment and recommendation may be very helpful to you. On the other hand, if his or her experience and learning happened in a very different situation, the value judgment may not be very helpful.

Consider the following conversation. Then jot down two values and resulting value statements which might be held by the two people involved (as implied by their statements).
Conversation:

    Bill: "Let's go over and help our new neighbors unpack."
    Sam: "Forget it. No one in the neighborhood helped us."
    Bill: "Come on. It will go so much faster if we help."
    Sam: "So what. We'll just encourage them to bug us every time they have a job to do."

Are any or all of the values and value statements which you wrote similar to ones you have? Based on your values and relevant value statements, how would you have responded to Bill?

Learning Experience

Distinguishing Fact from Inference

Another important skill in analytical listening is that of distinguishing fact from inference. By doing so, we can decide to what extent we can count on a person's statements as a basis for making decisions. It would be helpful if people indicated the difference in their messages with such phrases as "In my opinion" or "I infer that." However, few people do that.

A statement of fact can only be made after direct sense experience and is, therefore, limited to statements about past or present events. A statement of inference is a guess, sometimes reasoned, which goes beyond observation. An example would be the difference between "I saw Mary spend two hours in the library each night last week" and "Mary surely did a lot of studying last week." The first was observed directly and stated as "fact." However, the second could not have been observed directly and involves a personal interpretation. The person making the second statement went beyond what they saw or heard and made a statement of what the "fact" meant. It is very possible to sit somewhere looking very much like you are studying when you are not. Accepting that second inference as fact might not cause problems. However, consider this statement: "I can tell you what will be on the midterm because I had the course last semester." We all want to spend our study time on material which will be on the test. Based on this statement, how would you study for the test? This statement that the person knows what will be on *this* semester's midterm is an inference. It is based on the fact of what was on last semester's exam and on the unstated inference that the teacher will not change the test questions. If you treated that inference as "fact" without further investigation, you could be in for some disappointment. What additional facts would you want to collect to help make your study plans?

Learning Experience

Mark an F beside those statements below that could be made as a statement of fact. Mark an I beside those statements below that are examples of statements of inference. Explain your choices. Which are the more reliable statements?

"I heard the radio weatherperson say there is a 40 percent chance of rain tonight."
"There is a 40 percent chance of rain tonight."
"It will rain tonight."
"It is raining."
"John is sorry he yelled."
"John is angry."
"John is yelling."
"John is shaking his fist."

The acceptability of inferences is based on the quality of facts and reasoning used as well as the expertness of the person making the inference.

Even statements of fact have to be examined in terms of the qualifications of the observer. As discussed earlier, our frames of reference will greatly influence what we "see" in any situation. Therefore, *factual statements are more credible if they are supported by several individuals, especially if those individuals are experts in that particular area of sense observation.*

A continuum of the credibility of statements of fact and inference is represented in figure 13. As is shown in the continuum, facts and inferences become more reliable with the number of qualified individuals who support them.

FACT				INFERENCE			
(Made after sense experience)				(Goes beyond sense experience)			
Most reliable							Least reliable
Sense Data of Many Experts	Sense Data of One Expert	Sense Data of Several People	Sense Data of One Person	Support of Many Experts	Support of One Expert	Support of Many Nonexperts	Support of One Nonexpert

FIGURE 13

Learning Experience

Using the Fact-Inference continuum in figure 13, write one statement which would be an appropriate example of each of the points along the continuum.

Add other appropriate points along the continuum.

In summary, factual statements can be made only after direct experience. Inferences go beyond the facts to make an interpretation or judgment of what the "facts" mean. Also, inferences have some element of chance and cannot be treated as necessarily true. Both facts and inferences become more reliable as the number of experts supporting them increases.

Analysis through the Use of Criteria

Analytical thinking is appropriate any time that the message, value judgments being received or your response makes a difference—to you or someone else you care about. Perhaps the obvious exception would be a shouted message, "Duck!" (meaning move quickly). We usually trust the person sending the message and react before evaluation.

Most people do react to messages they receive by some form of evaluation. But it is usually a good–bad, right–wrong type of evaluation, based on their unspoken frames of reference. Such polarized evaluations usually lead to the sending of insensitive and inappropriate feedback. This type of feedback often encourages defensive reactions and eventually disagreements. It is very difficult to discuss openly such generally stated value judgments—even when someone takes the initiative to ask why someone thought something was bad or good. If someone does ask us, we are often in the difficult position of trying to state clearly our values so that others can understand them.

We are suggesting instead that you evaluate a given thing, decision, or event by the application of criteria. *Criteria* are *concrete statements of standards for evaluation* (usually in question form). Evaluation of the message is accomplished by applying the chosen criteria to the specific message. Such evaluations are more functional for decision making and also are more accurately understood by others. They indicate *degrees* of acceptance, some degree of rightness, not *either* right *or* wrong.

The potential specific criteria for evaluating messages are many and varied, depending on the specific nature of the message. *Seven general criteria* are listed which are applicable and important for most messages.

1. *Is the source qualified to make the judgment he or she is making?*
   This is a very basic criterion which should be applied to all messages. For example, you might agree that Dick Clark is well qualified to comment on the trends in music for the last twenty years, but you should question his authority on medical advances in the last twenty years. People certainly have a right to their own opinions, but you should be careful not to accept inferences based on little or no background in the area.
2. *What are the source's motivations in sending the message?* (Does the source have anything to gain personally by taking a certain stand on an issue?)
   Again, having a stake in the message certainly does not disqualify a person from having an opinion. However, certain motivations may

promote intentional or unintentional bias, such as salespersons who receive commissions on what they sell.

3. *Are the judgments in the message supported by evidence?*
Because there are usually several possible inferences that could be made regarding any situation, it is important to consider the amount and quality of evidence which supports each possible judgment. For example, because of the many contradictory predictions as to whether the world will run out of oil in a few years or not, panels of experts have been put together to consider the evidence. It is important that the evidence used to support a judgment be relevant to that judgment.

4. *Is the information used in the message up-to-date?*
People and situations change. Therefore, it is important that our messages reflect these changes by using as up-to-date information as possible. For example, you would want the most current information concerning job openings in a particular field before determining a college major.

5. *Does the message contain limited or false reasoning?*
Certainly as important as evidence supporting a given judgment is the reasoning which led to it or is built on it. Let's look at three types of reasoning that often are carelessly used.

Generalizing.   This type of reasoning moves from several specific instances to a general statement about the whole category of those types of instances. People use generalizations often because they are easier to remember than specific information. For example, having heard about the many dishonest actions of politicians associated with one political scandal, someone might generalize that all politicians are dishonest. Generalizations often have some probability of being accurate but should be applied carefully to new instances. Several helpful questions to ask in testing generalizations are (1) On how many instances is the generalization based? (2) Was there anything unusual about the instances which would lead to an inappropriate generalization (e.g., all gathered at a particular time of year)? (3) How many exceptions are there to the generalization?

Comparing.   This type of reasoning highlights the similarities and differences between two chosen things, events, and/or people to then conclude that one property which exists in one of the similar items also exists for the other item. For example, since Bob and Al are so much alike, it is safe to assume that if Bob enjoys his bicycle that Al could enjoy a bicycle. Comparisons are often helpful ways of thinking but should be checked by the following questions: (1) Are the two things, events, or people similar enough in important aspects to warrant further inferences about their similarities? (2) Are there important differences between the two items in relationship to the new area in which similarity is inferred? Comparisons and resulting inferences should become much more tentative as we move from things to events and finally to people.

Causal reasoning. This type of reasoning involves concluding that because something followed something else, it was caused by that which preceded it. For example, because a person fainted after seeing someone coming at him with a large snake, it is assumed that the person's act of coming with a snake caused the other person to faint. The basic limitation of this type of thinking and one which a listener should always check is that of the single cause. Most events, especially those directly involving people, are more complex than to be only caused by a single event. Usually there are several things leading up to a given result. So a responding communicator should ask: (1) Is the cause suggested too simple to have led to the result? and (2) Is the relationship correlative rather than causal? That is, some events occur together yet are not necessarily leading to each other. This can often be tested by checking to see if the two events *always* occur togther.

Consider the following comments in terms of the reasoning used. Underline any examples of weak reasoning. Describe for each underlined example why you think the reasoning was weak. **Learning Experience**

"I don't think the pass-fail system of grading will work at our college. Why, they tried that system at Merriman High School last year and their student record files are really messed up. We don't want to get into that kind of hassle here. Also, I had a friend who went to a college where they had a pass-fail system. She said that she just couldn't get motivated to really work hard because she knew she didn't have to. We could certainly learn from her experience and avoid the problem. Do you know that she finally dropped out of college because that grading system just didn't get her motivated."

6. *Does the sender use propaganda devices to gain acceptance of a message?*
   Typical propaganda devices include telling half-truths; name calling; using testimonials which represent one person's opinion; exaggerated claims; having well-known but unrelated people advertise a product; and trying to get us to do something by suggesting that "everyone is doing it." Such devices add color and variety to advertisement and other persuasive attempts; however, they should not be used as the basis for decision making. Being sensitive to such attempts to short-circuit thinking has been referred to as *crap detecting.* By applying several of the tests for limited or false reasoning you can identify the limitations of these devices. What messages other than product advertisements typically use these propaganda devices?

7. *What benefit or importance does the message have for you?*
   Each year we become more aware of the various kinds of pollution which are part of our environment. "Message pollution" can be added to the long list. Each day your attention is drawn to messages

that are loud, different, controversial, and even violent. Because of the number of messages that people are exposed to daily, there is increased concern for our right to privacy. By determining the potential benefit of the message, you can productively guide your selective attention to reduce the impact of message pollution on yourself.

Chapter 8

Communicating Effective Feedback Messages

Objectives

Your learning should enable you to:

1. Recognize examples of feedback being used as a corrective function in communication.
2. Define nondirective feedback.
3. Define directive feedback.
4. Recognize examples of nondirective and directive feedback.
5. State the general circumstances in which a responding communicator would choose to use either nondirective or directive feedback.
6. For a communicative situation:
   a. Set a feedback goal.
   b. Determine if nondirective or directive feedback would be more likely to accomplish your goal.
   c. Explain your choice of nondirective or directive feedback.
   d. Describe your exact feedback behaviors (what you would say and/ or do).
   e. Choose one of Gibb's communicative behaviors which will be most likely to help you reach your feedback goal.
   f. Explain how you would establish that behavior in this situation.

Outline

I. Feedback: Verbal and nonverbal messages sent by the responding communicator to the originating communicator as a response to the original message
 A. Occurs after setting listening goals and accurately decoding and analyzing the message
 B. Influences the communication process
  1. Influences content of sender's developing message
  2. Influences delivery of sender's message
  3. Influences later communication with sender
  4. Influences communication climate
 C. Main function of feedback is corrective
  1. Provides data to enable the originating communicator to determine the accuracy of the responder's decoding
  2. Based on feedback data the sender will make appropriate corrections in his or her message
II. Guidelines for Setting Feedback Goals
  1. Consider how feedback can influence your listening goals
  2. Consider how feedback can influence the sender
  3. Consider the implications your feedback could have on you
III. Nondirective and Directive Feedback Patterns
 A. Nondirective feedback describes, questions, or indicates receptive interest but does not evaluate
  1. Example: "How do you feel about that?"
  2. Guidelines for choosing nondirective feedback
   a) When responder wants more information
   b) When responder wants to help sender clarify meanings
   c) When responder wants a more open interaction
   d) When responder wants sender to make a personal choice without the influence of the responder's value judgments
  3. Guidelines for encoding nondirective feedback
   a) Make no reference to your opinion of message or sender
   b) Express interest and support
 B. Directive feedback states the value judgment of the responder
  1. Example: "I don't think you should go"
  2. Guidelines for choosing directive feedback
   a) When responder wants his or her frame of reference to influence sender's judgment
   b) After responder fully understands the sender's message
   c) When responder is qualified to make a judgment
   d) When responder wants to get involved in the sender's behaviors
  3. Guidelines for encoding directive feedback
   a) Make sure the statement is identified as an opinion
   b) Use supportive communication climates to counter defensive reactions
   c) Express the value for your judgment
IV. Feedback Channels
 A. Feedback can be sent through any of the human senses
  1. In some situations verbal feedback is inappropriate
  2. It is impossible not to send nonverbal feedback
   a) Typical nonverbal messages as responses:
    —leaning forward to show involvement
    —leaning back or away from sender to show noninvolvement
    —slight nod of head as understanding and encouragement to go on

  —puzzled look to show confusion

  —an open body position and arms uncrossed to show openness

  —arms crossed and legs crossed away from sender as evaluation and closedness

  —glancing at a watch as indicating desire for interaction to close

  —many subtleties of facial expression

  b) Be careful to avoid sending conflicting verbal and nonverbal feedback

 B. Consider feedback that should be avoided

V. Guidelines for Encoding Feedback

 A. Send feedback that is appropriate to the sender, message, and context

 B. Be certain the sender perceived the feedback

 C. Make certain the feedback is clear in meaning

 D. Send the feedback as soon after message as possible

 E. Be aware of overloading the system

 F. Delay any activity which has an unrelated and unintentional effect

VI. Assessing Feedback Effectiveness

 A. Observe sender's nonverbal reactions

 B. Ask sender to check accuracy

VII. Influencing the Communication Climate

 A. Responder's behaviors influence the communication climate

 B. Supportive communication behaviors lead to more accurate communication

 C. Review Gibb's communication behaviors in chapter 3

Reading

Feedback is *the verbal and nonverbal messages sent by the responding communicator to the originating communicator as a response to the original message.* Let's review the steps the responding communicator does before considering a response. After determining appropriate listening goal(s), the responding communicator actively decodes the message (using listening procedures to decode it as the sender intended); analyzes the message when appropriate (by considering implied values, fact vs. inference, and applying appropriate criteria); and finally encodes a response as feedback.

Feedback can be a significant influence on the developing message of the sender. Feedback can potentially influence (1) *what* the sender sends, (2) *how much* is sent, and (3) *how* it is encoded. The originating communicator, being sensitive to the responses of the responding communicator, will be able to infer if the message is being understood and/or accepted as it was intended. If the person gets feedback indicating that the interpreted meaning was not as intended, the message can be modified to clear up any uncertainty in the mind of the responding communicator. This is called the *corrective function of feedback. Feedback provides data to enable the originating communicator to surmise the understanding and misunderstanding of the original message and make appropriate corrections in the message.*

For most situations, therefore, a major feedback goal of the responding communicator would be to clearly communicate responses which indicate understanding or lack of it. If a sender doesn't know that the receiver doesn't understand, the sender might go on explaining and visualizing the idea. This happens in classrooms rather frequently. If a teacher does not know that you have misunderstood or not fully understood, another topic may be introduced and you may be expected to behave later as if you understood. If you don't understand something in class, what kinds of feedback messages might you send to communicate that?

Feedback not only can influence the immediate behavior of the sender, but also can influence later interaction between the individuals involved and help to set and maintain the climate for communication. In communicative situations where the senders and receivers do not have direct contact with each other, the same potential for the influence of feedback exists. Although feedback may not be able to influence the developing message (such as feedback to a televised message), it can influence later interaction, later messages, and certainly the communication climate.

Setting Feedback Goals

Because feedback messages have an important potential influence in communication, it is important for a responding communicator to consider what he or she wants to accomplish before responding to a message. The following potential influences should be considered when setting feedback goals for a given interaction.

1. How can your feedback message(s) assist the accomplishment of your listening goals?
2. What effect will your feedback have on the sender? Later messages? The sender's feeling about himself or herself? The sender's feelings about you?
3. What implications could your feedback have on you? Feelings about self, new obligations, and so forth?

In some communicative situations the appropriate type of response is implied in the sender's message. For example, someone might ask you, "Where is the cat?" A descriptive, direct reply seems appropriate. Someone might request, "Pass the honey." The intended reply would be the behavior of passing the honey jar. More often, however, a meaningful reply to a message received, decoded, and thought about is not a simple matter of a called-for behavior or a descriptive response. In these cases it is helpful to consider the alternatives of directive or nondirective feedback as potential feedback patterns. The terms of *directive* and *nondirective communication* have been developed by therapists to describe types of feedback to their patients. These types are appropriate for formal and informal, large group and interpersonal communicative situations. In the more formal or large group settings these feedback patterns are more often communicated nonverbally than verbally.

Nondirective and Directive Feedback

Nondirective feedback is that which *describes, questions, or indicates receptive interest* in relation to the topic area *and does not evaluate.* Feedback which describes stays as close as possible to the facts and identifies statements as being "how you see it" rather than "how it is." Such phrases as, "it seems to me," "based on what I know," etc., might be used to introduce your comments.

The intended result of nondirective feedback is that the sender of the original message feels comfortable to communicate and/or think further about the message. Such feedback does not evaluate and makes no reference to the responder's opinion of the message of the sender. Nondirective feedback expresses interest and support, while it encourages the sender to continue the message verbally or to continue his or her thinking about it. It is used in at least two situations: (1) when the responder wants to learn more about the sender's message or (2) when the responder wants to assist the sender to think through the situation and help the sender make his or her own judgment or decision. In the first situation the responder might ask a specific question or give nonverbal encouragement to go on, such as nodding the head, saying "uh-huh," or leaning forward with an interested facial expression. Repeating part of the original message ("only two people got an A?") also can lead to the sender continuing to explain what s/he is talking about. By repeating part of the message ("You want to quit school?"), describing part of the situation as you see it (remember, no evaluation!), or asking a specific question, the sender is encouraged to think or talk out the situation—perhaps by further clarifying his or her reasons.

Nondirective feedback usually is perceived as supportive (reducing defensiveness) and most often leads to more open interaction than is likely with directive feedback. Nondirective feedback is often used as an investigative procedure before moving to the use of directive feedback. An excellent situation in which to use nondirective feedback is while listening to an angry outburst. By repeating, describing, questioning, or indicating receptive interest, you'll probably help that person to calm down, talk openly, and resolve the difficulty. By evaluating in this type of situation, you usually will only "feed the fire" and be less helpful than you wanted to be.

Directive feedback is that which *states the value judgment of the responder and is based on personal values.* When people state their opinions they are making judgments based on their value(s)—which serve as reasons for their judgments. For example, if you and your best friend go downtown to buy a pair of shoes, you find a pair you like and you ask your friend's opinion. The person says, "I like them." There are usually several possible values, or combination of values, which lead to that opinion. He or she might believe that you have good taste in clothes; that you should make your own choice; that you should buy comfortable shoes; that you should buy fashionable shoes; that a person should spend very little time shopping; or there might be other values which could also lead to that opinion. The opinion will be seen as either positive or negative by you.

Directive feedback usually is used when the responder wants his or her own frame of reference to influence the originating communicator. A general guideline when considering the use of directive feedback is to make sure you understand the message and important related circumstances before offering a value judgment. You should also remember that, as Gibb suggested, *evaluation usually leads to defensiveness.* Certainly this is less true when the evaluation is positive, but even positive evaluations can lead to less open and less helpful interactions. Rogers and Farson suggest:

Passing judgment, whether critical or favorable, makes free expression difficult . . . it is a difficult lesson to learn that positive evaluations are sometimes as blocking as negative ones. It is almost as destructive to the freedom of a relationship to tell a person that he is good or capable, as to tell him otherwise.[1]

Another important realization is that giving a judgment (based on your value system) is not appropriate just because someone asks for an opinion. You may not be qualified to give an opinion or you may feel for some reason that it would be better to help the person work out a decision without the influence of your value system. According to an old Chinese philosopher, "If you give a man a fish, you feed him for a day; if you teach a man to fish, he can feed himself for a lifetime." Nondirectly helping people work through a decision may enhance their skills in life-long coping and feelings of independence.

Even though using directive feedback has many limitations, there are situations in which your judgment is requested, you are qualified to respond, and you feel such a response would not be harmful to the originating communicator or your relationship. In such situations, developing supportive communication climates (chapter 3) will greatly lessen potential defensiveness.

When considering and using directive feedback, apply the following guidelines.

1. Make sure the statement is identifiable as an opinion statement or value judgment. Don't assume the sender realizes it's "just your opinion."

---

1. Carl Rogers and Richard Farson, "Active Listening" in *Readings in Interpersonal and Organizational Communication,* 2d ed., ed. Richard Huseman, Cal Logue, and Dwight Freshley (Boston: Holbrook Press, 1974), p. 546.

2. Be ready to counter defensive reactions (responses to your responses) which are likely to occur—immediately or at some later interaction. Develop a supportive communication climate to reduce defensiveness. Chapter 3 indicated nonverbal indicators of defensive reactions.

3. Express the basis for your opinion (your values), not just the conclusion. For example, in the shoe buying situation discussed earlier, the friend might have said, "I like the shoes because they're stylish and inexpensive." If you were concerned about the durability of the shoes, you would then be notified that this opinion should not be pivotal in your decision.

In most extended interchanges a combination of nondirective and directive feedback may be appropriate. Be sure to consider the additional information gained by each new message (a response to your response if the other person is adapting to your feedback) as you determine the appropriate feedback response. Try to avoid directive feedback until that evaluation is appropriate. In most situations, beginning with a nondirective approach will lead to more accurate, meaningful, and helpful interpersonal relationships.

Consider the following example of nondirective and directive responses to a message.

> *Message:* "I can't understand how I flunked that test."
> *Feedback:*
> Nondirective—"What was the test like?"
> > *or*
> > "You seem really disappointed."
> Directive—"The test was probably tricky."
> > *or*
> > "You probably didn't study enough."

If the message sender was a close friend, which type of feedback would you use? Why? What effect would it be likely to have?

Once you have specified what you want to accomplish by your feedback message, select the pattern which will most likely accomplish your goal. In general, use nondirective feedback when you want to learn more about the sender's message without influencing the development by your opinion, to assist the sender in coming to a personal decision, or to be openly receptive to further messages. Use directive feedback when your goal will be best achieved by giving your opinion and only after fully understanding the message.

Feedback Channels

As with an original message, feedback can be sent through any of the human senses. Be sure to consider both verbal and nonverbal opportunities for sending feedback. In some situations (e.g., more formal or large group communication) continual verbal feedback to show response might be disruptive or otherwise considered inappropriate. In these situations you might use the following nonverbal behaviors which indicate typical responses to messages (they would be used in conjunction with verbal messages in other situations): leaning forward to show involvement; leaning back or away from the sender to show noninvolvement; slight nod of the head as understanding and encouragement to continue; puzzled look to show confusion; shaking of the head and furrowed brow to show disagreement; an open body position and arms uncrossed to show openness; arms crossed and legs crossed away from the sender as evaluation and closedness; glancing at a watch as indicating desire for the interaction to close; and the many subtleties of facial expression.

Before sending feedback consider those behaviors you want to be careful to avoid doing as well as those you want to do. The behaviors to be avoided can be determined by considering the list of potential feedback influences given earlier. To practice these ideas we suggest you do the "Feedback Pattern Selection" Learning Experience.

Feedback Pattern Selection Experience

Learning Experience

Consider the following communication situation and message. Then complete the questions following it.

A girl from down the hall came back from the library with a sheepish grin on her face. She said, "I've solved my problems of doing research for my paper." And she pulled from under her jacket three articles torn from recent periodicals. She glances at you for your reaction.

What would your goal be for sending feedback in this situation?

What feedback pattern would be most likely to assist in achieving your goal?

Why would that feedback pattern be most helpful?

Describe your exact feedback (what you would say and/or do). Specify verbal and/or nonverbal channels used. Also comment on behaviors you would refrain from doing and why.

Guidelines for Encoding Feedback

A primary feedback goal should be to communicate clearly your understanding (or lack of it) to the sender so that he or she can adapt the message accordingly.

Following are four guidelines for encoding effective feedback (some are adapted from suggestions by Barker[2]):

---

2. Larry Barker, *Listening Behavior* (Englewood Cliffs, N.J.: Prentice-Hall, Inc., 1971), pp. 123–24.

1. *Send feedback that is appropriate* to the sender, the message, and the context within which you are functioning. Inappropriate feedback will function as noise and reduce accuracy of communication.

2. *Send feedback as soon as possible.* If you send a delayed response, the originating communicator could be unsure as to what you are reacting to. To avoid such confusion, it may be helpful to clarify what you are responding to when you send delayed feedback.

3. *Clarify your intended meaning.* If you have the opportunity to send feedback verbally, use concrete symbols if possible. When using any combination of channels, be consistent in the feedback messages you send. Conflicting verbal and nonverbal symbols usually reduce the accuracy of communication.

4. *Make sure the feedback is received and understood.* Until feedback is received and understood it is not a usable part of an interaction. Carefully choose the channels which would be most effective for clear communication in a given situation. For example, in a classroom situation, if you had a specific question, orally asking the question would communicate more accurately than only nonverbally sending a quizzical look.

As it is impossible not to communicate nonverbally, you will be sending messages through nonverbal channels at all times during the interaction. Especially in situations where your responses could have long-range implications for you (as in a job interview), be aware of what you are communicating nonverbally. Let's look at the situation of a job interview. For example, if the interviewer asks if you could handle a challenging assignment with an irate customer and you say, "Yes, I am ready to handle that type of situation," while your voice is jerky and your toe is tapping nervously, then your nonverbal metacommunication is not consistent.

Let's use the four guidelines to change your response so that the nonverbal messages compliment and enhance the verbal answer. You would want to send the response as soon as possible and send the nonverbal feedback that was appropriate to your verbal message and would clarify your meaning. Having a firm voice, direct eye contact, and an initial nod of the head would really change the total message. Then, using the fourth guideline, you could look at the interviewer to see if he or she understood.

Estimating Effectiveness

Similar to overall listening goals, feedback goals provide the basis for estimating the effectiveness of feedback. Make as direct a check as is possible to determine if your feedback goals have been accomplished. In long-term interpersonal relationships openly ask others if your feedback is being perceived as you intended it. A specific point to remember is that it is the perception of the other person that finally matters. You may be sending what you consider to be positive directive feedback, but it may not be perceived as rewarding by the other person. In more formal situations you can infer the attainment of your feedback goal from the other person's nonverbal responses.

Overall Communication Climate for Responding

A listener–responder also must be concerned with the overall communication climate which is set by his or her feedback behaviors. Usually the initial choices which relate to the overall climate already have been made by the sender. However, a climate can be set by the verbal and nonverbal responses made.

Review the supportive and defensive climates researched by Gibb (chapter 3). Overall utilization of a supportive communication climate can maximize positively perceived messages and minimize the potential defensiveness encouraged by negatively perceived messages. For example, in a situation where directive-punishing feedback patterns are selected as the best way to reach set goals, an overall climate of empathy could minimize potential defensiveness.

Additional Learning Sources

Barker, Larry. *Listening Behavior.* Englewood Cliffs, N.J.: Prentice-Hall, Inc., 1971.

Clevenger, Theodore, and Matthews, Jack. *The Speech Communication Process.* Glenview, Ill.: Scott, Foresman and Co., 1971.

Devito, Joseph. *Communication: Concepts and Processes.* Englewood Cliffs, N.J.: Prentice-Hall, Inc., 1972.

Hess, Herbert, and Tucker, Charles. *Talking about Relationships.* Dubuque, Iowa: Kendall/Hunt Publishing Co., 1976.

Heun, Richard. "Inference in the Process of Cognitive Decision-Making." Unpublished Ph.D. dissertation. Department of Speech, Southern Illinois University, 1969.

Keltner, John. *Interpersonal Speech-Communication.* Belmont, Calif.: Wadsworth Publishing Co., 1970.

McCroskey, James; Larson, Carl; and Knapp, Mark. *An Introduction to Interpersonal Communication.* Englewood Cliffs, N.J.: Prentice-Hall, Inc., 1971.

Rissover, Fredrec, and Birch, David. *Mass Media and the Popular Arts.* New York: McGraw-Hill Book Co., 1971.

Ross, Raymond. *Speech Communication,* 4th ed. Englewood Cliffs, N.J.: Prentice-Hall, Inc., 1977.

Weaver, Carl. *Human Listening.* Indianapolis: Bobbs-Merrill Co., Inc., 1973.

Zimmerman, Gordon; Owen, James; and Seibert, David. *Speech Communication.* St. Paul: West Publishing Co., 1977.

Skill Test

This skill test will give you an opportunity to check your knowledge and skills in listening and sending feedback. Initiate and put yourself in the position of a responding communicator in a situation where a parent, teacher, or friend is explaining an idea to you. Select a situation where you can set a personally meaningful listening goal. We suggest that you do not let this person know you are doing this as an assignment until you are finished.

Before your communication experience, complete the precommunication form. Your instructor may want to talk about your preparation with you before the communication experience.

After the communication experience, complete the postcommunication form and share it with your instructor.

Skill Test Precommunication Form

On other sheets of paper, complete the following form.

1. State a specific, self-chosen listening situation (including description of the originating communicator and topic).
2. State a goal for your listening in this situation.
3. State two aspects of your frame of reference in relation to this specific listening situation.
4. Describe one likely effect of each aspect listed for your listening in this situation.
5. Plan three listening procedures which will help you accomplish your listening goal.
6. Describe the physical situation in which you will interact with the other person.
7. State any likely influences of the physical situation on the other person's message sending.
8. List any parts of the sender's frame of reference you already know regarding this topic that will help you to better understand the person's meanings in this situation.
9. State one goal for your feedback message(s) in this situation.
10. Select the main feedback pattern (directive or nondirective) that you will most likely use to assist you in accomplishing your feedback goal. Explain your choice.

Skill Test Postcommunication Form

On other sheets of paper, complete the following form.

1. State two parts of the other person's frame of reference, regarding this topic, which that person revealed during the interaction.
2. Describe one example of metacommunication you received during the interaction.
3. Write one value judgment the person made.
4. Infer the value statement which the value judgment was based on.
5. Write one statement of fact that the other person communicated to you.
6. Write one statement of inference that the other person communicated to you.
7. State two general criteria for analyzing the message(s) you received from this person.
8. Write a brief analysis of the message(s) using your criteria.
9. Describe your use of your chosen listening procedures and the accomplishment of your listening goal.
10. Describe your use of your chosen feedback pattern(s) and the accomplishment of your feedback goal.

Skills for the Originating Communicator

Overview

Message sending is a daily behavior. Some people, such as doctors and teachers, depend directly on their ability to call up accurate meanings in others. An important goal in your message sending situations is to have others understand your messages.

In this skill area, you will be developing skills in formulating, developing, and sending messages to specific listeners to attain high levels of understanding. When people think of speaking, they typically think of speaking to a public. Yet most speaking is done on an interpersonal level and would be better described as talking. For example, you try to explain your ideas on drugs to a friend or you try to help someone understand how to fix a flat tire. When we talk with ourselves, it is usually called "contemplation." In all of these examples of communication the central purposes are understanding and retention.

In these daily situations we've probably all been in a position to honestly say: "I would have spoken out, but I couldn't put my ideas into words." So many opportunities for initiating or improving human interaction are lost because of such reasons. Perhaps as many are lost because we do take the plunge to communicate and don't do so effectively.

In this skill area you will focus on encoding your ideas into effective messages and on decoding and using responses to your messages so that you may communicate more effectively. Also, these skills will enable you to communicate your ideas assertively. Assertive communication refers to the direct, clear, and appropriate expression of feelings, opinions, and ideas without undue anxiety and with respect for yourself and others. Assertive communication avoids the negative personal and interpersonal consequences of both nonassertive communication, which is emotionally dishonest, indirect, and self-denying, and aggressive communication, which is self-enhancing at the expense of another person. The basic principles you will learn in this skill area are applicable to any level of communication, whether sending messages with a date, your parents, a small group, or a large group.

Definitions

Accurate Communication
When the responding communicator (the listener-responder) decodes the message and calls up the same meaning as the originating communicator (the sender).

Assertive Communication
Speaking which is clear, direct, and appropriately expresses your own opinions without anxiety and with respect for others' opinions.

Communicator Credibility
The attitudes the receiver has toward the sender of the message regarding the person's friendliness, expertness, trustworthiness, and similarity.

Feedback
The message sent by the responding communicator to the originating communicator as a response to the original message sent.

Feedforward
The planning of the originating communicator in the form of setting goals, expectancies, and contingencies in order to be prepared to handle the various possible responses of the listener(s) to the message.

Feedforward Contingencies
The potential alternative message segments planned by the originating communicator to adapt to the many possible responses of the responding communicator(s) at selected important points in the development of his message.

Feedforward Expectancies
The originating communicator's prediction of how the responding communicator(s) will be responding at selected important points in his message.

Feedforward Goal
A statement, in terms of listener response, of what the originating communicator wants to achieve through a specific message or set of messages.

Originating Communicator
The sender of the original message and the receiver of feedback messages.

Rapport
The feeling of a harmonious relationship.

Responding Communicator
The receiver of the original message and sender of feedback messages.

Chapter 9

Formulating Ideas

Objectives

Your learning should enable you to:

1. Identify two specific, future situations where you might make
   a. a public statement of personal belief in your personal life.
   b. a public statement in your professional life.
2. After making a public statement of belief,
   a. use concrete symbols to clarify your meanings.
   b. indicate the value(s) which your belief implies.
   c. compare your belief to alternative views which have considerable support.
   d. indicate the implications of sharing this idea.
3. State at least four ways you could learn about a responding communicator's frame of reference for a given communicative situation.
4. Explain the relationship between a communicator's credibility and the acceptance of his or her messages.
5. For sending a specific message to a specific listener,
   a. determine your credibility.
   b. suggest specific ways to improve your credibility where needed.

Outline

I. Anticipating message-sending situations
   A. Anticipate intrapersonal, interpersonal, and public messages in your personal life
   B. Anticipate intrapersonal, interpersonal, and public messages in your professional life
II. Topics for message sending
   A. Most are determined by your expertise or responsibility
   B. Expand and stimulate what you think about with:
      1. books
      2. magazines
      3. organizations
   C. Develop skills in formulating ideas
III. Formulating ideas
   A. Make a full-sentence statement of your idea
   B. Change any of the abstract symbols to concrete ones or add an example for clarification
   C. List three or four reasons which explain why you believe as you do
   D. Cite evidence which leads you to hold this belief
   E. Indicate the value(s) that your idea implies
   F. State the alternative viewpoints to yours which have considerable support
   G. Reword your statements, including any appropriate qualifications
   H. Indicate the implications of sharing your belief with others
IV. Knowing your listener(s)
   A. Determine their frame of reference
      1. Talk with the person (or a member of the group)
      2. Talk to an opinion leader in the group
      3. Talk with someone similar to the person
      4. Read material they are reading
      5. Ask questions of the person who provided the contact
V. Communicator credibility: the attitudes the receiver has toward the sender of a message
   A. Factors influencing credibility
      1. Friendliness of the communicator
      2. Expertness of the communicator
      3. Trustworthiness of the communicator
      4. Similarity of the communicator to the receiver
   B. Suggestions for raising credibility
      1. Act in a manner perceived as friendly
         a) Talk with people beforehand
         b) React positively to feedback
         c) Show genuine interest
      2. Establish yourself as an expert
         a) Support your inferences
         b) Use careful reasoning
         c) Tell of your experiences and knowledge
         d) Borrow from authority of others by quoting
      3. Act in a trustworthy manner
         a) State the basis for your value judgments
         b) Clarify the difference between facts and inferences
         c) Use nonverbals which agree with your verbal message
      4. Show yourself to be similar to listener
         a) Verbalize similar concerns

        b) Mention similar acquaintances
        c) Mention similar experiences, groups
        d) Dress similarly

VI. Adapting message development to listeners
    A. Use information about frame of reference
    B. Remember frames of reference change over time
    C. Adapting to a number of listeners
       1. Search for commonalities
       2. Build on their reasons for being there

The ability to send messages which call up the intended meanings in others is a crucial communication skill and assumes that you have a clear intended meaning in your mind. Some messages are sent spontaneously with little preparation. Through feedback from others these ideas become clarified in the process of exchanging meanings. In other situations a more carefully thought-through idea is called for. Examples of this are your answers during an employment interview, your oral report at a business meeting, or your statement during a public speech. In these situations it is more appropriate to have your main meaning clearly formulated ahead of time. Many political candidates and businesses accomplish this important task through groups of people called "think-tanks," where campaign pitches and new products are carefully considered before going public with them. This chapter will assist you in developing skills in formulating an idea and understanding the person you will be sending your message to.

Likely Message-Sending Situations

Anticipating the message-sending situations in which you are likely to be personally and professionally involved will give you an important perspective for your skill development in the next four chapters. These situations will occur throughout your life. Within the next several weeks you may be asked to make a class speech, give an oral report of a committee's work, or speak to a community group. Many other situations will occur in the future. Take some time here to project your future message-sending needs.

First, consider your typical activities four or five years from now. Briefly describe the kind of activities you see yourself involved in. Now make a list of your likely personal and professional message-sending situations. You might use the following categories to assist your thinking.

Likely Message-Sending Situations

	Personal	Professional
Intrapersonal Messages	A	B
Interpersonal Messages	C	D
Public Messages	E	F

You will have six lists: (A) Intrapersonal messages in your personal life; (B) Intrapersonal messages in your professional life; (C) Interpersonal messages in your personal life; (D) Interpersonal messages in your professional life; (E) Public messages in your personal life; and (F) Public messages in your professional life. Examples of each might include:

A. Clarifying my personal values
B. Clarifying my professional goals
C. Having my children understand why I object to their using fireworks
D. Having the PTA understand my feeling on sex education in the schools
E. Having my officemate understand why smoking is bothersome to me
F. Having my students understand a class lecture

Try to include at least four likely situations in each list. You might talk this over with someone who might be in a similar situation in the future, or perhaps with someone you will share that future with.

Topics for Message Sending

What will you be talking about as you send messages to other people? You might go back to your six lists and place a "G" by those situations in which there will be a given or implied topic on which you would send messages. In many of the situations the issues on which you will speak are determined by some expertise or responsibility you have.

Your list may have included situations, such as talking with others at social functions or being asked to give an after-dinner speech, in which you may perceive yourself as "not having anything important to say." To come up with new ideas you can use new books, magazines, newspapers, organizations, and/or people to expand and stimulate what you think about. You also may work on developing skills in formulating your ideas.

Formulating Your Idea

After determining an idea you want to communicate, you can formulate a clear thought by using the following guidelines. At this stage, focus on creative exploration rather than structure or development of the idea.

1. *Make a full-sentence statement of your idea.* We would suggest completing the statement, "I believe . . ." to focus responsibility and ownership of the idea.
2. Is your statement sufficiently concrete so that others can learn what your idea is? Do you use abstract symbols like "good" or "right" to express your idea? Would a listener understand what your idea is? *Change any of the more abstract symbols to concrete ones or add a sentence which clarifies through example.*
3. *List three or four reasons which explain why you believe as you do.* Are each of your reasons actually different, or is one a restatement or a specific example of another reason? Work on your list of reasons until they are each different and clearly stated.
4. *Cite evidence which leads you to hold this belief.* How would you support it if questioned? Where did your belief come from? Do

additional research to clarify your idea and your reasons. Where could you discover this information? From whom?

5. *Indicate the value(s) that your idea implies.* Are your reasons actually statements of value?

6. *State the alternative viewpoints to yours which have considerable support.* Compare your belief to the other viewpoints. This will help you to anticipate questions or objections which others may have, leading them to misunderstand or distort your intended meanings.

7. Does your statement of belief apply in all situations? Would you want to qualify it in any way? *Reword your statement including any appropriate qualifications.*

8. *Indicate the implications of sharing your belief with others.* What are the implications for you personally? For those you share it with? Based on these implications, what specifically are the pros and cons of sharing this idea? What other guidelines would you add to help you think through an idea before expressing it? Try the following experience to develop your skills in formulating an idea.

Imagine yourself in the following situation. Make a statement of belief and apply the eight guidelines (plus any of your own) to that statement.

"Your father tells you that the doctor has just told him that your mother has only two months to live. He has decided not to tell her and asks for your opinion. What do you believe he should do?"

Learning Experience

Knowing Your Listener(s)

Many communicators encode messages in the way that they would find easiest to understand if they were listening. This is like talking to your own reflection in a full-length mirror. However, we know that no two people or their frames of reference for a situation are exactly alike. As people are increasingly different, the chances of accurate communication occurring become smaller. Similar understandings are possible only if you, as an originating communicator, choose to encode your messages in ways that adapt to your receivers as real and unique people.

The accuracy of any communication increases as the consistency of messages with the listener's frame of reference increases. Because of their frames of reference, listeners often will "not hear" or "mishear" what has been said. If listeners do not have the necessary experiences or vocabulary, they might not understand at all. People also might substitute or add additional meanings to what they hear. The process of *selective attention* leads individuals to focus on only parts of a message; *selective processing* to decode and think about that message based on personal meanings; and *selective retention* to remember only parts of a message and to remember them as they interpreted them. Since it is listener understanding that counts in most message sending, it is vital to adapt the message to each listener.

In order to adapt messages to specific listeners, it is necessary to know them so that you can anticipate how they will decode the message.

The process of knowing a listener means understanding his or her frame of reference for the communicative situation you will share. Reviewing from chapter 3, the parts of the frame of reference are: (a) stored information in the form of experiences, values, and attitudes; (b) important needs; and (c) perceptions of the communication situation. Let's explore some of the ways in which you could learn about a person's frame of reference.

If you are giving a speech to your classmates you will already know quite a bit about them. Some of what you have learned will be from what they have said and done in class and some from informal communication outside of class. In interpersonal communication, information about frames of reference is often shared in the early stages of a relationship. Answers to such questions as "Where do you live?" "How many in your family?" "Do you smoke?" and "What do you really get angry about?" lead to increasing mutual understanding.

Sometimes you will be sending messages in situations where you will not know your listener personally. Such examples may include a job interview or a public speech. Below are several ways to learn about and infer what your listener's(s') frame of reference is for a communicative situation.

1. Talk with the person (or one member of the group) prior to your message sending in another situation and share perceptions and experiences.
2. Talk to an opinion leader in the group who influences others' ideas.
3. Talk with someone quite similar to the person you will be communicating with.
4. Read magazines, newspapers, and books that they are reading.
5. Ask questions of the person who provided the communication opportunity (a friend who got you the job interview, the person who asked you to make the speech).

What other methods could you add to the list to discover the frames of reference of the people you will communicate with?

After you gather information and understanding about their frames of reference, infer the goals and expectations they will have for the communication situation you will be in. How might their goals and expectations lead them to selectively attend to, think about, and remember your message?

Communicator Credibility

One of the most important applications of people's expectations for a communication situation is how they perceive the people they are speaking and listening to. *The attitude which the receiver has toward the sender of a message* is referred to as *credibility*. When a listener receives a communication, the two dominant sets of stimuli he or she receives are the message and the originating communicator. Phrases such as *credibility gap* are common today to describe a situation—when our attitudes toward some people or offices are so low, we do not trust what they say.

Research studies have suggested that certain factors are among the most influential in determining a responding communicator's acceptance of the originating communicator. Some factors refer to a general image that the listener has of the sender and some to a more specific relationship of the originating communicator to the issue involved in the message.

Factors influencing communicator credibility are

Friendliness of the communicator;

Expertness of the communicator on this topic area;

Trustworthiness of the communicator on this topic area;

Similarity of the communicator to the listener.

In many situations your listener may not be aware of your expertness to talk about an idea or of other qualifications related to credibility. In other situations, your credibility may not be high due to certain perceptions your listener has of you. Because of the vital importance of that person's attitude toward you as she or he decodes and processes your message in both situations, it is important to raise the level of your credibility before communicating your ideas to that person.

Your credibility will be determined not only by what the responding communicator(s) knows about you from previous experiences, but also by how you function within a communicative situation nonverbally as well as verbally. For example, behaviors exhibiting friendliness might be perceived as more genuine than a verbal statement.

A CREDIBLE SOURCE...
"AFTER ONE COURSE IN PSYCHOLOGY?"

The following suggestions can assist you in improving your credibility in a given situation.

1. *Act in a manner that will be perceived as friendly by the listener(s).*
   Talk with people beforehand (if group).
   React positively to feedback.
   Show genuine interest.

2. *Establish yourself as expert enough to send your message.*
   Be ready to support your inferences.
   Use careful reasoning.
   Tell of your experience and knowledge about the issue.
   Borrow from the authority of others by quoting authorities *acceptable to the listeners.*
3. *Act in a manner that will be perceived as trustworthy by the listener.*
   State the basis of your value judgments.
   Clarify the difference between your statements of fact and inference.
   Use nonverbals which reinforce the verbal message, not contradict it.
4. *Show yourself to be similar in some way to the listener(s).*
   Verbalize similar concerns ("We all want to . . .").
   Mention similar acquaintances.
   Mention similar experiences, membership groups.
   Dress similarly.

Learning Experience

Consider yourself in the following communication situations. You are explaining to your parents your ideas on each of the topics listed below. Write first how your parents would assess your credibility on each topic, in terms of the factors listed in this part. Then suggest how you could raise your credibility if necessary.

Inflation
Poker
The Middle East

Adapting Your Message Development to Your Listeners

Based on the information and inferences you make about your receivers, you can adjust the development of your message and your sending behaviors to best fit their frames of reference. In the next three chapters you will be working on skills in developing your messages to adapt to particular frames of reference.

Caution is in order when we talk about learning a person's frame of reference. We are suggesting that it is important to understand a person at a given time, in relation to the *you* as perceived by the other person, and in relation to the topic and setting of the communicative experience being considered. But we don't suggest you assume their frame of reference will be the same another time. Each variable will have potentially changed. This realization is especially important and difficult to remember in an ongoing relationship. It is too easy to feel that we "know" someone we interact with a great deal. However, effective communication is more probable when we keep in mind the constantly changing frames of reference of the people with whom we interact.

Adapting to Groups of Listeners

There are specific challenges when you send a message to more than one listener, as each listener will have his or her own frame of reference toward that situation. In most situations, however, there will be a common element which brings that group of people together to listen to you.

You may only know your listeners as a *group* of college students, PTA members, or football players. But you will always know *something* about, or can *find out something* about, your listeners. Most likely they will have several qualities in common which would be related to your topic. For example, in dealing with a group of college students, you could infer several things about them: "most of my listeners come from rural areas"; "most of my listeners have not experienced extreme deprivation of food or clothing"; "most of my listeners are relatively conservative"; or that they are "interested in learning new things in order to expand their current understanding." In chapter 11 you will be working on skills in anticipating reactions and adapting to them. This is extremely helpful when you are talking with a group of people.

Chapter 10

Developing Messages

Objectives

Your learning should enable you to:

1. State seven principles of effective understanding.
2. Recognize examples of parts of messages which appropriately apply the seven principles of effective understanding.
3. Improve a message by applying the principles of effective understanding.
4. Create examples of the seven principles of effective understanding to adapt an intended meaning to a specific person.
5. State three principles of message retention.
6. Improve the likelihood that a message will be remembered, by applying specific principles to encourage retention.

Outline

I. Accuracy of communication is maximized by using principles of effective understanding
  A. Structure: People understand better when something is organized to fit their methods of decoding and thinking
    1. Structure refers to the relationship of message parts in a message
    2. Main parts of a message are the introduction, body, and conclusion
      a) Body
        (1) Organized to adapt to the way a listener thinks
        (2) Developed first in message preparation
        (3) Three main body structures
          (a) Chronological pattern: development of an idea by a step-by-step time sequence
            i) Approach uses a concrete description
            ii) Useful for receiver with little background on topic
          (b) Topical pattern: development of an idea by distinguishable and parallel parts
            i) Put more understandable parts first
            ii) Put more acceptable parts first
          (c) Inductive-Deductive pattern: development of an idea by reasons-leading-to-a-conclusion or conclusion-supported-by-reasons approach
            i) Use inductive with opposing listener
            ii) Use deductive with accepting listener
        (4) Preview the type of structure in introduction
        (5) Highlight main parts by preview and review
      b) Introduction
        (1) Usually prepared second
        (2) Purposes include:
          (a) Gain attention
          (b) Motivate listener
          (c) Introduce idea
          (d) Build credibility
      c) Conclusion
        (1) Usually prepared last
        (2) Purposes include:
          (a) Summarize important parts of the message
          (b) Reinforce parts to be remembered
  B. Attention: People understand better when their concentration is focused primarily on the material to be understood
    1. Use materials that are unusual
    2. Use materials that arouse feelings of uncertainty
    3. Use materials that get listeners involved
    4. Use materials that meet important needs
    5. Use materials that are concrete
    6. Maintain attention throughout message
    7. Example: tell a brief personal story
  C. Motivation: People understand better when they want to understand
    1. Motivation is goal-directed behavior
    2. Associate your message with important needs of the listener
    3. Reinforce important reasons for being there
    4. Example: ask who would like to reduce their study time

D. Visualization: People understand better what they can see or imagine
 1. Two ways to accomplish: building image with words or show actual physical object
 2. Use guidelines for selection
   a) Visualization should be appropriate
   b) Visualization should be vivid
   c) Visualization should be coordinated with other content
 3. Examples: a chart showing how poor people spend their money or a vivid description of poor family's house
E. Comparison: People understand better when they can compare something new to something they already know
 1. Compare an unknown idea with a known idea
 2. Example: comparing business cycles to riding a roller coaster
F. Repetition: People understand better when they experience something repeatedly
 1. Two forms of repetition
   a) Repetition in the same words
   b) Restatement in different words
 2. Summaries and transitions are helpful repetitions
G. Symbol Usage: People understand better when the language limits the range of potential meanings to be called up
 1. Word-for-word preplanning of symbols only done for very formal messages
 2. Use concrete symbols to call up intended denotative meanings
   a) Level of concreteness dependent on background knowledge of listener
   b) Specify qualifications when using the symbol "is"
 3. Choose symbols that will call up intended connotative meanings
 4. Use assertive symbols to communicate personal meaning
   a) Use "I" statements like "I think"
   b) Use supportive climates
   c) Use cooperative symbols like "we"
II. Retention of communication is maximized by using principles of effective remembering
 A. Repetition
  1. 4–5 repetitions are needed to encourage high levels of remembering
  2. Provide a handle so that repetition will occur often within listener's experience
    a) Connect an important part of your ideas with something the listener will experience often
  3. Review and preview
  4. Example: develop and use a catchy phrase throughout message
 B. Visualization
  1. Develop concrete picture they can see in their minds
  2. Use direct representation or vivid example
 C. Stress of Main Ideas
  1. Stress main ideas verbally
    a) Direct reference to point by transitions
    b) Repetition
    c) Place at beginning or end of message
    d) Develop and use key terms
  2. Stress main ideas nonverbally
    a) Change the loudness of delivery
    b) Pause before and after point
    c) Change body position before point
    d) Change in speed of delivery
    e) Maintain eye contact longer before point

In Skill Area One *accurate communication* was defined as *communication in which both the originating communicator and the responding communicator of a message called up the same meaning.* It was suggested that total accuracy, that is, for all participants in a communication exchange to call up the identical set of connotative and denotative meanings, is impossible. It is possible, however, to interact with others with an adequately high degree of accuracy, especially in denotative meanings. One of the most basic goals of most communicators is to have their messages understood by the other person. The likelihood of encoding a message which specific people will accurately understand is maximized by the utilization of the following seven principles of effective understanding.

1. *Structure*—People understand better that which is organized to fit their methods for decoding and thinking.
2. *Attention*—People understand better when their concentration is focused on the material to be understood.
3. *Motivation* (reward)—People understand better that which they want to understand.
4. *Visualization*—People understand better that which they can see or imagine.
5. *Comparison*—People understand better when they are able to compare a new concept with a concept they already know.
6. *Repetition* (redundancy)—People understand better what they experience repeatedly.
7. *Symbol Usage*—People understand better when the language in the message limits the range of potential meanings to be called up.

In communicating to inform, explain, describe or demonstrate, using these seven principles will help you to accomplish accurate understanding.

Structure

Structure refers to *the relationship of message parts within a message.* The overall message usually follows the sequence of introduction, body, and conclusion. While these aspects are more carefully worked out in pre-planned messages, all messages attempt to introduce the issue to be discussed, to develop that idea, and to close the communication. The message development, or body of the message, is the first part developed in pre-planned messages. This contains the main meanings you want your listener to understand.

Body

In this part of the message you actually communicate what you want the listeners to understand. Each part of the discussion usually is highlighted by flashback-and-preview transitions as described in Repetition. The discussion part of the message is completed when the responding communicators fully understand your idea.

The body of your message should be structured in terms of the way a receiver thinks. This makes it easier for the person to understand and retain your message. As you interact with people, you become more sensitive to the thinking processes they use. You could probably tell us the way each of your parents makes decisions. You could also typify some of the major thought patterns of your close friends or of your boss, if you've worked at the same place for a long time. You might recognize some of their ways of thinking in the following list. The typical ways in which people think about the information they decode: some people gather a lot of information and carefully sift through it, looking at it from many possible viewpoints; others make quick judgments based on already-held values and/or past experiences; others look for exceptions to what you are saying to better understand the idea; and others make one-to-one comparisons with other situations they're familiar with or other ideas they have. Each of the other principles of understanding that follow can be adapted to different thought patterns. Following are three main types of structure for the body of your message and suggestions for adapting them to various thinking patterns.

Chronological pattern.   This pattern refers to developing an idea in terms of a step-by-step time structure, i.e., what happened (or is to be done) first, second, third, and so forth. This pattern is most often used to explain something which would happen (or did happen) over a period of time such as an experience, event, giving directions. It would be most helpful with responding communicators who have little knowledge and/or experience with the area you are trying to help them understand because such a pattern tends to be very concrete and visually descriptive as well as providing the necessary links between bits of information.

Topical pattern.   This pattern refers to developing an idea in terms of distinguishable and parallel parts, i.e., three aspects of an idea, three reasons why you believe an idea, three suggestions as to how to handle a problem. If you use a topical pattern you would consider those parts of your idea that would be most understandable and/or acceptable to the responding communicators, based on their experiences, attitudes, values, and needs. Put those more acceptable and/or understandable points first in the message and then move on to more difficult and/or less acceptable points. This pattern provides a basis on which the responding communicators can more easily provide the mental links between your ideas and their own frames of reference.

Inductive or deductive pattern.   These patterns refer to developing an idea in terms of a reasons-leading-to-a-conclusion or a conclusion-supported-by-reasons approach. If you anticipate the responding communicator will have contrary attitudes toward your idea, then an inductive pattern (from examples to the reason or from the reasons to the idea) will be less likely to create the barriers of selective attention, processing, and retention. If, on the other hand, they appear to have no contrary attitudes toward your idea, then a deductive pattern (idea followed by reasons or reasons followed by example) will lead to understanding.

The decision as to which of these patterns, or many other potential patterns, to use should be based on your understanding of the frame of reference of your listener. This decision can be guided by these questions: (1) How does the listener usually process meaning? and (2) What pattern will fit into the listener's frame of reference in terms of his or her knowledge, attitudes, and values?

Learning Experience

To improve your skills in selecting an organizational pattern to help a responding communicator fully understand an idea of yours, complete the following analysis and structure development.

Write down an idea you have which is quite different from one your father/mother has.

Write down several ways in which you think your father/mother processes meaning when talking with you (e.g., makes snap judgments, takes a long time to think it out, has many good reasons for an opinion, and so forth).

Select one of the basic patterns discussed here or another you are familiar with and explain how that pattern would best fit your father's/mother's frame of reference and his/her meaning processing.

Provide some indication in the introduction to your message as to what type of pattern you will use. This might be a very casual, "Let me tell you how that fight with Joe developed," or a more formal, "Today I'd like to share with you three of the concerns I have about our present grading system and conclude with a recommendation for change." Such indications usually follow attention and motivation factors. After developing the body of your message, consider appropriate ways of introducing and concluding it.

"CONSIDERING POSSIBLE ORGANIZATIONS"

Introduction

During the introduction you help the responding communicator set his or her listening goals by previewing the topic to be discussed. A specific attempt is made in the introduction to gain the attention of the listeners, to motivate them to understand, to introduce the idea to be developed, and to build your credibility. (See part of this chapter for specific suggestions on developing Attention and Motivation and parts of the last chapter on building credibility.) The introduction is successful when the responding communicators want to understand your idea, are positive toward you as a sender, and have enough of an idea of what is coming to set their own listening goals.

Conclusion

The conclusion to your message should tie together its important parts and reinforce those parts to be remembered. A typical conclusion summarizes and suggests any further considerations or action. It may also include a direct request for feedback. One valuable way to provide closure for your message is to follow up on a common thread, story, joke, and so forth, you have developed through your message (see sections on Attention and Motivation for specifics.)

Attention

Attention can be defined as *a focus of the receiving senses* and is vital as a preliminary step to understanding. William James, one of America's most influential early psychologists, said, "that which controls attention, controls behavior." If you want someone to understand you—gain and hold his attention. Thus, your first task as an originating communicator is to gain the responding communicators' attention.

Attention and motivation are closely related. We pay attention to some things because our frames of reference lead us to perceive selectively. That is, we pay attention to things because they are important, vital, or useful to us. We also are drawn toward a stimulus because it is unusual and intriguing. People's attention is focused on materials which

1. are unusual
2. arouse feelings of uncertainty or curiosity
3. get listeners involved
4. meet important needs
5. are concrete rather than abstract

Conversation openers like, "Wait until you hear this," "You wanted a date for Friday, didn't you?" or using the person's first name are examples of interpersonal communication attention getters. In public communication a major goal of the introduction to your message will be to gain the attention of your listeners. Among the more successful openers to messages are those which immediately relate to the experience of your listeners and lead them to be curious about what follows. Openers like "Have you ever wondered what it would be like to actually . . . ?" or "Let me tell you a story about a person who might live very near you and you've never seen . . ." are examples. Another highly successful attention getter is to get listeners physically involved in the experience. Such openers as "Will all of you who have ever . . . , please raise your hands," "Please close your eyes for a minute and . . . ," or "In a minute I'd like you to all yell the worst word you can think of" are examples. These openers will usually lead the listeners to focus on you and your message.

> Assume you are going to explain to a group of children the rules for playing basketball. The setting will be you with a basketball in your hands in an elementary school physical education class. The message will take about three minutes. Write several sentences which probably would positively gain the attention of the children and direct that attention to your topic. Specifically use at least two of the earlier suggestions.
>
> Second, if their attention was distracted, write two or more sentences you could use during the messages to refocus their attention on the message content.

Learning Experience

Unfortunately, getting their initial attention is not enough. We have all heard messages that were all downhill after a good start. As you develop the rest of your message, use the above five suggestions for keeping attention. One valuable technique is to start a story, joke, or involvement experience at the beginning of your message and pick up on it several times during the message: "You remember that unknown neighbor I mentioned at the beginning of my message, well . . ." or "Remember how you felt when your eyes were closed earlier and you didn't know what was going to happen . . . well . . ." are examples.

Motivation

Being motivated really means being ready to do something to accomplish a goal. *Motivation* can be defined as *goal-directed behavior*. If you want or need to satisfy hunger, you're motivated to eat. If you want or need admiration, you'll dress, behave, wear your hair in ways that get you the desired admiration. If you want or need to feel you have accomplished something, you'll be motivated to finish the things you start.

A vital part of our frame of reference is our important needs. If you can let receivers know that your message will help them accomplish one of their important needs, you will have motivated them to pay attention to, think about, and remember your message. Consequently, an important question for you as an originating communicator is, "What are my listeners' important needs and how can my message relate to those needs?"

Ask yourself, "How can I motive my listeners to want to understand? Listeners will be motivated if you can show them that the information is vitally important or useful to them. Thus, in preparing to send messages, study your listeners to discover if anything in their frames of reference (attitudes, needs, desires, values, interests) could lead toward their wanting to understand the information. People usually are motivated to better understand themselves and the situations they are in.

For example, if you want to arouse interest in tornado safety procedures, you might describe vividly the effects of exposure to tornadoes and attempt to show that the information you are giving may be used to save the responding communicators' lives sometime. Or to interest a friend in understanding the use of credit cards, you could suggest that understanding your hassle with credit cards could prevent her or him from having the same hassle.

In many communicative situations the responding communicator's presence will indicate that he is already motivated to some extent. For example, a person asking for directions, a friend inquiring about your weekend, or a group of people coming to hear you talk about your recommendations for an environmental action group all bring some motivation to the experience. As an originating communicator you might then reinforce or focus the motivation that brought the responding communicators to the interaction.

But do not assume that a person's presence infers motivation. Individuals might be in a given communicative situation for a related purpose, but they might not be directly motivated to understand your message. For example, some students are motivated to attend class sessions to "pass the course" —or even more long-term motivation of "getting the degree." If the teacher's goal as originating communicator is to help students understand why hydrogen's qualities make it such a valuable substance, it would be vital to link that understanding to some part of the students' frames of reference so as to motivate them toward understanding hydrogen.

You probably have been in an interpersonal situation where another person has felt left out of a conversation. If you receive this nonverbal message, you might help that person discover a relationship between some aspect of his frame of reference and the conversation. If he discovers such a relationship, he would likely be more motivated to understand the ideas of other people involved in the conversation.

In each of these types of situations be concrete as you build motivation. For example, to motivate your brother to understand grammar which of the following would be more motivational: "It's important to be able to use grammatically correct English," or cite job application refusals or sales lost because of errors in grammar? Since a responding communicator does not understand well unless he or she wants to understand, you should plan to develop motivation early in your message and continue to maintain it throughout the interaction.

Visualization

When we attempt to visualize something we are trying to help others see or imagine what we are talking about. Two means of using visualization are: (1) to send a message through one of the senses other than that of hearing to actually show the receivers what we mean, or (2) to send the message through the sense of hearing by vividly describing what we are talking about so that the receivers can create a new image in their minds.

The most typical use of the first means of visualization is called a visual aid and includes charts, pictures, and artifacts. Visual aids can draw attention and provide memory aids as well as increase understanding. One of the most useful visual aids is the chart or model which simplifies a complex idea. For example, a simple bar graph showing varying grade point averages of freshmen, sophomores, juniors, and seniors would likely be more understandable and more memorable than a person telling those statistics. This is especially helpful because we know that people are different in the decoding skills they have developed. Some people are more skilled in listening, some in reading, and some in direct experience.

Draw a graph, chart, or model which visualizes the following information: Of a farmer's total income, 50 percent came from cattle, 20 percent from hogs, 25 percent from soybeans, and 5 percent from corn.

Show your visualization to another person in the course. Ask that person if he or she has any suggestions for improving your visualization.

Learning Experience

You might try using other senses to help a person to imagine what you are talking about. This is more often and more naturally done in dyadic communication, but it is equally vital in situations where there are many listeners. Direct contact with other senses is also more involving for the responding communicator, further enhancing the likelihood of that person fully understanding your idea. Remember when selecting such aids to understanding that they should be appropriate, easily understood, simple, and well coordinated with the verbal message.

"TELLING IT LIKE IT WAS"

The second means of visualization is accomplished through the use of highly descriptive, concrete symbols. Words like *oozing, slithery, velvety, rotted, prickly,* and so forth call up strong visual images in people's minds. A message on soil conservation was concluded using visualization as follows:

> "Without additional soil saving efforts on the part of the farmers and the government, we face a depressing picture for our future. Rolling fields that are now fertile and rich with topsoil will be eroded and cut by gullies. Good grazing land will be covered by a thin weedy growth. . . ."

Perhaps you have had the experience of someone describing something so well that you vividly felt the experience of the sender.

Comparison

People usually understand a new idea or thing by seeing how it relates to something they already know. For example, if you were describing a person to a listener who doesn't know the person, what would you do? Probably you would call to their mind a person they do know who is like the unknown person and then add or subtract characteristics to describe the unknown person. We often make comparisons in our everyday conversations, in describing new tastes, people, and experiences. In fact, it is almost impossible to talk about anything new without using comparisons.

Comparison is used here to refer to *communication in which a "new" (unknown) idea to the listener is compared or contrasted to an "old" (already known) idea.* Communication which compares two unknown ideas does little to facilitate understanding of either idea. When comparing two unknown ideas, such as the mating habits of the Three-toed Great Northern Woodpecker and the Peruvian Llama, a person might understand something of the differences between them but little about their respective mating habits. Often comparisons are attention getters as well, by pointing up similarities or differences which a receiver might not have thought of, such as comparing in some detail running a presidential campaign to running a marathon foot race.

Given are several topics and a brief description of the person you are trying to explain each topic to. In light of the description of the person, write down something within that person's frame of reference to which you could compare the new topic so he would better understand the new topic.

Learning Experience

New topic	Description of person	Familiar topic to compare with
Germination of soybeans	City dweller	
Car's electrical system	Politician inexperienced with auto mechanics	
Mulching a garden	Schoolteacher inexperienced in gardening	
Odor of industrial pollution	Someone living on a farm	

Repetition

We probably have all heard a parent, teacher, marriage partner, or police sergeant say something very much like, "But, I told him twice!" The meaning might have been "how could he have forgotten after I told him twice?" The person being talked about may have decoded the meaning but did not remember it.

Learning research tells us that individuals understand and remember best that to which they are exposed repeatedly. The effective communicator uses various types of repetition to reinforce his or her ideas. Repetition usually takes two forms: (1) repetition of the idea in the same words and (2) restatement of the idea in different words (or using a different channel).

Repetition helps to overcome the gaps in the listeners' overall understanding of your message which occur as they continually are refocusing their attention. Summaries and transitions are types of repetitions of main ideas as well as aids in structuring messages. The message is often organized so as to begin with a brief *initial summary* of the main points to be made, followed by the elaboration of those points, and followed, finally, by a more detailed *final summary*.

Throughout the message main ideas frequently are repeated or restated, sometimes through the use of flashback-and-preview transitions (or *summary transitions*). That is, when the sender finishes her discussion of one point, she repeats her core ideas and then leads into the next point by a brief summary of that point. Thus, at this point, we might say, "We have discussed how to use Structure, Attention, Motivation, Visualization, Comparison, and Repetition. The next important principle of understanding to be discussed is Symbol Usage." This summary-transition would aid in structuring a person's thinking and also help in remembering.

Symbol Usage

In chapter 1 you learned about the decoding process in which people attached denotative and connotative meanings to symbols they received. As a final step in the development of your message, select the symbols which will be most likely to call up your intended meaning.

Unless the communicative situation is very formal and the actual symbols you use are quite important, you'll not be likely to plan your message word for word. Examples of situations which might call for such careful planning are a United States presidential address or a public service announcement explaining tornado warning procedures. The decision on how exactly you need to preplan the symbols you use should be based on the consequences of inaccurate communication. In our first example, a consequence might be offending some nationality or cultural group; in the second, it could be the loss of life. When you make the choice to plan your message word for word, you must balance the gains of potentially more accurate communication with the loss of flexibility. Flexibility allows you to adapt to reactions of your listeners and also creates a more personal climate. In fact, even knowing the reason for the President's carefully preparing public statements, you have undoubtedly heard people criticize him for "reading the message." Some presidents, such as President Carter have risked misunderstanding by talking "off the cuff" to create a more personal communication climate.

As you consider the type of symbols you will use to communicate your meanings you will want to review your receivers' frames of reference with specific emphasis on the nature and level of their store of information (experiences, values, and attitudes); their perception of the communication situation; and their resulting expectations of you in that communicative situation. Let's examine each of those a bit more.

The most basic consideration is whether the listeners have the necessary background knowledge to understand the symbols you choose. You might not want to use a lot of new slang words with people from a foreign country who know only English from formal study.

Use of Concrete Symbols

People understand something better when the symbols used are *concrete*, with *specific references clearly related to the message symbols.* Symbol *concreteness* refers to *the use of symbols which stand for particular things rather than abstract ideas and objects.* Thus you reduce ambiguity by more clearly specifying your meaning. This often means using additional words to insure full understanding rather than a general statement which would assume that the responding communicator would fill in the specific meaning in the way the originating communicator intended him or her to. For example, you might make the somewhat abstract statement "students are mature enough to handle responsibility." It is very likely that, while a listener might have a general understanding of what you mean, each listener would probably attach different specific meanings for that statement. A listener might, for instance, think you meant that a student should have no restrictions, personally or academically; whereas you actually meant that a student should be allowed to take a major role in making decisions about his or her personal life, but not necessarily have free rein in his or her academic life.

Using *more concrete symbols* is also important *when* you are *communicating your feelings.* For example, the abstract statement, "I can't stand him!" could call up many and varied meanings in the mind of a responding communicator. The setting probably would give the listener cues as to your intended meaning but you could help to reduce the ambiguity by a statement more like, "When John arrives late for our date, I get really tense!"

Here is another example which gets at the importance of knowing a person's experiences and knowledge about your idea when determining the specificity of words to use.

A person experienced in carpentry would likely understand the more abstract statement in reference to constructing a porch, "Use appropriate reinforcing structures where there will be extra stress." A person with less experience would not be as likely to "call to mind" the specific meanings intended. The sender would need to use concrete language to specify "appropriate reinforcing structures" and to indicate likely places where extra stress is likely when building porches.

Therefore, the goal is to use enough sufficiently concrete words to adapt to the specific listener's level of stored information related to the idea. We don't mean that you should totally omit the beauty of abstract words like *love, peace,* and *joy,* but that you use them knowing that each person will have his or her own meaning for such abstract symbols.

Learning Experience

Choose one of the following tasks that you are able to do well enough to teach another person how to do it. (If you feel that none of them are appropriate for you, substitute one that is.)
   Planting a garden
   Changing the oil of a car
   Sailing a sailboat

Write instructions for someone who has a general knowledge of the topic area.

Now write instructions for someone who has no knowledge of the area. Go back to your first set of instructions and pick out any symbol or combination of symbols which might not call up a specific referent and use more concrete symbols in their place.

Try out your instructions on a person fitting each category. Do these people understand well enough to do the task?

Use of the symbol "is" to describe people and events is another abstraction that usually leads to inaccurate decoding, thinking about, and retention of messages. When you use the word *is* in a sentence to describe a person or event, the statement is so general that it implies that the person or event never changes.

Let's say that you worked with a person at an after-school job in high school. You say casually to a potential future employer of that other person, "Joe is a sloppy worker." It sounds as though you've described a permanent quality of Joe and you've told all about him as a worker; when actually all you could say was that based on your experience, at a particular time, in a particular situation, Joe, was, in your opinion, a sloppy worker. (This might also be an important place to use concrete language to identify what you mean by sloppy.) What is important here is how the receiver is likely to interpret your comment.

When using the word *is,* use the following qualifiers to clarify the actual meaning.

1. "In my opinion" to indicate that it is only one person's viewpoint.
2. Time-date the statement—Put the statement in an appropriate context by indicating the time or date to which the observation specifically refers. For example, "during the last month of my senior year in high school." Also describe the circumstances surrounding the situation.

We have been talking mainly about denotative meaning. That is, will the other person know what you are referring to by the symbols you use? Another important consideration is the connotative meanings that a particular symbol is likely to call up in that person's mind. Again consider the listeners' values and attitudes as well as their experiences. For example, the symbols, "woman," "chick," "gal," and "lady" may all denotatively refer to the same thing, but they all have quite different connotative meanings to many people. Using them interchangeably or inappropriately could lead to inaccurate communication for some people. Such unadapted symbol usage, even though unintentional, can lead to lowered credibility for you and distortion of your message.

In anticipating both the denotative and connotative meanings that your listeners could attach to your symbols, consider also the influence of their important needs and perceptions of the communication situation. An example of the former would be a person, who is deeply concerned about the illness of a friend, overreacting to a reference to carelessness about health checkups. An example of the latter might be a person's angry reaction to your using a private phrase to refer to him/her in a more public situation. Because it is not possible to be aware of all factors which will influence a person's meaning attaching, your skills in using feedforward (developed in the next chapter) are quite important.

After you have made decisions about the choice of symbols to best denote and connote your meaning, plan to use them assertively. Figure 14 suggests the kind of qualifying and connecting words that characterize assertive, nonassertive, and aggressive communication. Add several words to each list from your own experience.

Characteristics of Verbal Behavior		
Nonassertive	*Assertive*	*Aggressive*
Qualifiers like "I guess," "only," "just"	*"I" statements* like "I think," "I feel"	Threats like "you'd better agree," "if you don't watch out"
Fillers like "um," "you know"	*Supportive climates,* See Gibb, chapter 3	
Negaters like "you'll probably disagree," "this isn't really important, but . . ."	*Cooperative words* like "we," "let's"	*Putdowns* like "you must be kidding"
		Evaluations like "bad," "wrong," "right"
		Sexist or racist words

FIGURE 14

In summary, while it is usually not appropriate to plan your symbol usage word-for-word, it is helpful to choose the kind of symbols which are most likely to call up your intended meanings. This is done based on the listeners' frames of reference for that situation. Following is a list of criteria which will be helpful in making your choice of the kinds of symbols to use to communicate your meaning.

1. Would the person be likely to know the denotative meaning you are attaching to the symbol?
2. Is the symbol concrete enough to call up a meaning similar to yours? If it is not, what additional qualifiers would make it more concrete?
3. Has the person had past experiences with the symbol which would lead to unintended connotative meanings?
4. Will the current needs of the person lead to distortion of the denotative or connotative meanings of the symbol?
5. Will the person's perception of you as a sender lead to inappropriate meaning attaching?

What other criteria would you add to this list in determining the symbols you would use to communicate an intended meaning?

Improving Retention of Messages

Often it is important that listeners do more than understand the message; they should retain (remember) it. Several techniques are helpful to a sender in leading the listener(s) to remember the important parts of a message.

Repetition, discussed earlier, is perhaps the most valuable technique in improving retention of messages. Generally, the more often we hear something, the more likely we are to remember it. A research study was done with 253 college students to provide answers to questions of this kind. Messages were prepared which were seventy statements long. (The whole message might have been six to eight minutes in length.) The students were tested by recall immediately after the message statements. If the students' recall had been tested later, the percentages in chart 3 would most likely have gone down. For example, after only one hour people typically cannot recall a large percentage of what they initially remembered. Chart 3 indicates the varying degrees of effectiveness for holding attention and increasing memory of repetition and other methods of emphasis.[1]

CHART 3.   *Ranked effectiveness of modes of emphasis*

(Most   5 repetitions
Effective)_ 90%_ 4 repetitions
     _ 80%_ 3 repetitions
     _ 70%_ Primacy—first statement in the message
             Verbal emphasis before an idea ("Now get this")
             2 distributed repetitions (in the middle and far apart)
             Primacy—second statement in the message
             2 distributed repetitions in the message (in the middle and
                 close together)
     _ 60%_ Verbal emphasis—after an idea ("Did you notice that")
             Pause
             Recency—last statement in the message
     _ 50%_ Primacy—third statement in the message
             Recency—second from last statement in the message
             2 repetitions (together at the end)
             Loudness
             Bang
             Recency—third from last statement in the message
             Gesture
     _ 40%_ 2 repetitions (together at the beginning)
             Normal—statements intermediate between primacy and re-
(Least   cency, unemphasized
Effective) 30% Slowness of speech

Only two modes of emphasis (5 or 4 repetitions) led to 90 percent or more recall! Only three repetitions led to 80 percent or more immediate recall!

How can you use the information to help people remember your ideas? Why not give repetition a try? Four or five repetitions of an idea in the same words really works. Chart 3 indicates that two repetitions together (whether at the beginning or at the end of the message) were recalled by less than 50 percent of the students.

Direct repetition is often used within the structure of the message by preview and review methods. A catchy phrase related to the idea often is developed and repeated several items throughout the message.

It is also helpful to provide a "handle" for listeners which is repeated; that is, to connect the remembering of your idea with something they will likely do or see often and reinforce that connection several times. Select some aspect of their frames of reference and connect your idea to it.

Visualization also can improve retention of messages. People will remember better if they have a concrete picture of what you're talking about in their mind through a direct representation or an example.

---

1. Arthur Jersild, "Modes of Emphasis in Public Speaking," *Journal of Applied Psychology* 12 (1928): 611–29.

Stressing main ideas is a third essential method of helping people to remember your message. Highlight what it is you want them to remember. Reviewing from chapter 6, verbal indicators that an important point is about to be, or is being, made include (1) direct reference to the point by transitions, (2) repetition, (3) position in the message (usually the most important points occur at the beginning and end), and (4) developing and using key terms.

Nonverbal methods of stressing can also be used. Nonverbal indicators which will assist listeners in knowing an important point is being given include (1) change in the loudness-softness of delivery, (2) change in the rate of delivery (usually slowing down), (3) pausing before and after the point, (4) changing body position (leaning forward, moving to another position), and (5) maintaining eye contact for a slightly longer period of time just before making the point (often in conjunction with a verbal transition).

The following was one of the top five messages in a national oratory contest. Read through the message attempting to understand the meaning intended by the communicator. Then go back through it and underline examples of each of the principles you think she is using and name them in the margins. Comment briefly on the effectiveness of her choices, given that her listeners were a group of college students and teachers. Compare your analysis with another person in the course. Discuss similarities and differences. You might want to discuss this experience with your instructor.

Learning Experience

ANTS HAVE MORE SENSE

Judith I. Toombs

Southeast Missouri State University

Par. 1 L1   A recent Frank Sinatra movie entitled *Hole in the Head* features a catchy song with a catchier moral. The lyrics tell of an ant who wanted to move a rubber tree plant. And he kept trying until he did. You may remember one of the last lines of the song. It goes like this: ". . . so when you're gettin' low, stead of lettin' go, just remember the ant. Oops, there goes another rubber tree plant."

Par. 2 L1   You know, that's a heady philosophy for people. If we believe it, it tends to make us think we are unstoppable, a kind of little engine that could for our allotted three score and ten years.

Par. 3 L1   At the risk of sounding unAmerican, which I am not, or appearing to be an apologist for sloth, which I am not, or speaking as an apostle of mediocrity, which I certainly am not, I think we ought to reexamine the philosophy which teaches us that we can do anything if we work at it hard enough and long enough. Certainly you and I have been bombarded by that from the time of childhood. Most people can remember the little slogans their third and fourth grade teachers used to put

L9   on the board. They stood there as constant and obvious reminders to *strive*. I'll bet you remember some of these. They
went like this, "You Can Do Anything If You Put Your Mind to
It;" "You Can If You Think You Can;" and then, of course, the

L13 most cogent of them all "If at First You Don't Succeed, Try
Try Again." Now, there's a lot of good in these slogans. They
remind us to be diligent and persistent. And most of us need
reminders like that from time to time. But it is too bad, I think,

L17 that somewhere along the line, maybe in the 6th grade, or the
11th or 12th grade, or during the freshman year in college,
we don't have someone putting up slogans that remind us of
another important and related truth and that is, What any of

L21 us can do is limited by our capabilities. Let me give you an
example.

Par. 4 L1   The records of the counseling service of the State University of Iowa show that a few years ago a young graduate
student was referred in for counseling. It turned out that he

L4   had been a star athlete as an undergraduate, but his unusual
abilities along such lines were regarded with fine disdain by
his father. His family were first generation immigrants. They
were living in a neighborhood in which there was a generally

L8   accepted standard for the young men. They should all become lawyers, doctors, professors, or something equally re-
spectable. In the old country such professions had been vir-
tually closed to them or to their fathers and the families were

L12 fiercely ambitious for their sons. But this particular young
man had failed to pass the scholastic requirements for medical school. His father, however, would not permit him to give
up. So he entered graduate school majoring in physical edu-

L16 cation, but at the time, he was taking courses which were required for admission to medical college and he was failing.
The clinician wrote of him, "A battery of tests indicate he may
as well be trying to jump over the hospital."

Par. 5 L1   This young man did not have the capacity to be an M.D.
All the evidence should have been clear to him. But he
couldn't quit because in the back of his mind lurked the re-

L4   minder from a teacher, or a parent, or a slogan from a Dale
Carnegie writer that pushed and goaded him, "If at first you
don't succeed, try, try, again."

Par. 6 L1   Failure has been defined as the felt difference from what
one expected and what one gets. If what we expect is bound-
less because we are conditioned to believe we can do any-

L4   thing, we are in trouble.

Par. 7 L1   Feelings of inadequacy and failure are largely responsible
for attempted suicides on college campuses. And in 1966
suicide threats were made by more than 100,000 college stu-

L4   dents. Ten thousand tried it and it is among the first ten
causes of death. The magazine *Science News* reports that

365,000 people actually take their lives each year. That's
more than cholera, small pox, tetanus, and rabies combined.

L8 That's more than die in traffic accidents. Many of the suicides are due to frustration. Frustration is a disease in our
society. Last year in America $55 million went to people
pushing themselves beyond their own physical and mental

L12 capabilities.

Par. 8 L1   Despite all warning signs, there is no evidence that we are
becoming wiser, learning that we can't do everything simply
because we want to. It's true that occasionally, a famous lit-

L4 erary figure tries to teach us a lesson. Cervantes had to have
just this thought when he wrote Don Quixote, the story of the
comic knight errant who was an object of scorn because he
sought unattainable goals. You remember the tasks Quixote

L8 set for himself. Just to right all the wrong in the world. Cervantes in the 17th century was warning us in the 20th century
that it is futile to strive for impossible things. What has the
20th century done to that good advice? It has been turned

L12 into the fantastically successful musical "Man of La Mancha"
where, in an emotional scene, of the hero as he suggests as
a vital moral lesson "Dream the Impossible Dream . . . right
an unrightable wrong . . . follow a star, no matter how hope-

L16 less, no matter how far . . . ."

Par. 9 L1   Mr. Cervantes, I think would choke. He never made Quixote
a hero until, as you may recall, at the end when Quixote
comes to his senses and acknowledges that his mission was

L4 impossible. And yet, here we are in our culture distorting his
story so that it is consistent with our slogan, "You can do
anything if you put your mind to it."

Par. 10 L1   Let me emphasize again, there is nothing wrong with setting high goals and holding "high hopes" for their attainment. But that's not the lesson that you and I have been

L4 taught. I've never seen an ant carrying a rubber tree plant.
That's because ants have more sense. It's only humans who
insist upon trying to do the impossible. Somebody needs to
busy himself teaching people the value of accurate self-

L8 appraisal as it pertains to the achievement of life goals.

Par. 11 L1   In about a year I'll graduate from college with a degree in
education. I have already planned the sign for the board in
my room. It may get me in trouble with the P.T.A., but that

L4 sign is going up. And it will read, "If at first you don't succeed, maybe you should quit."

Chapter 11

Planning Feedforward

Objectives

Your learning should enable you to:

1. Define feedforward as it functions in communication.
2. Define the following parts of feedforward as they function in communication:
   a. feedforward goal
   b. feedforward expectancy
   c. feedforward contingency
3. For a specific message,
   a. specify your feedforward goal
   b. determine desired and undesired expectancies
   c. anticipate specific nonverbal communication which would indicate the occurrence of your expectancies
   d. plan two or more contingency messages for each of your expectancies.

Outline

I. Feedforward: planning done by a communicator before message sending.
   A. Done in terms of the receivers of the message
      1. Purpose is to be able to handle the likely response of receivers
      2. Based on what sender knows about the receivers
   B. Make up of the three components of goals, expectancies, and contingencies
      1. Feedforward goal
         a) Definition: The end result of the communication—what the sender wants to accomplish
         b) The result occurs in the receivers
         c) Usually stated in terms of understanding, agreement, or desired behavior
      2. Feedforward Expectancies
         a) Definition: The listener's likely reactions at important points in the message
         b) Usually occur at transition points of the message—after introduction, main points, conclusion
         c) Some are desired and some are undesired
         d) Communicator should predict which of a listener's verbal and/or nonverbal cues will signal each expectancy
      3. Feedforward Contingencies
         a) Definition: Alternate message segments designed to adapt to likely listener responses
         b) Contingencies are planned using conditional thinking in an "if-then" form
         c) Which message you actually use of your contingency alternatives will depend upon which of the predicted expectancies actually occurred
   C. Suggested procedure for developing feedforward planning for a specific situation
      1. What is your goal?—feedforward goal
      2. What must your listener understand or agree to before he or she will attain your goal? —following each are likely expectancy points
      3. What listener reactions are likely after each of these expectancy points?—feedforward expectancies
      4. What feedback messages will indicate that the expectancies have happened?—listener feedback messages
      5. How will you adapt to each of the likely listener reactions?—feedforward contingencies

Reading

Feedforward is *the planning done by a communicator in the form of setting goals, expectancies, and contingencies in order to be prepared to handle the various possible responses of the listeners to the message.* Use of feedforward will increase the chances that you will attain your communication goals. As a fringe benefit, you'll also feel much more comfortable and be able to respond assertively during the interaction if you've planned ahead of time the kind of things you expect to happen and have in reserve planned alternatives to help you adapt.

Attaining goals in communication is extremely important. It's much like some sports. In football, for example, a touchdown occurs only when the ball crosses the goal line. Or in golf, you've finished the game only when the ball is in the hole eighteen times. Being close doesn't count. Attaining the goal is essential. The same kind of thing happens in communication. Imagine that you are in a new town and are supposed to meet a friend who is giving you a ride back home. Since you weren't sure that you were going to ride with your friend, he told you he would wait until 6:00 P.M. and then leave. If you weren't there by 6:00 P.M., he would assume you were not going. At 5:45 P.M., you ask directions to your friend's address. The goal of the person you ask is to give those directions clearly enough for you to be able to get where you want. If that goal is not attained, it's unlikely you'll find the place you're looking for on time. If that sender is not clear because of failing to adapt to you or if you don't accurately understand some part of the message, then you're not likely to find the place without further assistance. And at 6:00 P.M. it really doesn't matter whether you are one block or one mile away.

Many times in our lives we really need to explain an idea to someone or to get someone to understand us. The criterion for success in this important message sending situation is the attainment of your goal, that the person fully understands. Feedforward can help attain this goal.

Three elements exist in the concept of feedforward: goals, expectancies, and contingencies. A *feedforward goal* is *what you want to accomplish by your message.* It is the desired listener response. The feedforward goal will be listener understanding or agreement or some specific desired listener behavior. *Feedforward expectancies* are *the listener's probable reactions at important points in your message. Feedforward contingencies* are *the alternative message segments planned prior to sending the message for adapting to the different possible expectancies.* The contingencies which *actually are used* during message sending are determined by the listener responses at the important points. You determine listener response from actual feedback, both verbal and nonverbal, at the expectancy points.

The emphasis of Skill Area Three is on sending *clear messages,* so the feedforward goals we will discuss here are understanding and retention of messages. (Skill Area Six is devoted to sending messages that change attitudes and behavior.) The most probable feedforward expectancies when sending messages to secure understanding are that your listener(s) will understand, not understand, misunderstand, be interested and motivated, or inattentive and unmotivated to listen.

The rest of this part discusses the three parts of feedforward in more detail and uses several examples of various expectancies to illustrate. Examples are drawn from messages that have the goal of gaining understanding and the goal of changing attitudes and behaviors.

Let's look more carefully at the second and third elements of feedforward: expectancies and contingencies. Expectancies are the various possible reactions of the listeners to your main ideas. For example, if you wanted to explain to your mother why you need an apartment of your own, your goal would be for her to understand your need. The expectancies for that message would relate to your reasons for the need. Suppose you intended to explain that you can't study at home because of lack of privacy and that you need the experience of budgeting and keeping up an apartment.

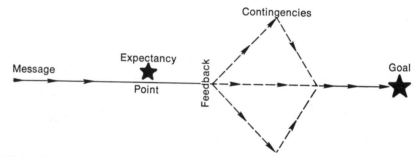

FIGURE 15

For the first point, your expectancies might include: (1) mother understands why it's impossible for you to study at home; (2) mother doubts that lack of privacy is why you can't study; (3) mother doesn't understand why you need more privacy for study; (4) mother misunderstands your reason and thinks you are complaining about how you are treated by the family members; and (5) mother misunderstands your reason and thinks you are just wanting to get away from home so you can party all night. Expectancies also could possibly include that your mother is not at all interested in the problem or that she will not listen carefully because she will be distracted by outside noise or concern with some other problem. As you plan for sending this message to your mother, you will need to determine which of these several possible expectancies are likely and plan for ways to adapt to them if they occur. When you do that, you are working on the third element of feedforward, contingencies.

Contingencies are planned message segments to handle possible expectancies (see figure 15). Contingencies are planned by using conditional reasoning in the form of "if-then" statements and are most often based on the consideration of alternative views. By considering the most common alternative views which are supported by others as you formulate your idea, you will have the basis for anticipating possible reactions to your idea.

The choice of which contingencies to actually use when sending the message depends on what expectancies do happen. For the example just cited, if you achieved expectancy 1, you would simply go on to the next point. If you got expectancy 2 from your mother, you'd have to decide some way to show you can or do study well when you have privacy. If expectancy 3 was the obtained response, you'd need some way to explain or show why privacy is necessary for study. If you received expectancy 4 or 5, you'd need to plan some way to counter the specific misunderstandings. If your mother's response was lack of interest or distraction, you might need to plan for choosing a different setting or time or some other means for getting her attention directed toward your problem.

Using Feedforward

The point of using feedforward is to be prepared for whatever listener reactions are probable, but not to use the contingencies unless they're needed. Often people spend long amounts of time explaining or illustrating when they don't need to, thus wasting both their own and their receiver's time. Equally, or more often, people fail to achieve the goals because they haven't responded to some specific listener reaction. Feedforward will not guarantee that you have thought of every possible problem you'll encounter in communicating, but it certainly improves the probability that you have.

In one-to-one and small group message sending settings, you'll have both verbal and nonverbal feedback to help you determine which expectancies have happened. In one-to-many message sending settings, you'll have to rely much more on nonverbal cues. If, for example, during a speech you noticed at the end of your introduction nonverbal signs that your listeners were not interested (e.g., lack of eye contact and turning bodies away from you), you'd know you have achieved an undesired expectancy. You would want to use a contingency to motivate them or otherwise gain their attention. If you had planned for this possibility, you'd be more able and comfortable in making the needed changes than if such disinterest catches you unprepared for it. Without such planned contingencies, speakers often plunge ahead without listeners' interest or become frustrated and upset, thus destroying the effectiveness of the remainder of their message.

Obviously if at the end of your introduction you achieve your desired expectancy, you'll notice nonverbal signs like leaning forward and eye contact that indicate interest. The most appropriate response from you then would be a transition into your first main point.

The communication concepts from Skill Areas One and Two are important here, especially those related to your understandings of nonverbal feedback. Directly related to use of feedforward is one of the most common barriers in communication, the lack of use of feedback for corrective purposes. Using feedforward helps overcome that barrier. The more you know about your receiver, the better you can anticipate his possible reactions and plan appropriate contingencies. Listener adaptation, as discussed in chapter 9, is important in the use of feedforward. To use feedforward effectively, you also need to use your understanding of frame of reference. Familiarity with a person's frame of reference is very important in determining expectancies and contingencies. Some ideas are very difficult for some people to understand because of their frames of reference. If you know the basic attitudes and experiences of your listeners, you can better predict what parts of your ideas may need more explanation or development to achieve the desired understandings.

When applying the concept of communication feedforward to a particular situation, five questions can be valuable.

1. What is your goal? (feedforward goal)
2. What must your listener understand or agree to before he or she will respond as necessary for you to achieve your goal? (The answer to this question determines the expectancy points.)
3. What listener reactions are likely after each of these expectancy points? (e.g., what are the feedforward expectancies?)
4. What feedback messages will indicate that the expectancies have happened?
5. How will you adapt to each of the likely listener reactions? (e.g., what will your feedforward contingencies be?)

Let's take a specific example to describe the application of these five steps in using feedforward. Let's refer back to that example of Don asking Donna to go to the movie with him that was used in chapter 4 to describe the communication process. If Don used feedforward, he might have planned as follows:

Q: *What is your feedforward goal?*
A: "Donna agrees to go with me to the movies."

Q: *What must your listener agree to or understand before you will attain your goal?*
A: "If she (a) is available, (b) hasn't seen the movie, or (c) would like to see the movie."

In answering question 2, Don applies what he knows about Donna. He plans to ask her about these three conditions. After each question is an important point—or fork—in the path of his planning. These are the points at which he must plan expectancies.

Q: *What listener reactions are likely at each of these points?*
A: (Possibles) "At point A, Donna could be free, not be free, or have plans she would be willing to break."

At each point, Don would indicate what is the desired expectancy and determine what he would need to do if he doesn't achieve it on the first try.

Q: *What feedback messages will indicate that the expectancies have happened?*
A: "Verbal agreement or disagreement to questions. Vocal emphasis that will indicate interest and anticipation or not."

Q: *How can I adapt to the feedback messages?* (e.g., what contingency message segments should I plan?)

A: (Possibles) "Regarding expectancy point A, for instance:"

Don has planned that if Donna says she is free Friday night, he will immediately ask question B, has she seen this particular movie? If she answers no, he moves to question C, does she want to see it? If her answer is yes, he'd probably either ask her if she wants to see it again or find a way to pleasantly end the conversation or change the subject. If Donna answered no to the first question, Don has planned to explain why he asked, that he wanted her to go to the movie with him and listen for her verbal and nonverbal feedback to determine if she wanted to see the movie badly enough to change her plans. As a result of his planning, Don is more likely to accomplish his goal and feel able to assertively handle any undesired expectancies he receives.

Let's look at another example. In this one the feedback wouldn't be verbal; therefore, knowing which expectancy was actually achieved would be much more difficult. Most human communication involves both verbal and nonverbal feedback, but some situations, like sermons and formal lectuers, have primarily nonverbal feedback. Since most people are less skillful at interpreting nonverbal than verbal feedback, these situations present special problems.

Let's say you are explaining to a large group of people why you believe we must have compulsory birth control (feedforward goal). You consider what would be important for listeners to understand and accept in order to accurately understand your total idea. You choose two ideas: if you understand that there are *too many people in the world* and that the *more people we have, the more problems we'll have,* you'll then understand the main point. At each of these points, your desired expectancy would be for the people to understand. Knowing something about your listeners, you predict possible expectancies after your brief explanation of each idea. Based on your prediction, you plan a contingency for each possible expectancy. For example, you might expect a reaction of hostility or doubt. Then you decide what feedback will indicate achievement of the three expectancies. Hostility might be indicated by hands on hips, lessened eye contact, leaning back in chair, crossing arms across chest, and raised eyebrows. Signs of doubt might be knit brows or a puzzled look. If listeners understand a point, they might nod, smile, and lean forward. Depending on the nonverbal cues actually sent following the statement and brief explanation of each idea, you would use the contingency segment planned for that particular expectancy.

Here's how it might work. You first give some examples and reasons why you believe that there are too many people in the world and then say, "so you probably agree with me that there are too many people in the world." At this point you desire agreement and look to your listeners for their feedback. Their feedback is shaking their heads, and talking in whispers to their neighbors which implies their reaction is hostility. You now use the message segment planned to cope with this possible reaction of hostility. You have carefully planned how to say this. If, after the contingency message and restatement of the idea, the reaction is nodding of their heads, you infer agreement and your contingency is a transition to the next idea—more people cause more problems. If instead, their feedback is knit brows, you infer they are still not in agreement and are doubting the idea. Your contingency would then be a contingency message planned to cope with doubt. After the message segment, you would again relate your idea and if you see nodding, you would use the agreement contingency. If, however, no apparent feedback is given, then the contingency would be a message segment to encourage feedback. You would continue using planned message segments until receiving the desired feedback, signifying that your listeners are reacting positively or until you give up.

In summary, planning ahead before sending messages is a vital part of accurate communication. It will enable you to better *use the feedback you receive for corrective purposes* and by doing so increase the chances that you will achieve your communication goals. Such planning is called *feedforward* and includes the following three parts: *goals—desired listener responses; expectancies—the listener's possible reactions at important points in your message; and contingencies—alternate message segments which you plan ahead of time to adapt to a particular expectancy.* The three parts are developed in terms of your knowledge of the specific listener.

Finally, we should emphasize that careful feedforward planning is important in all message situations. Many important interpersonal messages fail because of inadequate forethought. Use of the principles for effective understanding and retention, and sensitive sending help both originating communicator and responding communicator in sales, business, and personal conversation just as much as they do in public speaking.

On page 170 is a sample of feedforward planning. The development of the idea is on top. Then, sequentially on the bottom of the page so that they are useful for the communicator while sending the message are:

```
┌─────────────────────────────────────────────────────────────────────────┐
│  Restatement ────▶ Likely Feedback ────▶ Expectancies ────▶ Contingencies │
│  of the Idea       Responses                                              │
└─────────────────────────────────────────────────────────────────────────┘
```

FIGURE 16

The arrows in figure 16 represent the actual communication flow of feedback, decoding, thinking about, and correcting of the original message. In making your feedforward plans, however, you would reverse the second and third step of the sequence.

Feedforward planning does not, however, reduce the need for sensitive awareness of all cues to meaning in an interaction. Be careful of "missed cues" and "miscues," especially when feedback is largely nonverbal. Miscues are especially possible given the polite nonresponsive listening behaviors used by some audiences. We'll talk more about encouraging feedback in the next chapter. Your best efforts in encouraging feedback, however, are in developing a supportive communication climate, adapting to your listeners, and using the principles of effective understanding. They will react.

Sample Feedforward Form

[*Statement of Main Idea 1:* (optional—used in "deductive" approach) Data and analysis of population and population growth compared with natural resources indicates that there are too many people in both the U.S. and in the world].

Actual words of development and explanation of Main Idea 1: Population in rural farming areas like northeast Missouri is decreasing as young people go to cities for higher paying jobs. When they arrive, they are greeted with traffic jams and other indications of overpopulation—too many people. Paul Ehrlich, of Stanford University, has carefully studied population and natural resources and is convinced in his book, *The Population Bomb,* that the U.S. natural resources can support 150 million people and we already have over 200 million. This analysis indicates that the U.S. has too many people.

Many countries of the world have less natural resources than the U.S. and more population growth. The United Nations predictions indicate that the current world population of over 3.3 billion people will more than double to 6.8 billion by the year 2000. The well-to-do countries like the U.S. and Western European countries are predicted to go from .9 billion to 1.4 billion—a 50% increase, but the underdeveloped countries are predicted to go from 2.4 to 5.4—an increase of 125% so you can see why I say that,

Statement of Main Idea 1:	*Likely (Nonverbal)* *Feedback Responses**	*Expectancies** *(likely reactions of the listener)*	*Contingencies* *(alternative message segments designed to adapt to the listeners' likely reactions)*
"There are too many people in the world."	1) (Desired Feedback) nodding of head and leaning forward	1) (Desired Expectancy) There really are too many people in the world. (agreement)	1) "Now that we've agreed that there are too many people let's look at several of the results of the population size."
	2) shaking head lessening of eye contact	2) Every human life is important—there are never too many people. (disagreement)	2) "I would agree that every person alive is valuable. But as more and more people are born our styles of life change for the worse. The quality of living will go down as . . ."
	3) knit eyebrows and forehead	3) I'm really not sure that there are too many people in the world. (doubt)	3) "Let's review the highlights: Paul Ehrlich said 150 million was the maximum safe U.S. population. It is now over 200 million and predictions indicate about 300 million by 2000."

*NOTE: The categories of likely feedback and expectancies would be reversed in planning stage.

Now you try some feedforward planning.

Assume you're on your way to work and you're fifteen minutes late. You know you'll have to explain to your boss who greatly values punctuality.

You decide your first point will be: "I understand the importance of punctuality." Plan feedforward for this point using the following chart.

Statement of Main Idea 1:

"I understand the importance
of punctuality."

Likely (Nonverbal)
Feedback Responses	Expectancies	Actual Contingencies
(1)	(1)	(1)
(2)	(2)	(2)
(3)	(3)	(3)

Share your planning with another person in the course. Discuss any differences.

Now let's get some actual practice.

Prepare a short message concerning how to do a somewhat difficult task. Choose a friend who does not already know how to do that task. Plan expectations and contingencies for his feedback at each important step in your message. If you do not receive the desired feedback at important points, use your planned contingency until you get the expected feedback.

When you're finished (i.e., shared entire message, getting desired feedback at all points) have the person do the task. Discuss the message sending experience with the person. Did he/she feel he understood each important point before you moved on to the next?

Write down your results.

Chapter 12

Communicating Effective Messages

Objectives

Your learning should enable you to:

1. Select appropriate communication channel(s) to call up intended meanings for a message and specific receiver.
2. Adjust the physical situation for message sending to encourage accurate communication.
3. Determine means of developing rapport with listener(s).
4. Differentiate among assertive, nonassertive, and aggressive nonverbal communicative behaviors.
5. Encourage feedback from receivers.
6. Interpret and make decisions on adapting to receiver feedback for interpersonal and public communicative situations.
7. Develop questions to check the accuracy of your communication.

Outline

I. Overall suggestions for effective message sending
  A. Complete preparation appropriate to situation
  B. Be open to feedback for corrective purposes.
II. Choosing channels for communication
  A. Available channels for sending messages
    1. Sound—Example: yelling at a person
    2. Sight—Example: smiling at a person
    3. Touch—Example: kissing a person
    4. Smell—Example: wearing a person's favorite scent
    5. Taste—Example: giving someone a fresh loaf of homemade bread
  B. Choosing appropriate channels
    1. Consider nature of meaning to be communicated
      a) If talking about a sense, try to use that sense to compliment verbal message
      b) If talking about complex or large amounts of information, visualize it
    2. Consider the decoding skills of receivers
      a) If unskilled in using one sense, supplement with others
      b) If unskilled in handling type of information, present in different way
  C. Practicing chosen channels
    1. Facilitate accurate receiving and decoding by practice
III. Adjusting the physical situation
  A. Make sure all people can see and hear the communicators involved
  B. Be sure the seating is neither too hard nor too soft
  C. Seat people a comfortable distance from each other
  D. Make sure the temperature is within reasonable limits
  E. Select a room which is large enough to comfortably seat all the listeners
  F. Control potential noise sources
  G. Make sure any A-V support system you will use works
IV. Developing initial rapport
  A. Definition: the feeling of a harmonious relationship
  B. Develop a warm relationship
    1. Usually accomplished early in the interchange
    2. Usually accomplished by nonverbal behavior
      a) Touching
      b) Eye contact
      c) Smiling
    3. Make verbal reference to shared experiences
  C. Establish a supportive communicative climate
    1. Review supportive behaviors in chapter 3
V. Assertively communicating your message
  A. Definition: speaking which is clear, direct, and appropriately expresses your own opinions without anxiety and with respect for others' opinions
  B. Characteristics of nonverbal assertive behavior
    1. Good eye contact
    2. Strong, steady voice
    3. Comfortable, balanced stance
  C. Characteristics of nonassertive nonverbal behavior
    1. Downcast eyes
    2. Shifting of weight

        3. Whining, hesitant, or giggly voice tone
        4. Slumped body
    D. Characteristics of aggressive nonverbal behavior
        1. Glaring eyes
        2. Pointing a finger
        3. Raised, snickering, or haughty voice tone
VI. Encouraging and adapting to listener feedback
    A. Encouraging feedback
        1. In all communicative situations, by
           a) Adapting to the specific listeners
           b) Using a conversational, involved tone of voice
           c) Using principles of effective understanding and retention
        2. In interpersonal communication, by
           a) Asking questions and waiting for a response
           b) Pausing and maintaining eye contact for somewhat longer than usual
           c) Verbally interpreting nonverbal responses
           d) Showing appreciation for responses by nodding
        3. In public communication, by
           a) Using direct eye contact with as many receivers as possible
           b) Using rhetorical questions
           c) Using direct questions
           d) Acknowledging nonverbal responses of some listeners
           e) Moving about to come in closer contact with more listeners
    B. Interpreting feedback
        1. Review nonverbal communication in chapter 2
        2. Consider the specific receivers
        3. Consider the communication situation for feedback expectations
    C. Adapting to feedback
        1. In interpersonal communication
           a) Use each feedback message as basis for correcting messages and developing further messages
        2. In public communication
           a) When determined percentage of listeners are not sending desired feedback, use appropriate contingency messages in concise manner
           b) If less than determined percentage are not sending desired feedback, encourage later interaction with those listeners and move on
           c) Determine percentages
              (1) Consider the importance of accurate communication
              (2) Consider the situation
VII. Use of notes and practicing
    A. When to practice
        1. After outline is completed
        2. Several days before message sending, then shortly before message sending
    B. Where should you practice
        1. In setting where you will be communicating
    C. How should you practice
        1. Don't focus on specific wording
        2. Use sequence which focuses on ideas
           a) Read through outline slowly
           b) Read through outline out loud
           c) Read outline aloud stating all the likely feedback responses after each main idea
           d) Read outline again adding contingencies for all expectancies

       e) Without outline, go through message from beginning to end without stopping

       f) Reread outline again to yourself

       g) Practice aloud again, going straight through with a friend, using appropriate contingency messages

       h) Continue steps f and g until you feel in control of your message

  D. Choice of notes

    1. Phrase outlines are most helpful to use during message sending

    2. Write out direct quotes and statistics on note cards

  E. Pretest your message and contingency plans on listener similar to actual listener

VIII. Checking results

  A. Measured by your listener's understanding and retention of intended meanings

  B. Tested by questions that don't encourage guessing or reveal the desired answer

  C. Provides basis for further message development

  IX. Dealing with your feelings about sending messages

  A. Increased skill development leads to confidence and comfort in communicating with others

Reading

Many messages that have been effectively encoded do not call up intended meanings because of ineffective sending behaviors. You considered some of the potential barriers involved with sending messages in chapter 4. The best overall way to minimize communication barriers and feel good while sending messages is to have a level of preparation appropriate to the communication situation and be open for feedback to enable corrections.

There are specific communication skills you can improve to help you send messages more effectively. In this chapter you will be working on choosing and using appropriate channels for sending messages, developing an appropriate physical setting, developing rapport with listeners, speaking assertively, encouraging and adapting to feedback, practicing and using notes, dealing with your feelings about sending messages, and assessing your results. These are important during intrapersonal, interpersonal, and public communication.

Choosing and Using Channels for Communication

The available channels for sending messages correspond to the channels for receiving: sound, sight, touch, smell, and taste. You can send messages through each of the channels. For example, yelling at a person (sound); smiling at a person (sight); kissing a person (touch); wearing a person's favorite after shave or perfume on a date (smell); or giving someone a loaf of freshly baked homemade bread (taste). However, we usually use a combination of channels to call up our intended meanings.

In most communicative situations sound and sight will be the main channels used. Sound aspects of message sending refer to qualities of loudness, clarity, speed, and variety as you say the words. Sight aspects are nonverbal messages that you send through the use of yourself and your spatial relationships to other things, as well as actual visualizations you use to supplement your verbal message. The senses of touch, smell, and taste are more likely to be used in intrapersonal and interpersonal message sending.

The choice of message channels will be based on the nature of the meanings you want your listeners to understand and your listeners' decoding and thinking skills. Let's look at an example of how each could affect your choice of channels. If you are talking about sounds, textures, smells, or tastes, having your listeners use the sense you're talking about will lead to great understanding of your meaning. If you are talking about a highly specific, complicated, or very different object or procedure, you could provide your listeners with a visualization through a picture, model, diagram, and so forth. This not only provides another basis for attaching meanings, but allows them to get the whole picture at once, as your words only describe a part at any one time. In terms of the decoding and thinking skills of your receivers, many people have difficulty decoding, thinking about, and remembering certain kinds of symbols through a particular channel. For example, if you plan to use numerical data, it may be helpful to visualize that data on the board or in a prepared chart. Many people are better able to understand numerical concepts visually than by hearing them.

After selecting appropriate channels for sending your message, plan and practice the use of those channels to facilitate accurate receiving and decoding by the listener. This might include oral practice to keep an understandable speed of delivery or the manipulation of visual aids so that they can be seen by all listeners.

Adjusting the Physical Setting

In chapter 2 we discussed the influence of physical environments as nonverbal communication. In many situations you can adjust the physical setting to facilitate accurate communication. Following are guidelines for maximizing the physical setting before message sending:

1. Make sure all people can see and hear the communicator.
2. Make sure the seating is neither too hard nor too soft.
3. Seat people a comfortable distance from each other.
4. Make sure the temperature is within reasonable limits.
5. Select a room which is large enough to comfortably seat all the listeners.
6. Control potential noise sources. This could mean not sitting too close to the band at a disco if you want to talk or removing distracting elements from around the podium when you speak.
7. Make sure any support system you will use works.

What other aspects of the physical setting would you check to encourage accurate communication?

Developing Initial Rapport

Rapport describes *the feeling of a harmonious relationship.* We all communicate more accurately when we are comfortable. Comfortableness depends partly on the personal relationship between people and partly on the supportiveness of the communication climate involved. If you establish a warm relationship and facilitate a supportive climate, people will feel comfortable and more open to understanding your message. You might review the suggestions for developing supportive climates in chapter 3.

In your initial contact the basis for a warm relationship is usually established through nonverbal behavior. In interpersonal communication this might take the form of touching. This may mean a playful jab at a friend's arm, placing your hand on a shoulder as you join your friend, a handshake, hug, or kiss. Make sure such touching behavior is as acceptable to the other person as it is to you. The nonverbal reactions will be good indicators of its acceptability. As this is an area many Americans are not comfortable with,

you may have to be careful in using this channel. A smile, a good joke, or a reference to an earlier good experience together can accomplish the same goal. Remember that, unless the expectations are clear and acceptable that you are about to make a lengthy comment on something, interpersonal communication implies sharing; and you should provide many opportunities for it to occur. The other person may have feedback on your message or something they want to say.

In more public communication, where you are expected to be making a statement, establishing rapport starts also with the initial nonverbal contact you make with your listeners. They are likely to be looking expectantly in your direction. Before you say anything, take a few seconds to get comfortable with the new perspective you have as you face a number of people. It's a powerful feeling, and at this minute your body and head are making an important decision as to who's in charge. Even the most experienced public speakers face this moment. We have found it valuable at this point to take an easy, but full breath, make direct eye contact, and smile.

Assertively Communicating Your Message

In the overview to this skill area we defined *assertive speaking* as *that speaking which is clear, direct, and appropriately expresses your own opinions without anxiety and with respect for others' opinions.* Assertive speaking avoids the negative influences of either nonassertive or aggressive communication. You have already begun developing skills in formulating and developing a personal opinion. Clearly state your idea in a way that supports it but leaves room for others to hold different ideas. You also have worked on choosing symbols which characterize assertive speaking. Another skill in speaking assertively includes the nonverbal ways in which you communicate your message. Figure 17 provides examples of nonverbal sending behaviors which indicate assertive, nonassertive, and aggressive sending behaviors. You might review figure 14 in chapter 10 concerning the verbal indicators of each of these communication styles. To develop skills in using assertive sending skills, it might be helpful to work with another person who could provide feedback about how you come across in specific situations.

CHARACTERISTIC NONVERBAL BEHAVIOR

Nonassertive	*Assertive*	*Aggressive*
downcast eyes; shifting of weight; whining, hesitant, or giggly tone of voice; slumped body	good eye contact; strong, steady tone of voice; comfortable, balanced stance	glaring eyes; pointing a finger; raised, snickering, or haughty tone of voice.

FIGURE 17

With one or more people, try sending the following message using each style of sending behavior in figure 17. Communicate the message assertively, non-assertively, and aggressively. As you know, the language symbols would also change with each type. The message here is written assertively.

Message:
"I would rather you didn't smoke in this small room. I feel uncomfortable. We could go outside if you would prefer."

How did you feel sending each type of style? Get feedback from others on their reaction to each type of sending behavior.

Encouraging and Adapting to Listener Feedback

The corrective function of feedback is one of the most important concepts in communication. You need receiver response so you know what feedforward contingencies to use to adapt to your listeners and attain accurate communication. Originating communicators should not just look for feedback, they should actively seek it. Even sources who don't have face-to-face contact with their listeners when sending messages (i.e., letter, radio, television), usually try to get receiver response. Telephone numbers to call and prepaid return envelopes seek response. Mass media use elaborate systems of ratings, contests, and surveys to measure listener response. Even though the feedback secured is usually delayed, it's better than getting no feedback at all.

In all communication situations, encourage feedback by:

1. sharing your concern for receiver understanding;
2. adapting to the specific listeners;
3. using a conversational, involved, tone of voice;
4. using principles of effective understanding and retention.

In interpersonal communication you could encourage feedback by:

1. asking questions and waiting for a response;
2. pausing and maintaining eye contact for somewhat longer than usual;
3. verbally interpreting nonverbal responses: "You look like you have a question." "You don't seem to understand. What isn't clear?";
4. showing appreciation for responses by nodding.

When you have more listeners than you can verbally interact with personally, you still can encourage feedback. In public communication situations encourage feedback by:

1. using direct eye contact with as many receivers as possible;
2. using rhetorical questions (questions for which you don't expect an oral answer but that will cause listeners to answer to themselves);
3. using direct questions;

4. acknowledging nonverbal responses of several listeners (others will often feel included);
5. moving about to come in closer contact with all listeners that you can.

Greater challenges are faced when you are sending a message to a large group of listeners. With only one listener you can choose and send alternate message segments based on his or her feedback alone. If you aren't sure what a single listener's feedback is indicating, you usually can stop and ask for clarification. But when you have many listeners, it is unlikely that they will all react in a similar manner. You are then placed in the position of trying to decide whether you are getting enough of an undesired type of feedback to warrant using an alternative message segment. Also, if you are not receiving feedback from a few, do you stop and encourage feedback even though the majority are already reacting?

There are no rules for handling such situations. However, the following suggestions should help.

1. Continuously encourage feedback by using rhetorical questions, casual sending behaviors, asking for hand raising, pausing, relating to their experiences, etc. so you will have a basis for making decisions.
2. If more than __ percent of your listeners are not sending the desired feedback, use appropriate alternate message segments. If they are concise and to the point, they will not bore those who are already with you.
3. If less than __ percent are not sending the desired feedback, try encouraging later interaction with those people who are not with you by saying, for example, "One or two of you look like you disagree. . . . Can we get together and talk about that later?" By such techniques you can maintain the continuity of your message, while not ignoring those who are not "with you."

You will be able to fill in the blanks regarding percentages by considering the importance of the understanding for each listener (e.g., an instructor in a medical school might decide 100 percent understanding was necessary when explaining a surgical technique to medical students).

Feedback always should be interpreted in light of your knowledge of the specific listeners and the situation in which the communication is occurring. Be aware of the receivers' goals and expectations for the communication situation. They may give a certain response because they think it's expected. You may have to probe for reactions beyond what a listener believes to be socially or otherwise appropriate. Your feedforward preparation will provide a sound basis for your adapting to feedback.

During your next casual conversation with a friend, give that friend five pieces of paper with one of the following feedback messages on each: agreement, understanding, disinterest, disagreement, and misunderstanding. Shuffle them so your friend has the pieces of paper in random order. Ask him/her at vari-

Learning Experience

ous points in the conversation to send feedback messages which indicate the message on the sheet on top of the pile. The person should go through the five messages keeping them in the same order. Each time you think one of the messages is being sent, write down the message. Compare your list with the order of the sheets after the conversation. Do this with several people to begin noticing individual differences. You will find, however, that there are basic similarities.

Write down your results.

Use of Notes and Practicing

In some important intrapersonal and interpersonal and in most public communicative situations, using notes which summarize your preplanning and practicing your message sending ahead of time may be helpful. Practice can facilitate natural message sending, facilitate the use of feedforward, and increase the chances of accurate communication. When practice is appropriate, this discussion may be helpful. *When should you practice?* Not until you have finished your message outline on paper, for until then your sequence of ideas is most probably not clear and complete. For shorter messages (2–7 minutes) do your best to practice the first two or three times, earlier than 24 hours before you communicate your message. This gives you sufficient time to incorporate further changes if these first practices suggest minor improvements. Your later practices probably will come the night before the message is sent. An excellent technique to help you remember your message is to review your outline silently just before falling asleep. In the morning, one last practice ordinarily is very good.

How should you practice? For your practice, use a setting very similar to the one you will use for actual message sending. Practicing in the setting in which you will speak can increase your feeling of comfort in the actual communicative situation. Somehow even a room which is quite familiar to you, such as a classroom you have been using for several weeks, can look totally different when you stand up in front as opposed to sitting as part of a group. If you're going to give a report in the board room of a company, see if you can get into the room and stand or sit as you will during your report. Get used to the setting from that perspective. This also will give you an excellent opportunity to determine how loud you should speak to be heard clearly and help you anticipate difficulties in using other aids in your message. Locate nearby electrical outlets, for example. Regarding the loudness of your voice, remember that when the room is filled with people, you will need to speak louder than in an empty room.

In your practicing, try the suggested procedures listed below and follow them specifically for your first messages and later change them to fit your own individual requirements. The following procedures are based on the psychological concept that memory and retention are enhanced by concentrating on the message as a whole rather than specific parts. Your wording and examples will change with each practice. Don't try to remember your message word for word. The procedure is also oriented to direct your major attention toward the sequence of ideas rather than specific phraseology.

Get Acquainted with the General Pattern of Ideas

Wording should change—avoid verbatim memory.

1. Read through your message outline silently, slowly, and thoughtfully from beginning to end. Do it again. Don't backtrack for details or for any other reason . . . get the feeling for the total message.
2. Read the outline aloud thoughtfully, without hurrying.
3. Read the outline aloud stating all of the likely feedback responses and expectancies after each main idea.
4. Read the outline again adding contingencies for all expectancies.
5. Abandoning the outline, go through your message from beginning to end. Don't stop or repeat, even if you know that you forgot a major idea or expectancy.
6. Reread silently your message outline once again.
7. Practice aloud again, without stopping or backtracking. Practicing with a friend and adapting appropriate contingencies to his responses is quite helpful.
8. Repeat steps 6 and 7 until you feel that you have good control of your message.

Once you have control over your thought sequence, you can then attend to reviewing specific points and contingency messages. Let's emphasize at this point that we are NOT suggesting that you write out the whole message. Indeed, we suggest just the opposite. Even when you must give speeches in public, extemporaneous speaking is the most effective style of message sending. Manuscripts almost always are a factor making the sending of the messages less effective than it would otherwise be. Some speakers rely on manuscripts because they haven't taken sufficient time in preparation; but this situation is a negative factor in effective communication and should be recognized as such.

Neither should you memorize your message. Aim instead for mastery of your sequence of ideas. *Phraseology should vary* as you practice and when you send the message. *Brief notes* are often helpful, using key words to remind you of the sequence of ideas. Many people like to use a phrase outline. Note cards can be used to help you quote important statistics or quotations or other detailed evidence you plan to use. It's worth noting that if you can't remember statistics you plan to use, perhaps your receivers won't be able to either, and you might need to plan for some visualization if you think the data are important to the total message.

An excellent test of your feedforward preparation is to *pretest your message sending.* Choose a person as much like your actual listeners as possible. Ask your pretest listener to role-play your actual receivers and try to give you the feedback as those receivers might. Send the message to your role-player, watch for positive and negative feedback, especially at expectancy points. Afterwards discuss his/her reactions. Find out if your receiver was reacting to sending variables or to the content. Use this pretest to determine if you need to make any changes in your message or the style of sending.

Checking Results

As always we check the success of our communication by comparing our results with our goals. Your goal is to attain a high degree of accurate communication as measured by your listeners' understanding and retention of your intended meanings. Specifically, you want them to understand your overall purpose and main ideas or reasons for your belief. In addition, you will want them to understand and remember the basis for your main points, which could include facts, examples, comparisons, and visualizations.

The best way to test their understanding and remembering is to ask them and compare their answers with those you intended. To validly measure understanding and retention, it is desirable to ask questions that don't encourage guessing or lead the listeners to the correct answer even if they didn't know it. Thus, questions which have one word answers, such as "yes" or "no," don't accurately measure understanding. For example, if we were to ask you, "What were the four components of credibility that we described?" your answer would indicate the degree to which you remembered those components. If you remembered three of the four, that would indicate a 75 percent goal attainment. On the other hand, if we asked, "The four components of credibility we described are friendliness, expertness, trustworthiness, and similarity, aren't they?" your answer probably would be "yes" from which we would inaccurately infer 100 percent goal attainment. This inaccuracy would help us to feel successful but wouldn't provide helpful data for determining how to improve the less strong points of our message on credibility. It also wouldn't provide corrective feedback to further development of your accurate learning of the four parts of credibility.

In summary, questions like "What were my three main ideas?" or "What were the four components of credibility we discussed?" avoid the problem of guessing or leading and enable you to both accurately measure your degree of communication accuracy and to identify parts of your message that were not fully accomplished.

Dealing with Your Feelings about Sending Messages

We decided to talk about this important area last in this skill area because we believe that the basis for most uncomfortable feelings about communicating with others is the lack of skill development. It is quite reasonable to feel uncomfortable about doing something that you aren't fully skilled in yet. Therefore, by applying and practicing the basic skills involved in the first three skill areas, we are confident that you will begin seeing yourself as a person who has something to say and possesses the skills to communicate in a way that others will understand.

Additional Learning Sources

Becvar, Raphael. *Skills for Effective Communication: A Guide to Building Relationships.* New York: John Wiley and Sons, 1974.

Clevenger, Theodore, and Matthews, Jack. *The Speech Communication Process.* Glenview, Ill.: Scott, Foresman and Co., 1971.

Connolly, James E. *Public Speaking as Communication.* Minneapolis: Burgess Publishing Co., 1974.

DeVito, Joseph. *Communication: Concepts and Processes.* Englewood Cliffs, N.J.: Prentice-Hall, Inc., 1971.

Flew, Anthony. *Thinking Straight.* Buffalo, N.Y.: Prometheus Books, 1977.

Hess, Herbert, and Tucker, Charles. *Talking about Relationships.* Dubuque, Iowa: Kendall/Hunt Publishing Co., 1976.

Holtzman, Paul. *The Psychology of Speaker's Audiences.* Glenview, Ill.: Scott, Foresman and Co., 1970.

Keltner, John. *Interpersonal Speech-Communication.* Belmont, Calif.: Wadsworth Publishing Co., 1970.

Mudd, Charles, and Sillars, Malcolm. *Speech: Content and Communication,* 3rd ed. New York: Thomas Crowell Publishing Co., 1975.

Taylor, Anita; Rosegrant, Teresa; Meyer, Arthur; and Samples, B. Thomas. *Communicating.* Englewood Cliffs, N.J.: Prentice-Hall, 1977.

Skill Test

This skill test will consist of a two-step experience in communicating to gain understanding. You will first prepare a message that explains to a specific self-chosen person an idea about which you feel strongly. When you have completed your planning using the steps which follow, your instructor will go over your planning with you. You will then communicate your idea to that self-chosen person. When you think you have achieved your feedforward goal ask that person to complete the listener response form. This form will contain questions you have developed to test your listener's understanding.

After achieving the agreed-upon level of understanding with this person, you will then adapt that same idea to a group of your classmates in this course so that they will be able to understand fully your idea. To do so, use the suggested steps which begin on page 189. Your instructor will want to go over this planning with you also.

You will arrange with your instructor for a time to send your message with a group of other students in the course. When you think you have achieved your feedforward goal, ask your listeners to complete the listener response form.

At this time you will also be a receiver for the other students. Use appropriate active listening to:

a. Send feedback reflecting your understanding of the message you receive.
b. Write the main meaning of the sender's message.
c. Write the main points (reasons) of the sender's message.
d. Answer, in writing, the two questions asked by the sender following his/her message.

You may take notes but don't let note taking interfere with your sending feedback.

Remember, as you prepare your messages and listen and respond to others' messages, the sender's goal in this situation is that messages be *understood,* not that you agree with the points being made.

In both situations send your message by communicating it in a normal conversational manner (don't read or memorize your message). Be aware of and interpret feedback in light of the specific receiver(s) and the situation and adapt your message by using appropriate contingency messages. If you are not receiving clear feedback, use appropriate methods to encourage better feedback. In your public communicative situation, you will receive mainly nonverbal feedback.

After each experience you will assess your own message sending. You and your instructor may want to develop additional or alternative skill tests to check your skills in communicating accurately with others.

Precommunication Form: Part I

On separate sheets of paper, complete your message preparation for your chosen listener by doing each of the substeps listed below for *Formulating Your Idea, Knowing Your Listener, Developing Your Message, Anticipating Feedback, Planning for Message Sending,* and *Assessing the Results of Your Communication.* Share your completed message preparation with your instructor before sending your message. This careful preparation will enable a very high degree of understanding.

Formulating Your Idea

1. State, in one sentence, a personal idea you are really concerned about by completing the sentence, "I strongly believe . . . ." (Work on this statement until it is sufficiently concrete to communicate your main meaning.)
2. List three or four reasons which explain why you believe as you do. Work on these reasons until each is a clearly stated different reason.
3. State evidence that supports your idea. List the resources you used.
4. State one or more values (or partially developed values) which lead you to hold this idea.
5. Describe major alternative ideas on this issue which have support among others.
6. State any qualifications you would make concerning your idea in terms of its application to people and situations.
7. State the implications for you and your chosen listener of your sharing this idea at this time.

Knowing Your Listener

Write the name of a real person whom you want to understand your idea. This person should be *someone who does not understand* what you believe *before you talk with him or her* and someone you can get together with after you have gone over your preparation with your instructor.

8. State the relevant stored information that your chosen listener has which will influence his or her processing of your message. State both the information and the influence in terms of that person's experiences, attitudes, and values.
9. State the important needs that your chosen listener has which will influence his or her processing of your message.
10. State how your chosen listener will likely perceive the communication situation.

11. State any goals or expectations your chosen listener may have for this communication situation.

12. Estimate your credibility with this person as you talk about this particular personal idea. Do this in terms of his or her perceptions of your friendliness, expertness, trustworthiness, and similarity.

Developing Your Message

This message development will involve your application of each of the seven principles of effective understanding and the three principles for increasing retention, as they specifically apply to your chosen listener.

13. For each of the seven principles of effective understanding (Structure, Attention, Motivation, Visualization, Comparison, Repetition, Symbol Usage), state how you will use that as your message development and why. The "how" should be specific (for example, "I will compare living with a physical handicap to driving a car without headlights—in terms of the many things that you can't do and the many adaptations that have to be made"). The "why" should explain your choice in terms of how it will increase understanding for your chosen listener (continuing with the above example, "My listener drives a battered up old car and constantly complains about the things he can't do because of it. This will help my listener to better understand the limitations that a physically handicapped person has at all times").

14. Select from the principles to increase retention and explain how you will assist your listener to remember important parts of your idea.

15. Develop a phrase outline of the body of your actual message. Begin with your three or four main reasons for holding your belief and use each of your plans, indicated in 13 and 14 above, within your outline. Include your evidence at appropriate places. Each of your main reasons should be fully developed so that your chosen listener will call up the intended meanings. If your outlining skills are not fully developed, check with your instructor for materials which will help you.

16. Develop an introduction and a conclusion to your message.

Anticipating Feedback through Feedforward Planning

17. For each main part of your message (your introduction, each of your main points, and your conclusion) plan for at least three potential reactions of your chosen listener. Put the desired expectancy first. We have found it helpful to place a sheet of paper with the headings indicated below along side your developed outline and prepare feedforward for each main part.

	Expectancies	*Likely feedback indicating expectancies*	My contingency message
1		1	1
2		2	2
3		3	3

In anticipating the likely feedback which would indicate that each expectancy had occurred, it is likely that your chosen listener will use both verbal and nonverbal feedback.

Plans for Sending Your Message

18. Indicate the physical setting you will use to send your message, including any adjustments you will make.
19. State the channels you will use to send your message.
20. Indicate two ways you will encourage feedback.

Assessing the Results of Your Communication

So that you can assess the results of your communication, ask your listener to complete a Listerner Feedback Form on which that person will write down the main meaning of your message, the reasons you had for believing your ideas, and the answers to two questions which test his or her understanding of your message.

21. Write two questions about important parts of your stated idea, other than asking to list your reasons, which test your listener's understanding. Avoid yes/no and one-word answers as they usually do not test understanding. Write the answers which would express understanding of your message.

Postcommunication Form: Part I

Complete the following on separate sheets of paper and share it with your instructor along with your Listener Response Form.

1. Briefly describe the influence of the physical situation as you communicated your message to your chosen listener.
2. Describe briefly any verbal responses you received as you sent your message (or following your message). Comment on how you interpreted and handled these responses using feedforward contingencies.
3. Describe briefly any nonverbal responses you received as you sent your message. Comment on how you interpreted and handled those responses using feedforward contingencies.
4. Describe and explain any differences between the answers you received from your listener on the Listener Response Form and those you wanted.
5. Comment on the overall accuracy of communication as you explained your belief to this person.
6. Write and explain two specific changes in your message which would have increased the accuracy of communication with this listener.

Precommunication Form: Part II

On separate sheets of paper, complete your message preparation for your class members by doing each of the substeps specified on pages 189–91. Each time those substeps refer to "your chosen listener," answer those questions for "your classmates." Use the same personal idea, but adapt it to this audience. Some parts of your preparation may be the same. Substeps 1–6 of Formulating your Idea may well be the same. If so, indicate "same" on your preparation sheets. Substep 7 will be likely to change. Some of your message development for your chosen listener may be used in your message for your classmates. Aspects of it should change, however, as the development should be based on the listeners' frames of reference, and your class members' collective frame of reference will be different from your chosen listener. In Substep 18 you may not have a choice over the physical setting. Indicate any adjustments of the setting that you could make to enhance understanding. You may choose to use the same questions developed in Substep 21 if they worked well for you in checking the understanding of your chosen listener.

After completing each of the substeps in preparation for your message to your classmates, share your preparation with your instructor. You will then determine a time to send your message.

Postcommunication Form: Part II

Complete the following on separate sheets of paper and share it with your instructor along with your Listener Response Forms.

1. Describe briefly the nonverbal feedback you received. Cite any differences between feedback and feedforward.
2. Describe briefly your use of feedforward contingencies during your message. How did they influence the accuracy of communication in this situation?
3. Describe and explain any differences between the answers you received from your listeners as a response to your questions (ones prepared to test their understanding).
4. Assess your own sending behaviors and their influence on communication accuracy in this situation.
5. Comment on the overall accuracy of communication as you explained your idea to your classmates.
6. Write and explain two specific changes in your message which would have increased the accuracy of communication with these listeners.

Skills in Solving Problems

Overview

Hardly a day passes without our having to face and resolve a large number of problems. For example, a family owns only one car. One parent must get to and from work, the other parent needs to drive the car to a meeting, the son wishes to go to the beach, and the younger child wants to be driven to a friend's house. What sort of schedule can satisfy everyone's needs? . . . A man is not doing as well as he would like in his school work. The end of the semester is only three weeks away. What would be the best way to improve his functioning in school during that time period? . . . And the list could go on and on. Usually we manage to resolve most of the problems that face us. Many times, however, we realize that we forgot to consider an important variable or for some other reason decided on a solution that did not fully solve the problem or one that introduced new problems into our life. Consider how much more is at stake when community leaders are attempting to resolve a strike by city employees or when world leaders are trying to resolve an energy crisis.

Problem solving is one of the most common activities which people do when they get together in small groups. By doing so, they have decided that involving several people will lead to a more effective solution than just one person. A group of people can lead to effective problem solving when new ideas are needed, when different points of view are needed, and when the decision of the group will personally involve a number of people. *Group problem solving takes more time, but the solution is usually worth it.*

This skill area will assist you in developing skills which will allow you to efficiently and effectively solve problems. As a great deal of your life will also be spent in problem solving with others—whether in an organized committee or a family determined to find meaningful solutions together— this skill area will be directed toward developing skills in problem solving through communication with others. You will be applying all of the communication skills you have acquired in the core communication skill areas.

Definitions

Brainstorming

A technique of cooperative group thinking used to stimulate the production of ideas and facilitate their expression. It involves a *free-wheeling* contribution of new ideas (or combinations and improvements on previously stated ideas) with *no evaluation.*

Conflict Management

The resolution of disagreements in a way that members are satisfied and are able to continue working together in a mutually productive manner.

Criteria

Standards by which something can be evaluated (in group discussions, they are most often used to evaluate solutions).

Directive Feedback

Feedback which states the opinion of the responder.

Group

A collection of two or more individuals, consciously aware of each other, interacting, working toward a common goal(s).

Group Consensus

The maximum possible agreement by all group members on a given point.

Group Discussion

A collection of two or more individuals who conspicuously identify with each other, interacting dynamically working toward a common goal(s), chiefly through the medium of oral communication.

Group Leadership

Any group member's behavior that helps the group identify and achieve shared goals.

Nondirective Feedback

Feedback which describes or questions but does not evaluate. It is used to encourage the sender to continue explaining, to further think through the message being sent, or to offer general support.

Nonverbal Communication

The process by which meanings are called up by nonword symbols.

Problem-Solving Process

A format for process which assists efficient progress toward a goal without eliminating important considerations.

Chapter 13

Organizing Problem Solving

Odjectives

Your learning should enable you to:

1. Specify the advantages of using an organized process for problem solving.
2. List and describe the basic steps of a problem-solving process.
3. Differentiate between discussion questions which are likely to lead to effective problem solving and those which are not.
4. Describe the use of brainstorming in problem-solving discussions and the rules for using it.
5. Define group consensus and indicate at which steps it is important within a problem-solving process.
6. Solve a personally chosen problem by using the steps of a problem-solving process.

Outline

I. An organized problem-solving process increases goal accomplishment
   A. Goals are reached more efficiently
   B. Important considerations are not overlooked
II. Four group thinking patterns have been found effective
   A. Creative thinking pattern
      1. Careful description of current problem
      2. Brainstorming for solutions
   B. Reflective thinking pattern
      1. Four-step procedure
         a) Awareness of problem
         b) Description of problem
         c) Analysis of problem
         d) Solutions for problem
   C. Single question pattern
      1. Single question developed which is most basic to solving this problem
      2. Subquestions developed and researched
   D. Idea solution pattern
      1. Focus on developing the best solution to satisfy all involved
      2. Used especially in arbitration
III. A process which integrates the four patterns follows—used flexibly by determining the necessary steps and substeps for a given question and group.
   A. Step one: *Preparation*—the group clarifies the goal of the group and establishes atmosphere and format
      1. Determines goal (States form of solution based on the power of the group)
      2. Determines necessary information and research
      3. Determines potential barriers
      4. Determines procedures for participation
         a) Leadership
         b) Seating
         c) Place
         d) Time
   B. Step two: *Description*—the group determines the current status of the problem
      1. Defines terms within the question
      2. Identifies facts related to the problem, differentiating between facts and inferences
      3. Identifies points of view of those involved
      4. Determines previous action taken
      5. States what is unsatisfactory about present situation
   C. Step three: Analysis—the group determines why the problem exists
      1. Determines why the problem developed
      2. Determines what has kept the problem from being solved
      3. Determines the most basic causes of problem
         a) Differentiates between symptoms and causes
            (1) Keeps asking "Why" to each potential cause to get at the most basic causes
         b) There are seldom single causes for complex problems
   D. Step four: *Proposals*—the group suggests many possible solutions
      1. Brainstorms solutions: a process of temporarily suspending critical analysis and suggesting many possible solutions
         a) No criticism allowed, verbal or nonverbal

        b) Quantity is the objective

        c) Building off earlier ideas encouraged

    2. If arbitration, group determines ideal solution

        a) A solution in which all participants can win essential points

        b) Difficult, as parties usually have predetermined ideal solutions

  E. Step five: *Selection of "best" solution*—the group determines standards by which solutions can be judged and selects the "best" solution

    1. Develops criteria for assessing solutions

        a) Based on what standards a solution must meet to be acceptable

           (1) Example: Our solution for redecorating the apartment must not cost more than $120.

        b) Ranks criteria based on importance

    2. Chooses "best" solution of those brainstormed

        a) Should solve problem

        b) Should get at basic causes

        c) Should meet criteria

        d) Should not create other difficult problems

  F. Step six: *Implementation*—the group works out plans to implement the chosen solution

    1. Develops specific plans

        a) Who will be involved

        b) How much it will cost

        c) What is the best time to implement

        d) Specific steps planned

    2. Determines potential obstacles

    3. Makes plans for overcoming obstacles

IV. Wording a problem-solving question

  A. To promote open and productive discussion

  B. Done prior to or during the Preparation Step

  C. Guidelines

    1. The problem should be stated in the form of an open-ended question

        Example: "What should the company's policy be to reduce employee absences?"

    2. The problem should be limited in scope

        Example: "What can college students on this campus do to reduce the amount of fuels used for heating?"

    3. The problem question should be unbiased

        Example: "What should the school's policy be toward a final exam week?"

V. Group consensus

  A. Definition: the maximum possible agreement by all members on a given point

  B. Overall goal is consensus on "best" solution

  C. Consensus should be reached after each step in a problem-solving process (avoids backtracking)

  D. Approached in terms of individual integrity

VI. Problem-solving assessment

  A. In-progress Analysis

    1. Done during a discussion

        a) Problem-solving steps reconsidered

        b) Interpersonal atmosphere considered

    2. Important in on-going group

  B. Post-discussion analysis

    1. Done after a discussion; each process step checked for thoroughness

  C. Structured and unstructured assessment used

    1. Structured: responding to predetermined checklists

    2. Unstructured: spontaneous interaction

Reading

Group Process

Two typical goals for groups are learning and problem solving. The *success* of such groups usually is defined in terms of the *degree to which the specific goals were met* by the group and *quality of the product.* In learning, the group goal usually is to describe and understand something, i.e., a problem, an idea, themselves. In problem solving, the goal is the development and implementation of a "best" solution. This chapter focuses on the problem-solving discussion.

Research concerning productive discussion groups suggests that an organized yet flexible process for discussion increases the likelihood that a group will reach its goals most efficiently, while not overlooking vital considerations.[1]

A variety of patterns has been developed to promote quality solutions. Four basic group thinking patterns include (1) creative thinking pattern, (2) reflective thinking pattern, (3) single question pattern, and (4) ideal solution pattern. A brief description of each pattern follows.

The *creative thinking pattern* is characterized by (1) a careful description of the current problem and (2) brainstorming for solutions. The *reflective thinking pattern* follows the steps for individual problem solving and highlights careful thinking through a movement from awareness, description, analysis, to solution, as developed by John Dewey, a famous American educator. An integral part of the pattern is the use of carefully determined criteria for assessing possible solutions.

The *single question pattern* focuses on the single question which, when answered, means the group is able to accomplish its purpose. This includes the development of subquestions and research to answer each question. The *ideal solution pattern* highlights the consideration of the points of view of all those who would be affected by the solution. It is especially helpful in a case of arbitration or when several points of view are directly in conflict.

Following is a suggested problem-solving process which integrates essential aspects of each pattern. It is not meant to be followed exactly but to be used flexibly by a specific group based on which phases or parts of phases would be most functional toward accomplishing the group goal. The unique interaction between the group members and the discussion problem question would influence the emphasis placed on various steps and substeps.

A Problem-Solving Process

Problem Question

I. *Preparation* (The group clarifies the goal of the group and establishes atmosphere and format.)

---

1. John Brilhart, *Effective Group Discussion* (Dubuque, Iowa: Wm. C. Brown Co., 1974), p. 98.

What is the specific group goal?

What information and/or research will be necessary to reach the goal?

What important question(s) must be answered in order to accomplish the group goal?

Are there any specific barriers we may face in problem solving?
  —strong individual member attitudes toward problem?
  —an important point of view not being represented in the group?

What procedures for participation will best lead to our goal?
  —time, seating, place
  —leadership: shared, designated, or leader-in-reserve

II. *Description* (The group determines the current status of the problem.)

What terms within the problem question need to be defined and/or clarified?

What are the facts related to the problem?

What are the points of view of those involved in the problem?

What previous action has been taken to attempt to solve the problem?

What is unsatisfactory about the present situation?

How serious is the problem?

III. *Analysis* (The group understands why the problem exists.)

Why did the problem develop?

What specific factors have kept the problem from being solved already?

What are the most basic causes of the problem?

IV. *Proposals* (The group suggests many possible solutions.)

What are all possible solutions (brainstorm without evaluation)?

or

What would be the ideal solution from the point of view of each person (or group) affected (useful in arbitration or when several definite views are in conflict)?

V. *Selection of "best" solution* (The group determines standards by which solutions can be judged and selects the "best" solution.)

What specific criteria must the solution meet?
  —What are all the necessary standards which the solution to the problem must meet?

What solution is "best" ("best" should answer all four below)?
  —Which solution solves the problem?
  —Which solution eliminates the basic causes?
  —Which solution meets the criteria?
  —Which solution does not create other problems?

VI. *Implementation* (The group works out approaches to implement the chosen solution.)

How can the chosen solution be put into action?
  —Who must be involved? Cost of implementing? When is best time?
  —What is the best general approach to implementing the solution?

What obstacles may come up to hinder the implementation?

What approaches are most likely to overcome the stated obstacles?

Preparation

Preparation by a discussion group prepares for the entire discussion. The goals for preparation are to set a clear goal, get to know each other, discover vital questions, find specific potential barriers, determine necessary research, and set procedures for reaching the goal. During this time a group also establishes relationships and sets communication patterns.

Much of this is done nonverbally as individuals interact with each other and establish their roles. It is *vital* at this early stage that *each member of the group make an oral contribution* to the group. Research has shown that if a person hesitates to get involved at this early stage, that person will be less likely to communicate later. All members should be aware of this—not only to make sure you communicate at this stage but also to assist another person.

Within the context of realistic goal setting, it is important for a group to be fully aware of its potential "power" in carrying out a determined solution. Therefore, a group will want to consider during this initial phase what form the solution will reasonably take, i.e., a set of recommendations, direct action by the group, and so forth.

As most productive problem-solving groups are characterized by the withholding of judgment until being fully informed, groups will often take a "break" after the first phase of awareness–ventilation to do necessary thinking and research once the boundaries for the discussion have been set.

To organize your research and thinking preparation before a problem solving group, it is recommended that you prepare an outline which parallels the steps the group will use. The outline-type preparation has been found to be helpful for participation in the free-flow of a discussion. Having ideas too fully written out tends to lead to speeches rather than flexible interchange when a bit of information and/or analysis is pertinent to the group. You are also more quickly aware if parts of your preparation have already been offered by another group member.

Description

When the group moves into the *description phase* of problem solving, the members are asking the question, *"What is the situation now and what is unsatisfactory about it?"* Before leaving this step the group members should be sure they fully understand what the situation surrounding the problem is. Facts and inferences should be clearly differentiated. It is important to identify the influential people who must be considered and any prior attempts at solving this problem. Also, considering the seriousness of the problem will suggest to the group important considerations such as the amount of time they have to implement a solution and other problems which the central problem influences.

Analysis

When the members feel confident that they have fully described the present situation, they move on to the *analysis phase*—determining why the situation developed. Analysis is one of the most important phases of discussion in problem-solving groups and one that may take up much of the group's time. Groups often spend their time dealing with symptoms rather than causes. For example, let's say Sam is trying to solve a problem of low grades. He decides he spends too much time at the union and chooses the solution of spending more time at the library. He may still find himself wasting time at the library and/or working harder and not getting better grades. Time could be his basic problem, but it is usually a symptom. By asking "why do I spend so much time at the union," the student may really get back to more basic reasons—displeasure with courses, feelings of inadequacy, worry with personal problems—which are the real causes of the problem. Only by dealing directly with these basic causes will the student be likely to raise his grades.

There are seldom single causes for complex problems. Usually the interaction of several preceding factors led to the problem. Occasionally, there will be problem situations which do not necessitate determination of causes to reach a meaningful solution. An example would be a community trying to decide how to handle a drought. It would be difficult to determine the cause for such a situation. The number of problem situations in which it would not be profitable to consider why the problem exists, however, are small.

Learning Experience	Consider a personal problem you are facing currently. Briefly describe that problem.
	Now attempt to list the likely causes of the problem you described.
	Go back to each of the listed causes and ask yourself "why?" Then go back to each of your whys and ask why to each of those. Continue this process as long as you are learning more each time about the reasons for the problem.

Possible Solutions

After the group members have fully analyzed the problem, they attempt to *offer all possible solutions to solve the problem.* The great challenge here is to avoid being tied to typical solutions that have been offered in the past. To assist cooperative thinking by the group which results in the production of many and varied possible solutions, the technique of brainstorming was developed. *Brainstorming is a process of temporarily suspending the critical analysis of ideas and quickly suggesting as many possible solutions as the group members can think of.* The following *rules for brainstorming* should be followed carefully:

1. No criticism of ideas is allowed, verbal or nonverbal.
2. "Free-wheeling" is encouraged.
3. Quantity of ideas is the objective—the more the better.
4. Building from and combining earlier offered ideas is encouraged.

A relaxed yet alert attitude in participants produces the best results. The group should be sure someone is writing down the solutions suggested. In summary, brainstorming encourages creative development of many solutions to the problem. During the process no concern should be given to the practicality of any given solution. Ideas should be verbalized quickly with no evaluation at that time by other members or the person offering the idea.

Each member probably will bring potential solutions as a result of his pre-planning; but hopefully the group product will reflect more than what the individual members brought to the discussion. It will also reflect their creative interaction during the process of discussion.

When the problem-solving situation is one brought about by the direct conflict of clearly stated opposing views, it usually takes the form of determining the best solution agreeable to all parties involved. This is typical in labor-management contract arbitration or situations where professional arbitrators are called in to assist with problem solving. In such cases the focus is on compromise among the potential solutions. The group attempts to find a combination of solutions in which each party can "win" whatever is essential to them. If this approach to a "best" solution is used, both of the conflicting groups will have chosen their "ideal" solutions ahead of time, as well as "how far they will go" in compromising. Each group will base their acceptance of possible compromises on their own previously decided and private criteria.

Choose the Best Solution

After developing as extended a list of potential solutions as possible, the group determines criteria for assessing each solution. Each criterion should be clear enough that each group member interprets it basically the same way. You have already used criteria to analyze others' messages. In a problem solving process, criteria are used to assess solutions to a problem. When you develop criteria, you are asking the question, *"What standards must a solution meet to be acceptable?"* Criteria can be stated in question or statement form. For example:

Statement: Our solution for redecorating the apartment must not cost more than $120.

or

Question: Does our solution for redecorating the apartment cost less than $120?

To make the criteria as definite and concrete as possible, it is often better if the group puts the criteria in statement form so that they become a checklist for evaluating solutions. Most of us use criteria when we are about to make an important decision, whether it's choosing the best date, car, or course to take. For example, before you buy a used car, you probably would make a list of requirements (criteria) for finding the best car for you. You might include:

1. It must have a radio.
2. It must not cost over $450.
3. It must not have any rust on the body.
4. It must not have over 20,000 miles on the tires.

Realizing that you may not be able to meet all your criteria in one car, it is helpful to *rank your criteria* in terms of which is most important. So you may decide that you would put the radio as the last criterion and would accept a car if it had all other things. As you go to look at various cars you would then evaluate each car by your criteria and choose the one that best met them. Criteria are then functional in helping a person make personal decisions.

Criteria take on additional importance when the best solution will be determined by group interaction. Imagine a couple choosing a car. Much time, effort, and disagreement could be avoided if the people involved in choosing a solution determined criteria before going out and buying.

Learning Experience

Consider the personal problem you analyzed on page 205. Develop four criteria which a personally workable solution to this problem must meet.

Go back and reconsider each criterion. Specify each so that it is usable in assessing possible solutions.

The group will then examine the advantages and disadvantages of each brainstormed solution. Some will be discarded quickly. If the group has reached agreement after each phase of problem solving and developed clear criteria, the step of choosing the best solution (or combination of solutions) should not be a difficult task. The *solution chosen as best* should *solve the problem, eliminate the basic causes, meet the criteria,* and *not create other more difficult problems.*

Implementation

The sixth phase—that of *implementation*—may well be a most crucial one for a given problem. Here a group considers the practical concerns of *putting the best solution into action.* A general approach to implementation is planned. First, the group considers who must be involved (e.g., who will write and present the group's recommendations), the cost of implementation, and the best timing for implementation. The group then considers specific obstacles to implementing the solution and works out specific approaches to overcoming the obstacles. Such approaches would involve utilizing effective communication skills.

Effective Problem-Solving Questions

As most productive discussions are characterized by individual prediscussion preparation, it is usually helpful to determine the question ahead of time and allow time for the individual members of the group to do necessary research and thinking related to the problem question. The *problem question* should be clearly *worded* in such a manner as to promote open and productive discussion, leading to maximum group agreement on the solution. This is especially important in problem-solving groups. The following guidelines will be helpful in *phrasing problem questions.*

1. The problem question should be stated *in the form of an open-ended question.* Open-ended questions are those that don't restrict the range of answers and, therefore, encourage communication of many possible answers. Questions that begin with "what" are usually open-ended questions and have the advantage that they state the goal but don't state a specific answer in the question. Avoid questions that can be answered with a "yes" or "no," as these imply a solution and, therefore, lead to debate rather than discussion.

   Example: "What should the company's policy be to reduce employee absences?"

   rather than

   "Should the company cut the pay of employees who are absent repeatedly?"

2. The problem question should be *limited in scope.*

   Limited questions are those that adapt to the time, resources, and member skills available to any problem-solving group. This usually takes the form of adding appropriate qualifiers or limitations to problem questions.

   Example: "What can college students on this campus do to reduce the amount of fuels used for heating?"

   rather than

   "What can college students do to reduce the energy crisis?"

3. The problem question should be *unbiased.*

   Symbols which call up strong favorable or unfavorable connotative meanings should be avoided in problem-solving questions. Descriptive symbols are preferred and will help to avoid the distortion of the members' selective perceptions.

   Example: "What should the school's policy be toward a final exam week?"

   instead of

   "What can we do about the time wasted by final exam week each term?"

Group Consensus

Consensus means agreement. *Group consensus* in problem-solving discussions refers to *the maximum agreement possible by all group members on a given point.* The overall goal of such a group is to reach maximum consensus on a "best" solution. In order to facilitate this overall goal, it is most functional to move toward group consensus at every step. Each step becomes consecutive, in that it is important to reach consensus at that step before going on to the next step. It saves time to work out agreements along the way. For example, if one member disagrees on how the terms are defined and consensus is not reached, it may be necessary to discuss definitions so that the group can achieve an honest consensus on the best solution.

Consensus is approached within the context of individual integrity. Realistically, it is not always possible for all members to agree on aspects of a discussion. In fact, it is unlikely, given the variety of people in a group representing different points of view. Sometimes groups, such as the Supreme Court, are not able to reach consensus on a best solution and a "minority report" is made by some group members. Most often, however, by using appropriate conflict management skills and working for agreement at each step, an honest consensus on a best solution is possible.

Problem-Solving Assessment

In-progress Analysis. Essentially this type of analysis involves a group (or individual) pausing in-progress toward its goal to ask, "Is the current process most productive?" "Are we being stifled by too strictly following a process?" "How do we feel about the discussion?" and "Can the atmosphere be improved to facilitate progress?" This type of assessment is increasingly valuable if a group works together over a long period of time. Any ongoing group must make periodic evaluations of its progress.

Post-discussion Analysis. This type of analysis consists of asking whether the goal was reached. Each step of the process is considered briefly, perhaps after some lapse in time, to check its thoroughness. If a group identifies problems in the process used, such analysis of both process and interaction will help to avoid future problems and improve current product.

Within both approaches to analysis, *structured* and *unstructured* assessment is helpful; often a combination is best. Structured analysis would involve the members responding to predetermined checklists or questionnaires regarding the process and/or product of the group. Such structured instruments could then be discussed. Unstructured analysis would involve spontaneous interaction of the members about how they reacted to the group's process and/or product.

Chapter 14

Interacting with People in Problem Solving

Objectives

Your learning should enable you to:

1. Identify six characteristics of small groups.
2. Specify the conditions which indicate that group problem solving would be more effective than individual problem solving.
3. Identify nonverbal symbols within small group interaction that would signify agreement, disagreement, involvement, and noninvolvement.
4. For a specific discussion situation, determine whether directive or nondirective feedback would be most effective.
5. For your small group interaction, specify two membership responsibilities that you would find most difficult to accomplish and suggest specific methods for developing those skills.
6. For specific group discussions, determine whether a single leader or group-shared leadership would be appropriate.
7. Identify the characteristics of effective discussion leaders.
8. For a specified area of group leadership skills (e.g., initiating discussion or regulating participation), list several specific leadership skills.
9. Describe the role of conflict in a group problem-solving discussion.
10. Indicate steps for managing a specific task conflict.
11. Indicate specific means of avoiding interpersonal conflict in group discussions.

Outline

I. Characteristics of small groups
   A. Each group is a collection of unique individuals
      1. People adjust their uniqueness enough to have a productive and satisfying role
      2. Unique combinations of interests, abilities, and personalities lead to varied functioning of the group
   B. A group develops structure
      1. Basic patterns develop
         a) Leadership and influence system develops
         b) Communication networks develop
         c) Members take on roles
         d) Affection patterns develop
      2. Individual participation differs in each group
         a) Based on initial or earned status
         b) Roles played consistently
   C. A group develops norms
      1. Definition: rules for conduct which lead to stable and predictable patterns of relationships
      2. Examples of norms
         a) Standards of acceptable productivity
         b) Acceptable communication patterns
         c) Acceptable methods and procedures for functioning
         d) Acceptable language
   D. Groups vary in cohesiveness
      1. Definition: unity felt within the group based on attractiveness of group for members
      2. Factors influencing cohesiveness
         a) Size
         b) Tasks
         c) Type of organization
         d) Status of group
         e) Recognition and satisfaction of individual's need for security
      3. Characteristics of cohesive groups
         a) Friendliness
         b) Loyalty
         c) Less friction
         d) More "we-ness"
         e) More conformity
   E. Groups vary in sociability
      1. Definition: friendliness among group members
      2. Varies with task orientation of group
   F. Groups establish group goals
      1. Groups form to satisfy needs of members
      2. Groups are more productive if individual goals are compatible with group goals
      3. Individual and group goals are more compatible in cohesive groups
II. Deciding when to use a group for problem solving
   A. Groups can waste time on jobs that could be better done by individuals
   B. Conditions necessary for group problem solving
      1. When fresh ideas are needed
      2. When different points of view are needed

       3. When time is not an essential factor

       4. When a group of people must act on a decision

III. Review of core communication skills necessary for group interaction

    A. Skill Area One

       1. Skills in using verbal and nonverbal symbols to call up intended meanings

       2. Nonverbal communication important especially in areas of involvement and agreement

          a) Indicators of involvement

             (1) Leaning forward toward the group

             (2) Eye contact with members of the group

             (3) Purposeful body movement

          b) Indicators of noninvolvement

             (1) Leaning back away from group

             (2) Lack of eye contact

             (3) Body movement unrelated to group

             (4) Silence

          c) Indicators of agreement

             (1) Nodding of the head

             (2) Open body position

             (3) Legs crossed toward person agreeing with

             (4) Purposeful body movement

          d) Indicators of disagreement

             (1) Crossed arms

             (2) Body orientation away from person disagreeing with

             (3) Furrowed brow

             (4) Nervous body movements

       3. Determining frames of reference is important

          a) Anticipating the influence of your own frame of reference

          b) Anticipating others "hidden agenda"—unspoken goals for the group

    B. Skill Area Two

       1. Active listening to understand other points of view

       2. Assessment of others' messages to determine appropriate solution

       3. Sending effective feedback is done in terms of group goals

          a) Directive feedback to express your opinion

          b) Nondirective feedback to fully understand others' views

    C. Skill Area Three

       1. Sending clear messages to call up intended meanings

IV. Membership skills for group problem solving

    A. Group members should have adequate preparation for participation in the discussion

       1. Research and think through each subquestion of the process prior to the discussion

       2. Outlined preparation is usually helpful

    B. Group members should work to develop group goals and procedures that all members can work within

       1. Develop a goal that is meaningful and "do"able

       2. Develop procedures for interaction that will facilitate goal accomplishment

    C. Group members' participation should be active and involved—verbally and nonverbally

       1. Encourage everyone to make a verbal contribution several times during the Preparation step

    D. Group members should use the supportive communicative behaviors described in chapter 3

       1. Established early in the discussion and continued

       2. A means of avoiding interpersonal conflict and managing task conflict productively

    E. Group members should assist in developing group cohesiveness

       1. Use communication skills to help members feel

       a) that the problem is relevant to them
       b) that the chosen goal is meaningful, and
       c) that their contribution is important
  F. Group members should adopt a critical attitude toward the quality of group thinking
    1. Review criteria for analytical listening in chapter 7 for guidelines for messages and feedback
    2. Use supportive climates to reduce defensiveness
    3. Change your ideas when appropriate
  G. Group members should work to achieve the maximum degree of consensus consistent with integrity of personal beliefs
    1. Verbalize disagreements and questions as they occur
  H. Group members should share responsibility for the group process and product
    1. Important even if the group has a specific leader
V. Group leadership skills
  A. Definition: any behavior which helps the group achieve agreed upon goals
  B. Selecting leadership for a group
    1. Advantages of a single leader
      a) Goal is usually reached faster
      b) Responsibility for reaching goal is fixed
      c) Details and arrangements are clearly assigned
      d) Proper division of labor
      e) Discipline is easier
      f) Someone to be impartial in conflict management
      g) Procedural details won't distract other members
    2. Advantages of group-shared leadership
      a) Draws upon total leadership potential of the group
      b) Leads to greater involvement
      c) Reduce barriers of status
      d) Self-discipline is effective
      e) More direct interchange among members
      f) Maximum opportunity for leadership development
      g) All are equally likely to participate
      h) Problem solving will be more thorough
  C. Characteristics of effective leaders
    1. Have a good grasp of the problem
    2. Are skilled in organizing group thinking
    3. Are open-minded
    4. Are active participants
    5. Are democratic and consultative
    6. Have respect for and sensitivity to others
    7. Are self-controlled
    8. Can take on distinctive roles
    9. Share rewards and give credit to the group
  D. Specific leadership skills
    1. Leadership in process matters
      a) Prediscussion
        (1) Distribute information
        (2) Arrange appropriate setting
        (3) Consider the needs and skills of group members
      b) Initiating discussion
        (1) Provide transition from previous meeting
        (2) Help members to know each other
        (3) Get each member to contribute early

          (4) Get agreement on common goal

          (5) Get members to share personal feelings

     c) Making process suggestions

          (1) Facilitate determination of most useful process

          (2) Encourage members to assume appropriate tasks

          (3) Act as timekeeper

          (4) Check for consensus after each step

          (5) Provide summary/transitions between steps

     d) Clarifying

          (1) Give concrete examples of generalizations

          (2) Make relationships between contributions

          (3) Rephrase comments for greater clarity

     e) Promoting creative and critical thinking

          (1) Contribute fresh ideas

          (2) Use open-ended questions

          (3) Promote constructive conflict

          (4) Critically analyze the ideas of others

          (5) Get support for inferences

          (6) Apply criteria for assessing messages

     f) Summarizing

          (1) Indicate progress of group often

          (2) Verbalize consensus

          (3) Provide transition to next meeting

  2. Leadership in interpersonal interaction

     a) Climate making

          (1) Establish informality

          (2) Develop supportive climates

          (3) Provide emotional support

          (4) Maintain motivation

     b) Regulating Participation

          (1) Draw out less active members

             (a) Ask specific questions after nonverbal involvement

             (b) Sit directly across from person

             (c) Use direct eye contact and body behavior

          (2) Prevent people from monopolizing

             (a) Sit next to a person and avoid eye contact

             (b) Ask people for brief summary

             (c) Ask others for reactions to their comments

          (3) Managing conflict constructively

             Note: given separate consideration because of central importance

VI. Conflict Management Skills

  A. Definition: the resolution of disagreements in such a way that members are satisfied and are able to continue working together in mutually productive manner

  B. Conflict is essential to realistic problem solving

    1. Conflicts should be managed, not avoided

    2. Conflict should be dealt with directly

  C. Two types of conflict in discussion

    1. Interpersonal conflict

     a) Example: a person using inappropriate language

     b) Rarely helpful to group

     c) Steps in managing interpersonal conflict

          (1) Avoid it

             (a) Consider potential clashes prior to meeting

    (b) Use seating, allocation of responsibility, and climate making to avoid clash

  (2) Use supportive communication behaviors

  (3) Use task conflict management steps

2. Task conflict

 a) Example: difference of opinion on group goal

 b) Potentially helpful to group

 c) Steps in managing task conflict

  (1) Determine if the conflict is real or imagined

  (2) Determine the nature of the conflict

   (a) Level of opinion

   (b) Level of reasoning

   (c) Level of evidence

   (d) Level of values

   (e) Level of group goals

 d) Translate the conflict to a win-win basis

  (1) Assist the group to go through a problem-solving process regarding this conflict

   (a) Review the six steps for solving problems in chapter 13

Reading

It is likely that you spend a great deal of your time interacting in small groups. You have probably recognized that each of the groups you're involved in takes on its own unique character. Things which are acceptable within some groups would not be in others. And you may be a somewhat "different person" given the group you are in. Let's look at some of the factors which lead to a unique kind of interaction for each of the groups we join.

Characteristics of Small Groups

Each group is a collection of unique individuals. Groups are made up of individuals who affect the character of the group and who are in turn affected by the group. You enter a group as a unique person and then you adjust your uniqueness as far as you have to, or want to, in order to find a productive and satisfying role for yourself. Sometimes you decide not to adjust and leave the group. The varied combinations of individual interests, abilities, and personalities lead to varied group functioning.

A group develops structure. No group exists without some kind of structure. Group structure involves the leadership and influence system, communication networks, the patterns of roles the members take, and the patterns of affection. Certain individuals, because of initial or earned status or prestige, assume responsibility for certain functions of the group. You tend to assume roles which you play more or less consistently, although your role may vary from one group to another.

A group develops norms. Norms are "rules" for conduct which usually lead to stable and predictable patterns of interpersonal relationships. They are usually established by custom, leadership, or are gradually developed by the group. Member adherence to norms is regulated by positive and negative reinforcement by other members. Norms of groups might include standards of acceptable productivity; acceptable communication patterns (who may talk to whom, under what circumstances); acceptable methods and procedures for getting something done; and acceptable language.

Groups vary in cohesiveness. Groups vary in their attractiveness to their members. The attractiveness of a group depends upon such properties as size; tasks; programs; type of organization; status in the community; recognition and satisfaction of the individual's need for security. Highly cohesive groups are characterized by more friendliness, greater loyalty, less friction, more "we-ness," and more conformity.

Learning Experience

Consider the groups to which you belong. List one group which you consider highly cohesive and one group which you consider significantly less cohesive. Then consider what led the groups to differ in their cohesiveness and, finally, what specific differences occur in each group's functioning because of varied cohesiveness.

Why are there different levels of cohesiveness in the groups? Note specific factors.

Cite several ways in which the different cohesiveness affects group functioning?

Groups vary in sociability. Some groups are primarily concerned with friendliness among group members, such as a conversation at a party. Others are primarily concerned with task accomplishment, such as a business conference.

Groups establish group goals. Groups form in order to satisfy the needs of the members. A group will probably be productive to the extent that individual member goals are compatible with the group goals. Individual member goals are most likely to be compatible with the group goals in highly cohesive groups. In this skill area we are focusing on task-oriented groups.

When to Use a Group

Small group discussion is a particular type of group functioning using oral communication as its major form of interaction. Group discussion is used when a specific goal can best be reached by the interaction of *several people,* rather than by the individual thought of a single person.

It is important to carefully consider whether group discussion is the appropriate method for reaching specific goals. Much time is spent in committee meetings doing tasks that could better be delegated to individuals. Several conditions which would make group discussion more effective than individual decision making are when fresh ideas are needed, when different points of view are needed, when time is not an essential factor, or when a group of people must act on or comply with the decision to be reached.

In chapter 13 you developed skills in using a problem-solving process. We're now going to work on skills which facilitate the effective functioning of that process. As indicated earlier, the small groups which we will be most

"SEVERAL HEADS ARE NOT ALWAYS BETTER THAN ONE!"

concerned with are those that will work together on solving a problem. In this situation, effective interpersonal interaction becomes a means to an end, rather than an end in itself. It is, however, of primary importance in determining the success of the group's goal accomplishment. Through the use of interpersonal interaction skills, a diverse group of individuals can work together effectively. Each of the skills you have already developed through Skill Areas One, Two, and Three will be essential here. Let's review some of those communication skills in the context of small group interaction.

In Skill Area One you developed skills in using verbal and nonverbal symbols to more accurately communicate with others. Those skills become highly important in problem-solving discussions. Nonverbal communication takes on special importance due to the number of people in the group who will not be verbally communicating at any one time, yet they will be sending continual nonverbal messages which will provide valuable cues to their level of involvement and agreement. Reviewing some of these indicators, *nonverbals indicating noninvolvement* would include leaning back in a chair, lack of eye contact, body movement unrelated to the discussion, and silence. *Involvement,* on the other hand, would be suggested by leaning forward toward the group, eye contact with other members of the group, and purposeful body movement. *Disagreement* would be suggested by crossed arms, body orientation away from the individual disagreeing with, furrowed brow, and nervous body movements. *Agreement,* on the other hand, would be suggested by nodding of the head, an open body position, legs crossed toward the individual agreeing with, and purposeful body movement.

Further, in Skill Area One you developed skills in getting to know your own and others' frames of reference and in developing communication climates which facilitate sharing of perceptions. Both of these skills are crucial in problem solving. As the people in a group will be likely to have something at stake in the resolution of the problem, there may be some hesitancy in revealing one's personal goals and expectations. These kinds of "hidden agendas" can lessen the likelihood of a group resolving the problem in a way that all can win.

In Skill Area Two you developed skills in listening, assessing, and giving feedback based on others' messages. Each of these skills is essential in problem-solving discussions. You might have found yourself in groups where, rather than openly listening to what someone else is saying, you are already mentally encoding your own message and waiting for the moment to get in your "two cents worth." Sometime later you realize that you never really understood the person's meaning. This is one of the reasons why some group meetings take so much longer than they need to. Without listening and using feedback for corrective purposes, a great deal of repetition, backtracking and unproductive conflict occurs.

Active listening is an important communication skill in group discussion. Consensus within a group should be based on honest agreement and the *first step to agreement* is understanding the messages sent by the others in the group. Review *appropriate listening behaviors* which will help you reach your listening goals in a group discussion. In a discussion you will be listening more than you will be talking. Note taking will be especially helpful in remembering what is agreed on.

Critical thinking—*assessment of others' messages*—is vital to reaching a meaningful solution. And finally, *the sending of effective feedback* will be vital to the group's progress. The consideration of your feedback goals should always be made in light of the group goal. *Directive feedback* should be avoided until you fully understand another's point of view. Also it is vital in group discussions to support your directive (evaluative) comments by evidence or reasoning. *Nondirective feedback* is given when you do not fully understand the point of view of another person or when you want to encourage that person to fully think through the suggestion he or she has made.

In Skill Area Three you worked on sending messages which call up intended meanings. Obviously this is an important skill in group problem solving. It avoids the time spent by a person who has something valuable to say, but can't quite get it together in a way that communicates to others. Use the principles of attention, visualization, comparison, repetition, structure, symbol usage, and motivation to maximize the likelihood that your messages will be understood.

In addition to using basic communication skills, there are membership and leadership skills which become important in group problem solving. We are making a distinction between leadership and membership skills, although each member's contribution during a discussion may function as a leadership skill. *The distinction between membership and leadership skills is perhaps more accurately the difference between skills which are continually used in groups and specialized skills which you may use at given times during the interaction.*

Membership Skills

Members should have adequate preparation for participation in a discussion. The important questions to answer and research to be done will be determined during the Preparation step of the problem-solving process. You should then do the necessary research and thinking to answer each of the subquestions of the process. Most people find that preparing a phrase outline, including the specific facts and inferences that they have researched, is most helpful for later participation in the discussion. Such an outline will be easy to refer to while not losing track of the flow of the discussion.

Members should work to develop group goals and procedures that all members can work with. This is very important in a task group, especially if time is limited. The important focus is to develop a goal that is meaningful and "do"able and procedures for interaction that will facilitate its accomplishment.

Group members' participation should be active and involved, both verbally and nonverbally. We've all been in task groups in which some people aren't doing their share. It's frustrating. In problem-solving groups it is vital that each member be willing to share his or her ideas and participate without urging. A reluctant group member takes much time and energy from the task to be done, as other members continually need to work to get that person involved. A helpful procedure to encourage all members' participation is to be sure everyone makes a verbal contribution several times during the Preparation step of the process.

Group members should use supportive communication behavior as described in chapter 3. In this atmosphere you and others will feel "safe" to share your perceptions and ideas regarding the problem. It is important to establish this supportive climate early in the discussion and work to maintain it. This is an important part of the Preparation step of a problem-solving process, as you get to know each other. Being open and supportive does not mean you have to agree with everyone. In fact, productive problem solving needs a conflict of views. By being supportive, however, you will help to avoid conflict between people, which is seldom productive, and to manage task conflict in a productive way.

Members should assist in developing group cohesiveness. Earlier we described cohesiveness as a feeling of unity within the group. This feeling is encouraged if all members feel that the problem is relevant to them, the chosen goal is meaningful, and their contributions are important in the group reaching its goal. You can assist in the development of that feeling by the use of your developed communication skills.

Group members should adopt a critical attitude toward the quality of group thinking. As discussed in chapter 7, we usually talk in terms of inferences and value judgments without specifying the basis for such statements. To reach a realistic solution to your problem it is vital that the facts and opinions used in the process are supportable. You might review the criteria for analytical listening given in chapter 7 and use them as guidelines both for your statements and those of others. By using supportive communication behaviors as you encode your messages and feedback messages you will keep the focus on the message itself, rather than the person who sent it. Often this may mean changing your own mind if the information and group thinking suggest that another point of view is more appropriate.

Learning Experience

Consider the following excerpt from a problem-solving discussion in terms of the quality of the reasoning. Given only the information you have, write any examples of poor reasoning or careful reasoning within the interaction.

Sam: Well, if Professor Smith is against it, it's likely the rest of the faculty will be too.

Betty: I suppose you're right.

Jerry: Maybe we're moving too quickly. Could we talk to more faculty members?

Sam: Come on, Jerry, we don't have time to do that. The last time we tried to talk to the faculty about making changes, nothing happened. They never listen.

Go back and improve the dialogue at places where you indicated poor reasoning to reflect more careful reasoning.

Group members should work to achieve the maximum degree of consensus which is consistent with the integrity of their own beliefs. As indicated in chapter 13, the overall goal of a problem-solving group is to reach common agreement on a best solution. To accomplish this, consensus should be reached at each step of the process. To facilitate consensus you can verbalize disagreements and questions as they come up in the discussion. You might also solicit such responses from others if you see signs of nonverbal disagreement or questioning. This will help the group to avoid later backtracking to discover why consensus on a given step is not developing.

Group members should share responsibility for the group process and product, even if the group has a specific leader. It takes all members working together to help the group reach its goal.

In summary, effective interpersonal interaction in group problem solving is a means to an end. It calls for each member to apply appropriate communication skills and accept membership responsibilities.

Leadership Skills

One of the most important aspects of interpersonal functioning in a problem-solving group is the exercise of leadership. *Leadership* is considered here as *any behavior which helps a group achieve agreed on goals.* During any discussion each member may fulfill a leadership function at some time.

The advantages in having either a single designated leader or group-shared leadership are indicated below.

Advantages in having a single designated leader:

It is usually faster in terms of reaching the goal.
Members know more clearly where they stand; with a single leader, the responsibility for getting something done is fixed.
There is proper division of labor; people do what they are skilled in doing.
Discipline can be easier to maintain.
There is someone to act impartially to manage conflict.
External details and arrangements are clearly assigned.
With procedural problems taken care of, the group can concentrate on the problem.

Advantages of group-shared leadership:

It draws upon the total leadership talent of the group.
It will elicit greater involvement in group interaction.
Barriers to communication decrease as status among members is more equal.
Self-discipline is more effective than that from authority.
There is free flow among members—more direct interchange rather than through a leader.
There is maximum opportunity for the development of leadership attributes in all.

All can participate—with a single leader, that person is limited in his participation.

There is less likelihood that someone or something will be overlooked.

The most effective leader usually will be the one who functions democratically and utilizes the leadership capability of each member in the group. Even the single leader could then function as a "leader-in-reserve," generally overseeing the group's functioning and encouraging the development of individual member roles to accomplishing the necessary leadership functions. Shared or shifting of the leadership role will more often occur in a group that meets over a period of time or an ongoing group. When there is to be only one meeting of the group, a single leader is more likely to emerge (if not appointed) and more directly control the group's functioning.

Brilhart summarizes the characteristics of effective leadership supported by research. You will note that the majority of characteristics are also basic to effective communicators.

Effective discussion leaders
   —have a good grasp of the problem facing the group;
   —are skilled in organizing group thinking;
   —are open-minded;
   —are active in participation;
   —are democratic and consultative;
   —have respect for and sensitivity to others;
   —are self-controlled;
   —can take on distinctive roles;
   —share rewards and give credit to the group.[1]

Following is a list of some important leadership skills in both process and interpersonal areas.

Leadership in Process Matters

1. *Prediscussion*
   —distribute information
   —arrange appropriate setting
   —consider needs and skills of group members
2. *Initiating discussion*
   —provide transition if group has met before
   —help members to know each other
   —get each member of the group to contribute at the beginning
   —assist in agreement on a concrete goal
   —get members to share personal feelings on topic
3. *Making process suggestions*
   —facilitate determination of the most useful process
   —encourage members to assume appropriate leadership tasks
   —act as timekeeper, when appropriate

---

1. John K. Brilhart, *Effective Group Discussion*, 2d ed. (Dubuque, Iowa: Wm. C. Brown, 1974), pp. 128–32.

—check for consensus after each step

—provide summary transitions between steps

4. *Clarifying*

    —give concrete examples of generalizations

    —point to relationships between what members are saying

    —rephrase comments for greater clarity

    —use nondirective feedback to encourage clarification

5. *Promoting creative and critical thinking*

    —contribute fresh ideas

    —provoke original thought in others with open-ended questions

    —promote constructive conflict

    —critically analyze the ideas of others

    —ask for support for inferences

    —apply criteria for assessing messages

6. *Summarizing*

    —indicate progress of the group frequently. Don't let a group go for long without knowing what they've accomplished. This is also a good way to check for consensus. For example, "Are we all agreed that the basic causes for the problem are . . . ?"

    —verbalize consensus both as positive reinforcement and as an opportunity for people to question

    —provide transition if group is to meet again

Leadership in Interpersonal Interaction

1. *Climate making*

    —establish informality

A circle is ideal. If this is not possible, try to seat less active members in the dominant positions to encourage interaction. Even in a circle arrangement you can increase the interaction of more reluctant members by seating them directly across from very active members, such as a leader.

    —develop a supportive climate using Gibb's supportive communication behaviors

     —provide emotional support and help keep members off the defensive
     —determine when motivation begins to lag and suggest a break or alternative activity to get members back in the mood

2. *Regulating participation*
     —drawing out the less active members
     asking specific questions after nonverbal involvement
     sitting directly across from that person
     using direct eye contact and body behavior to that person
     —preventing people from monopolizing the discussion
     sitting next to the person and avoiding eye contact
     asking for brief summary of their contributions
     asking others for their reactions to the dominator's comments to draw others in

3. *Managing conflict constructively*
    Because of the integral nature of conflict in group interaction we will consider this skill in more depth below.

Conflict Management Skills in Problem-Solving Discussions

    Constructive conflict is essential to realistic problem solving. If a group moved through a problem-solving process without disagreement, we might assume that there was no problem to begin with, that group members were not chosen to reflect conflicting views, or that the climate didn't facilitate full expression of the members' ideas. Therefore, *it is appropriate to consider how to manage conflict rather than how to avoid it.* Conflict should be handled directly and constructively rather than indirectly. *Conflict management* in problem-solving discussion refers to *the resolution of disagree-*

ments in such a way that members are satisfied with the resolution and are able to continue working together in a mutually productive manner.

There are two general types of conflict: task conflict and interpersonal conflict. Examples of the former are related to differences concerning the process of the discussion, including selection of the process steps, relevance of facts, gaining consensus, and choosing group goals. Examples of interpersonal conflict are related to differences between "personalities," including a person's choice of symbols, someone dominating the discussion, not agreeing with the group consensus, or being absolute in opinions. While task conflicts are potentially productive to a realistic group solution, interpersonal conflicts rarely are. Let's talk about handling those first.

Managing Interpersonal Conflict

The best procedure for managing interpersonal conflict is to avoid it. Using the communication skills developed in the first three skill areas, you should be able to avoid most of these conflicts. It is helpful to consider the potential interpersonal clash of members beforehand and use seating, allocation of positions of responsibility, and climate making to avoid problems. We believe that the use of Gibb's supportive communication behaviors can be a major factor in avoiding interpersonal conflicts. As a leader you could establish these climates early in the discussion by restating comments, which might represent defensive-producing behaviors, into supportive statements. For example, if a member said, "Obviously, we've got to look at it from the perspective of the union members!" (representing certainty); you could respond, "_____, do you mean that it's likely that most people will expect us to do that?" (representing provisionalism). You can set the tone of the discussion and help members to avoid idea possessiveness. If an unavoidable interpersonal conflict does occur, you might use some of the approaches suggested below for managing task conflicts.

Managing Task Conflicts

The following steps are helpful in managing task conflict in problem-solving discussions.

1. *Determine if the conflict is real or imagined.*

   Some conflicts are only real on the verbal level. It might be that the people involved are misunderstanding the other's point of view. Have the members involved in the conflict paraphrase what they think the other's point of view is. Many times feedback can clarify a misunderstanding.

2. *Determine the nature of the conflict.*

   Dean Barnlund and Franklyn Haiman[2] suggest that people can disagree on any of five levels: the level of opinion, the level of reasoning, the level of evidence, the level of values, or the level of

---

2. Dean Barnlund and Franklyn Haiman, *The Dynamics of Discussion* (Boston: Houghton-Mifflin, 1960), pp. 164–77.

group goals. This step of conflict management is accomplished when members understand what the conflict is.

3. *Translate the conflict from a win-lose basis to a win-win basis.*

Assume that step two revealed an actual conflict at one or more of the levels of disagreement, the next step is directed at establishing the concept that all parties can win. If members feel that some have to lose in order for others to win, effective use of conflict is impossible.

The accomplishment of this step involves assisting the group members to follow a mini problem-solving process to resolve the identified conflicts. By accomplishing the two steps listed above, you have actually completed the steps of Preparation and Description. Continue by determining why the conflict occurred, setting up the necessary criteria which both agree on (thus allowing both to win) and implement the conclusion. The solution to the conflict will be a compromise.

Developing leadership skills for discussion is valuable and challenging. The application of such skills varies in terms of the individuals involved in the group and the task.

Learning Experience

Ask three to five other students to work with you in problem-solving practice sessions in which you will attempt to reach the best solution to a chosen problem. Develop problem-solving questions which reflect meaningful problems to those involved and meet the guidelines for wording a question. Develop enough questions so that each member of the group will have an opportunity to lead a problem-solving session. Work with problems that are quite narrow and do not necessitate extensive research, so that you may concentrate on your leadership skills.

Each leader in turn should plan for the session (time, place, prior member preparation, etc.) and function as leader during the session. It would be helpful to tape (video and/or audio) your discussion sessions so that the entire group can comment and learn from the experiences. When you are not functioning as leader, work on your membership skills.

As a result of your experiences, write two leadership responsibilities that you handled especially well.

Write two leadership responsibiilties that you need to work further on.

Also, write two membership responsibilities that you handled especially well.

Write two membership responsibilities that you need to work further on.

Ask for others' perceptions of your leadership and membership behaviors. How did they compare with yours?

Additional Learning Sources

Bormann, Ernest, and Bormann, Nancy. *Effective Small Group Communication,* 2d ed. Minneapolis: Burgess Press, 1976.

Brilhart, John K. *Effective Group Discussion,* 2d ed. Dubuque, Iowa: Wm. C. Brown, 1974.

Cathcart, Robert, and Samover, Larry. *Small Group Communication: A Reader,* 2d ed. Dubuque, Iowa: Wm. C. Brown, 1974.

Davis, James. *Group Performance.* Reading, Mass.: Addison-Wesley, 1969.

Filey, Alan. *Interpersonal Conflict Resolution.* Glenview, Ill.: Scott, Foresman and Co., 1975.

Keltner, John W. *Interpersonal Speech-Communication.* Belmont, Calif.: Wadsworth Publishing Co., 1970.

Phillips, Gerald, and Erickson, Eugene. *Interpersonal Dynamics in the Small Group.* New York: Random House, 1970.

Skill Test

During this skill test you will work in a group with others to select the best solution to a group-chosen problem and plan for its implementation. After the group discussion you will analyze the group's process and product. The objectives for this skill test are indicated below.

In an initial meeting with group members, you will jointly:
1. Select a discussion problem which all members agree can be solved by the group (enough information available, time, member interest).
2. Word a discussion question concerning the chosen problem which will lead to open and productive discussion.
3. Complete the Preparation Step of a problem-solving discussion process. (Share the above with your instructor before going on.)

Between the two group meetings, you will individually:
4. Prepare an individual process outline covering the remaining five steps of the process. (Share your outline with your instructor before participating in the group.)

In a second problem-solving session your group will together:
5. Solve the stated problem using a process approach and plan the implementation of the chosen best solution.
6. Complete a problem-solving report form.
7. Have each member accomplish two leadership tasks during the discussion which move the group toward accomplishing its goal.
8. Allow each member to fulfill appropriate membership responsibilities during the problem-solving session.

After the second problem-solving session, you will individually:
9. Assess the group's achievement of its stated goal.
10. Assess your participation in the group by:
    a. Describing your accomplishment of two leadership tasks.
    b. Assessing your handling of membership responsibilities.

Prediscussion Form

On separate sheets of paper complete the following form. Step I will be done with your group. Steps II–VI will be done on your own.

I. Preparation

1. Write the specific group goal.
2. Write an effectively-worded question for the problem of your choice.
3. Indicate the form your solution will take based on the power that your group has.
4. State the important questions that must be answered in order to accomplish the group goal.
5. State what research will be necessary to reach the goal.
6. List potential barriers to your having a productive discussion.
7. Determine means for overcoming the barriers.
8. Specify the time, place, leadership type, and seating arrangement you will use for your discussion.

(Share the above with your instructor before each group member begins his or her individual preparation.)

II. Description

9. Define needed terms within the question.
10. Describe the present situation.
11. List relevant facts concerning the problem.
12. State the points of view of all people involved.
13. Indicate what previous action has been taken regarding the problem.
14. State what is unsatisfactory about the present situation.

III. Analysis

15. State why the problem developed.
16. State what specific factors have kept the problem from already being solved.
17. List the most basic causes of the problem (be careful not to list symptoms).

IV. Proposals

18. List as many brainstormed solutions as possible.

V. Selection of the Best Solution

19. List and rank specific criteria that the solution must meet to be acceptable.
20. Write the solution that best meets the criteria, solves the problem, and yet does not create other major problems.

VI. Implementation

21. Write specific plans to implement the solution, including who will be responsible and the steps for implementation.
22. Identify potential obstacles to your implementation plan.
23. List specific ways to overcome the listed obstacles.

Group Discussion Report

To be filled out by the group right after finishing the discussion. One copy of the report will be shared with your instructor.

To: (Write the person or group to which your report would be sent.)
Regarding: (Write the group's problem-solving question.)

We believe the basic problem is (summarize your description of the problem).
We believe the basic causes of the problem are (list the group-determined basic causes).
Based on the following criteria:
We feel that the best solution would be:
The following steps are suggested for implementing the problem:
We anticipate the following barriers to implementation:
and suggest the following plans for overcoming those barriers:

Signed: (signatures of group members)

Postdiscussion Form

Complete individually on a separate sheet of paper.

1. Assess the group's achievement of its stated goal.
2. Describe and assess your group's thoroughness in using the problem-solving process in reaching its goal. Indicate any weaknesses.
3. Assess your participation by the following:
   Describe your accomplishment of two leadership tasks during the group discussion and explain how they assisted the group in reaching its goal.
   Comment on your handling of membership responsibilities, especially those you predicted would be most difficult for you to accomplish.

Skills in Interviewing

Overview

A very important concern for people is getting jobs. Whether the job be for summer employment, a part-time job, or for a life-long position, the communication relevant to getting a job may be among the most important of your professional career. Getting a job is very difficult. In one state over 2500 people applied for 10 job openings as conservation agents. Quite typically, people applying for teaching positions discover that the school system may have had hundreds of applications for one position. Companies are swamped by applications for summer jobs. The disappointments which result from nonsuccessful attainment of your communication goals can be extreme. Because it is very difficult for employers to make a decision based on your personal records, interviews are used as part of the hiring or employment procedure.

You will participate in many kinds of interviews during your personal and professional lives. This Skill Area is designed to enable you to develop all of the key skills necessary to perform the interviewer role, as well as to be successful in the interviewee role. These understandings and skills will be applicable to the wide variety of interview situations you will experience the rest of your life.

Definitions

Basic Differentia	Those skills or abilities which best distinguish between excellent or poor people for a particular position.
Closed-ended Questions	Questions which restrict the E's choices, are usually answered in few words, and provide very specific information.
Funnel Sequence	A series of questions which begins with a broad question and continues with progressively more narrow questions.
Interview	Planned interaction between two people for the purpose of attaining agreed-upon or understood goals by mutually focusing on a particular area.
Interviewee(E)	The person in an interview who helps accomplish the interview's goal by providing information.
Interviewer(R)	The person in an interview who is responsible for the results of the interview.
Inverted Funnel Sequence	A series of questions which begins with a narrow question and continues with more general questions.
Open-ended Questions	Questions in which the nature and extent of the answer is chosen by the E, are usually answered in many words, and provide more general information.
Rapport	The condition of a harmonious relationship that reflects the feeling of common goals.

Chapter 15

Giving Interviews

Objectives

Your learning should enable you to:

1. Explain the advantages of the interview process over written communication.
2. Explain why the interviewer goals in an interview are sequential.
3. Sequence interviewer goals for a hiring interview.
4. Define basic differentia.
5. Indicate alternative ways to determine basic differentia for a specific position.
6. Develop examples of basic differentia for a given position.
7. Distinguish between open- and closed-ended questions.
8. Develop questions to test basic differentia.
9. Develop sequences of questions.
10. Assess behaviors to determine their effectiveness for accomplishing specific R goals.

Outline

I. Interview: a planned interaction between two people for the purpose of attaining agreed-upon or understood goals by mutually focusing on a particular area.
  A. Interviews are used in a variety of situations
    1. Examples: bank loan officers, teachers, police officers
  B. People involved in the interview
    1. Interviewer (referred to as the R) is the person who is responsible for the results of the interview
    2. Interviewee (referred to as the E) is the person who helps accomplish the interview's goal by providing information
  C. Types of interviews
    1. Problem-solving types
      a) Appraisal: to discuss previous performance and set new goals
      b) Performance: to identify anticipated or actual problems and relevant solutions
      c) Reprimand: to identify problem, consequences, causes, and corrective action
      d) Grievance: to investigate a person's complaint
      e) Counseling: for a person to express feelings and work through problems
      f) Termination: to identify areas for organizational improvement
    2. Informative types
      a) Information seeking: to discover facts, attitudes, and ideas
      b) Hiring: to assess a prospective employee's basic knowledge and skills   / *Match*
      c) Information giving: to delegate responsibility, clarify details of a task, or communicate data
    3. Persuasive types
      a) Sales: to sell a product
      b) Recommendation: to sell an idea
  D. Advantages of interviews
    1. Enables the R to understand the thoughts, feelings, values, and other in-depth personality characteristics of the E not learned through written application forms
    2. Involves a realistic lifelike communicative situation which reveals E's current knowledge and skills
  E. Guidelines for R handling the steps of the interview process
    1. Interview goals are sequential; each step must be accomplished for later steps to be successful
    2. Attainment of each communication goal is in terms of the E's communicative behavior
  F. Overview of the steps of the hiring interview
    1. Planning the Interview
      a) Determine the goals for the interview
      b) Select communicative procedures to insure attainment of the goals
    2. Opening the interview
      a) Develop rapport
      b) Clarify the situation and the interview's goals
      c) Communicate that the E's feedback is important
    3. Exploring the content
      a) Ask questions relevant to the goals
      b) Relate answers to the question's purpose
      c) Ask follow-up questions
      d) Support the E
    4. Closing the interview

a) Give a short summary; allow for clarification

b) Describe the future disposition of the interview data

c) Show termination behaviors to end the interview when the goals are accomplished

5. Making the decision

II. R's behaviors in accomplishing each step of the hiring interview

A. Planning the Interview

1. Types of behaviors R can use to make final selection

a) Asking questions

b) Processing verbal and nonverbal feedback

2. Hiring interview goals are set in terms of basic differentia

a) Definition: those skills or abilities which best distinguish between excellent or poor people for a particular position

b) Methods for determining basic differentia

(1) Task analysis study: observing and categorizing the actual things people do for a particular position

(2) Comparative personnel study: comparing people who do the job most effectively to those who do the job least effectively, to identify their job-related differences

c) Basic differentia are the best predictors available to determine success on the job

d) Basic differentia include both general abilities and specific abilities relevant to a particular task

e) Examples of general basic differentia

(1) Enthusiasm and motivation

(2) Ability to communicate orally

(3) Emotional stability

(4) Aggressiveness and initiative

(5) Self-confidence

(6) Moral standards

(7) Leadership potential

(8) Pleasant personality

(9) Writing skills

(10) Poise during the interview

(11) Interest in people

(12) Good personal appearance

(13) Good scholastic record

(14) Preparation for the interview

(15) Formulated long-range goals and objectives

3. Questions are developed by R based on the specific basic differentia which will determine if the person has the relevant knowledge and skills

a) Information gained by questions includes descriptions, perceptions, attitudes, feelings, or values

b) Two types of questions used

(1) Open-ended questions: those in which the nature and extent of the answer is chosen by the E, are usually answered in many words, and provide more general information

(a) Questions which begin with the words "what," "how," and "why" are usually open-ended questions

(b) Example: "Why did you choose your major?"

(c) Advantage of open-ended questions is that they don't directly imply the basic differentia or the desired answer

(2) Closed-ended questions: those which restrict the E's choices, are usually answered in few words, and provide very specific information

(a) Questions which begin with the words "are," "have," "did," or "do" are usually closed-ended questions

        (b) Example: "Are you highly motivated?"

        (c) Disadvantage of closed-ended question is that it implies the basic differentia and the desired answer

    4. Questions are sequenced to enable following up and determining an in-depth understanding of the E's knowledge and skills

      a) Funnel sequence: a series of questions which begins with a broad question and continues with progressively more narrow questions

        (1) Typically opens with an open-ended question and uses follow-up questions to enable in-depth understanding

        (2) Each basic differentia is investigated before going on to the next

        (3) Strongest for investigating E's thoughts, feelings, values, and skills

      b) Inverted funnel sequence: series of questions which begins with a narrow question and continues with more general questions

        (1) Typically opens with an easy, closed-ended question

        (2) Often used at the beginning of the Exploring Content phase of the interview

        (3) Strongest for investigating specific information, descriptions of activities, and behaviors

    5. Nonverbal communication is planned by the R

      a) Appropriate environment is determined

      b) Appropriate dress of R is determined

B. Opening the interview

    1. Rapport is developed

      a) Definition: a condition of a harmonious relationship, reflecting the feeling of common goals

      b) Developed by R sharing some perceptions to enable the development of trust

        (1) Use of supportive communication behaviors (see chapter 3) are helpful

      c) Helps to overcome E's anxiety

    2. The situation and interview goals are clarified

      a) Responsibilities and duties of position clarified

      b) R doesn't state the specific basic differentia

    3. The R communicates that the E's feedback is important

      a) Communicates interest in learning about the E

    4. Steps are sequential and accomplishment is indicated by E's nonverbal and verbal behavior

C. Exploring content in the interview

    1. R asks questions related to the interview's goals

      a) Questions test the basic differentia

      b) Questions are specifically worded and used as prepared in the interview

        (1) Misunderstandings occur when questions are reworded after they've been asked

    2. R relates E's answers to the questions purpose

      a) In hiring interviews answers are related to the basic differentia

    3. Follow-up questions are asked if the answer didn't meet R's goal

      a) Planned or partially planned funnel sequence used

    4. The R supports the E

      a) Minimizes effect of control and evaluation that E perceives

      b) Accomplished verbally by sharing personal experiences using supportive climates

      c) Accomplished nonverbally by smiling and leaning forward

D. Closing the interview

    1. Done after sequential attainment of all goals

    2. R gives a short summary and allows for clarification

      a) E's feedback is used to correct original impressions

      b) Follow-up questions are asked as needed

    3. R describes the future disposition of the interview data

a) R determines specific means of communicating with E
4. R shows termination behaviors to end the interview when the goals are accomplished
E. Interview follow-up behaviors
1. Notes are translated into a report
2. Decision is made in terms of highest ratings on the basic differentia
3. Candidates are informed of decision
4. Another level of interviews may occur with top E's
a) Involve more R's and more specific basic differentia

The *interview* may be thought of as *a planned interaction between two people for the purpose of attaining agreed-upon or understood goals by mutually focusing on a particular area.* We face interviews in a wide variety of situations. Some of these situations might involve bank loan officers, salespeople, teachers, doctors, or police officers. These situations involve agreed-upon or understood goals, though your goals and the other communicators may be different. In each of these important situations your verbal and nonverbal communication will greatly influence the degree to which you can accomplish your goals.

The two people in an interview are called the interviewer and the interviewee. The only difference between these two words is the last letters, R and E, and these last letters will be used to represent the two participants in these materials. *The R (interviewer) is the person in the interview who is responsible for the results of the interview.* In the hiring interview the college

recruiter is the R. *The E (interviewee) is the person in the interview who helps accomplish the interview's goal by providing information.* The E would be the applicant in the employment interview or loan situation, the student in the interview with the teacher, the patient in the interview with the doctor, or the witness in the police interview. Both people, R and E, talk and listen and communicate nonverbally. One of the main characteristics of the interview is the dynamic and involved interaction between the participants.

Types of Interviews

There is a wide variety of interviews in which you will be involved during your life. A number of these are represented in figure 18, which categorizes the types of interviews under three main headings: problem solving, informative, and persuasive. These three types are defined in terms of the interviewer's goals for the interview. One of the most important kinds of interviews is the hiring or employment interview. As you can well imagine, the E's purpose for the hiring interview would be *both* informative and persuasive.

Type	Purpose
Problem Solving	
Appraisal	to discuss previous performance and set new goals
Performance	to identify anticipated or occurring problems and relevant solutions
Reprimand	to identify problem, consequences, causes, and corrective action
Grievance	to investigate (formally and/or informally) a person's complaint
Counseling	for a person to express feelings and work out problems
Termination	to identify areas for organizational improvement
Informative	
Information seeking	to discover facts, attitudes, and ideas
Hiring	to assess a prospective employee's basic knowledge and skills
Information giving	to delegate responsibility, clarify details of a task, or communicate data
Persuasive	
Sales	to sell a product
Recommendation	to sell an idea

FIGURE 18

The next two chapters will primarily focus on the hiring interview, as it will probably be the next major interview you will face. Because your first and important role in the hiring interview will be as the interviewee, we will focus both chapters from the perspective of you as the E. Many of the interviewer skills you will work on, especially that of asking questions which accomplish your intended goal, will be extremely valuable to you in many communicative situations.

The Hiring Interview

Interviews are almost always used as a part of the hiring or employment process, even for part-time jobs. They are used even though the interviewer will probably find the interview to be expensive in terms of his or her time. To minimize the expense, Rs typically conduct a 15–30 minute "screening" interview to determine the most promising applicants for a particular position, and then conduct more lengthy interviews with those Es. You might wonder why interviews are used when all Es put together carefully prepared, very elaborate application sheets or resumés which contain informative descriptions of the applicant as a person, his or her educational background, and previous work experience.

Advantages of Interviewing

Two main advantages are typically given to explain the expense in terms of time and effort on the part of the employing organization. The first advantage is that *the interview enables the R to understand the thoughts, feelings, values, and other in-depth personality characteristics of the E* which cannot be learned from written application forms. The opportunity to ask follow-up questions, which enable the R to get an understanding of the E, justifies the expense. A second major advantage is that *the interview involves a realistic lifelike communicative situation which reveals E's current knowledge and skills.* In order to be an effective employee a person must be able to both communicate effectively and to use her or his knowledge and skills immediately in actual situations. Effectively designed interviews enable the R to observe these skills in actual operation.

Major Steps in the Hiring Interview Process

There are five steps the R goes through in the interview process. These are **planning** the interview, **opening** the interview, **exploring** content, **closing** the interview, and **making** the decision. Figure 19 represents these five areas along with component subgoals. At the end of chapter 16 is a sample interview which you might use to assist you in visualizing how these goals are attained through the hiring interview process.

There are two guidelines of crucial significance for the R in handling the interview. The first guideline is that *the interview goals are sequential.* That is, if subgoal 3, "Develop Rapport," isn't adequately attained, then later goals are increasingly less likely to be fully attained. Rapport describes a harmonious relationship and is facilitated by use of the supportive climates discussed in chapter 3. If the interviewer doesn't develop rapport, the E will be nervous and the E's answers will less accurately reflect his or her knowledge and skills, making it more difficult for the R to accurately assess the potential value of the E as a job applicant. It is very important to adequately attain each goal in the interview.

STEPS AND COMPONENT R SUBGOALS FOR THE HIRING INTERVIEW

PLANNING THE INTERVIEW
1. Determine the goals for the interview.
2. Select communicative procedures to insure attainment of the goals.

OPENING THE INTERVIEW
3. Develop rapport.
4. Clarify the situation and the interview's goals.
5. Communicate that the E's feedback is important.

EXPLORING THE CONTENT
6. Ask questions relevant to the goals.
7. Relate answers to the question's purpose.
8. Ask follow-up questions.
9. Support the E.

CLOSING THE INTERVIEW
10. Give a short summary; allow for clarification.
11. Describe the future disposition of the interview data.
12. Show termination behaviors to end the interview when the goals are accomplished.

MAKING THE DECISION

FIGURE 19

The second guideline is that *the attainment of each communication goal is in terms of the E's communicative behavior.* Thus, adequately attaining each goal will be reflected in terms of E's nonverbal and verbal behavior. Specifically, if the E feels that subgoal 3 has been attained and feels at ease, the E's feedback (primarily nonverbal) will represent that. Your understanding of nonverbal communication will enable you to identify E's feelings of knowing what the interview is about and feeling that the R is positive toward him/her as a person. Specific nonverbal indicators might include a relaxed body, leaning forward, and direct eye contact. In addition, the absence of tightly held hands, a twitching or tapping foot, and physical tension further communicate the E's feeling of comfort. If the E feels uncomfortable or anxious at the beginning of the interview, it would be the responsibility of the R to identify those nonverbal indications and continue to work in developing a supportive communication climate to enable the development of rapport.

Let's take another example of the importance of these two guidelines. The fourth subgoal is to "Clarify the Situation and the Interview's Goals." If this step is successfully accomplished, the E will understand the purpose of the interview, an important step before the R explores the content of the interview. What are some of the E's nonverbal behaviors that would indicate understanding? You will find it helpful in preparing to be an interviewer if you identify, for each substep, two nonverbal behaviors that would clearly represent the attainment of that substep and two nonverbal behaviors which would indicate that the goal had not been attained. Thus, for example, two nonverbal behaviors for understanding might be a smile and a nod of the head. Whereas, two behaviors for not understanding might be a furrowed brow and tilting of the head to the side. Because of the importance of interviews, it is possible that the E will communicate understanding even if the person doesn't. Accordingly, it is desirable for the R, on occasion, to request verbal confirmation to supplement the nonverbal.

Planning the Interview

There are two basic subgoals the R performs in planning the interview. These are to "Determine the Goals of the Interview" and to "Select Communication Procedures to Insure Attainment of the Goals." *The overall goal of the hiring interview is to select the best possible candidate(s) for a particular position.* Figure 20 indicates the sequence of planning for the hiring interview. The R has two major types of behavior he or she can use to make

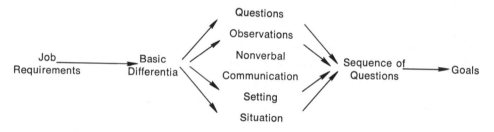

FIGURE 20

a selection. They are asking questions and processing verbal and non-verbal feedback. In *The Peter Prescription,* Laurence Peter wrote the "Peter Particular: Define the job clearly before the candidate is selected or promoted."[1] The underlying idea is to determine what things a person must do well in order to be effective in a particular job. This can be done either through what is called a *task analysis study which involves observing and categorizing the actual things people do for a particular situation* or by a *comparative personnel study which compares people who do the job most effectively with people who do the job least effectively to identify their job-related differences.*[2]

Certain knowledge and skills are required in order to ensure success in an employee. *Basic differentia* are *those skills or abilities which best distinguish between excellent or poor people for a particular position.* The

1. Laurence J. Peter, *The Peter Prescription* (New York: William Morrow & Co., Inc., 1972), p. 170.

2. Edgar H. Schein, *Organizational Psychology* (Englewood Cliffs, N.J.: Prentice-Hall, Inc., 1965), chapter 2.

idea is that the people having the skills are going to be excellent in the position and the people without the skills will be poor.

A job's task analysis or comparative personnel study identifies the basic differentia and, from these, the R designs questions which will determine whether or not the person has the relevant knowledge and skills. Finally, sequences of questions are designed to enable following up and determining an in-depth understanding of the E's knowledge ad skills. In addition to preparing the verbal communication for the interview, the R also plans the nonverbal communication. As we've indicated earlier *the nonverbal feedback will greatly influence* the R's *feelings* about the E. If an interview happens in a comfortable environment, with a warm personal distance of two to three feet with no unnecessary noise or distractions, the interview will work most effectively. In addition, there may be certain organizational policies for the dress of the R. IBM, for example, was known for years to require white shirts and dark ties of their sales personnel. The absence of a tie on a male interviewer may enhance the comfortableness and ease of an interview.

Basic Differentia

Basic differentia are defined as *those skills or abilities which best distinguish between excellent or poor people for a particular position.* Essentially, these are the best predictors available to determine success on the job. These could be either very general or quite specific abilities, knowledge, and skills relevant to a particular position. Two of the most common general abilities are communicating and learning. In fact, Chester Barnard, one of the first leadership theorists, said that the main task of the executive

---

GENERAL BASIC DIFFERENTIA

1. Enthusiasm and motivation
2. Ability to communicate orally
3. Emotional stability
4. Aggressiveness and initiative
5. Self-confidence
6. Moral standards
7. Leadership potential
8. Pleasant personality
9. Writing skills
10. Poise during the interview
11. Interest in people
12. Good personal appearance
13. Good scholastic record
14. Preparation for the interview
15. Formulated long-range goals and objectives

FIGURE 21

is communication. *The ability to learn is very important as organizations train employees for particular jobs.* It is probably the main reason why organizations are so concerned about high grade point averages in hiring for jobs in the professions. The wider your experience in learning effectively and efficiently in other-directed and self-directed learning situations, the more likely you are to be able to learn new skills on the job. Figure 21 represents one such list of general basic differentia. As the description of a job becomes more specific, more specific basic differentia are determined by task analysis or comparative personnel studies. These are the best predictors of job success. Figure 22 represents the type of basic differentia large corporations use for interviewing people going into merchandising management. Figure 22 is a form for using the basic differentia.

Select the job you most want. Imagine you are the college recruiter who is interviewing you for that job. Write the four basic differentia the interviewer believes are the most essential for success in that job. How did you select them? What sources of information were most helpful to you?

Learning Experience

Questions

The two major kinds of interviewer communicative behaviors to assess the E's development of the basic differentia are asking questions and processing feedback. Questions enable the R to get a wide variety of information. This type of information can include descriptions, perceptions, attitudes, feelings, or values. To accomplish this there are basically two kinds of questions. The first kind is called open-ended. *Open-ended questions* are *questions in which the nature and the extent of the answer is chosen by the E.* Typically, open-ended questions don't restrict the range of answers and hence enable a wide range. Open-ended questions usually are answered with a large number of words and provide more general information. *Closed-ended questions are questions which restrict the E's choices, are usually answered in one or few words, and provide very specific information.* A question which can be answered either yes or no is one example of a closed-ended question. Both types of questions directly parallel the types teachers can ask on exams. True-false, multiple choice, and other "objective" questions are examples of closed-ended questions. Essay, case analysis, or problem-solving questions are examples of open-ended questions. In objective questions the choices are limited by the teacher, and in nonobjective questions you have a wide range of choices.

Questions which begin with the words "what," "how," and "why" are usually open-ended questions. Questions which begin with the words "are," "have," "did," or "do" are usually closed-ended questions. Let's say, for example, the R is trying to find out your level of motivation as a general basic differentia. If the R asks "Are you highly motivated?" or "Do you see yourself as highly motivated?" or "Have you ever had periods of low motivation?" or "Do other people see you as highly motivated?" the person is

FIGURE 22.

Interviewer Worksheet
Merchandising Management Trainee

Candidate's Name _____   Date _____

Selection Factor	Comments And Documentation	Evaluation (check one)			
		Shows Little Evidence Of	Shows Adequate Evidence Of	Shows Good Evidence Of	Shows Strong Evidence Of
Motivation — The Desire And Reasons For Actions That Individual Has Taken Or Is Taking					
Leadership — The Ability To Accomplish Results Through The Efforts Of Others By Guiding, Directing And Coaching Them					
Communications — Ability To Express And Interchange Ideas Orally And In Writing					
Learning Ability — Desire And Capacity To Acquire Knowledge And Skills Through Study And/Or Experience					
Teamwork — Evidence Of Ability And Desire To Work With People In A Group Effort					
Competitiveness — Desire To Excel By Directing Efforts To Accomplish Personal And Organizational Objectives					
Self-Confidence — Strength Of Belief In Own Abilities To Accomplish Personal And Organizational Objectives					
Decision Making — Rational Development In Terms Of Weighing Alternatives And Acting In A Manner Appropriate To The Situation					
Determination — Maintenance Of Composure And Rational Thinking In Situations That Are Demanding Or Difficult					
Numerical Ability — Understanding Of Arithmetical Concepts And Dealing With Routine Numbers, Decimals, Percentages, Etc.					

Position	Geographic Preference	Date Available	School	Interviewer
		/ /		Location
Recommendations		Date	Referred To	
☐ Invite ☐ Employ		/ /		
	Date	Explain if not apparent from above		
☐ Reject	/ /			
Other Comments				

Guides For Interviewer Worksheet
Merchandising Management Trainee

Purpose
Interviewer Guides are intended to provide guidance to those who are responsible for interviewing and hiring candidates for the Merchandising Management Trainee Position.

Description
The Guides contain ten selection factors which have been determined by store personnel experts as important to successful performance in the Merchandising Management Trainee Program and to good performance as a Merchandiser.

Use
Rarely will all of the items for each selection factor apply to any one individual. The interviewer may find evidence of proficiency in a factor from indicators under any of the categories listed.

Preparation for Interview
This worksheet provides a method for planning and organizing the information that the interviewer needs to obtain. This will often vary based on the candidate's background, information gaps, and the amount of information the interviewer already has.

Comments, Documentation, and Evaluation
These parts are used to evaluate the candidate, and jot down indicators and facts that led to the evaluations. It is important to make note of them since, when interviewing many candidates, it is difficult to later remember the specifics of each interview.

The comments do not have to be lengthy; they are only notes and indicators. A single word or phrase will often be adequate. When other documents are available such as a resumé, they may be referenced on the Worksheet (i.e., "see paragraph 2 on resume").

The Interviewer Worksheet will not solve all of our selection problems. Any candidate's potential performance is much more than the sum of the facts, impressions and reactions obtained in a pre-employment interview. However, these, along with a practical understanding and use of interviewing techniques, knowledge of the job, and a solid commitment to developing the skills, abilities, interest, and needs of individuals will go a long way in ensuring qualified associates in each position.

Caution
These Guides were developed only for the Merchandising Management Trainee Position and may not be applicable to other positions.

asking closed-ended questions which would be answered with very short answers.

There are advantages and disadvantages to both kinds of questions. One disadvantage of closed-ended questions is that they typically imply the Basic Differentia and the desired answer. The E's analysis of this type of question might go like this: the R must be asking about this characteristic because it is considered important; therefore, I'd better indicate I have that characteristic.

Questions like, "Why did you choose your major?" or "How did you finance your college education?" or "What do you plan on doing five years from now?" are open-ended questions which would be used to measure motivation. "Why" questions are especially helpful in finding out people's frames of reference. One advantage of open-ended questions is that they don't directly imply the Basic Differentia or the desired answer. The guidelines you used in the skill test for Skill Area Three will also be helpful in designing questions. Field testing questions can eliminate confusion regarding their meaning. If you are ever interviewed in a Gallup, Harris, or Roper poll, those questions will have been field-tested.

Learning Experience   Let's imagine that you were to be given a gift of a free secretary for a year. What skills would that person need in order to be most helpful to you? How would you state those skills as basic differentia? Now here is the toughest part. Without any tests of physical performance, what is one open-ended question for each basic differentia whose answer would enable you to decide if a candidate had the basic skill?

Figure 23 visualizes open-ended questions to measure job-related basic differentia.

Sequences of Questions

Usually more than one question is needed to tap the in-depth information on a basic differentia. A *funnel sequence* is a *series of questions which begins with a broad question and continues with progressively more narrow questions.* Typically the funnel sequence begins with an open-ended question and may end with several close-ended questions. The open-ended question is like an exploratory oil well, to be followed by other drilling. Follow-up questions enable more in-depth and detailed investigation of a particular content area. Each Basic Differentia area is carefully investigated before going on to the next one. The funnel sequence is strongest for investigating the E's thoughts, feelings, values, and skills. Figure 24 visualizes an example of a funnel sequence.

An *inverted funnel sequence* is a *series of questions beginning with a question which is narrow in scope and continuing with more general questions.* One advantage of an inverted funnel sequence is that it begins with an easy answer and, hence, is often used at the beginning of the Exploring

FIGURE 23

Job Title	Basic Differentia	Questions
Public Accountant	1. Questioning skills	"What three questions would you ask me if I were applying for this position?"
	2. Personal integrity	"What would you do if you discovered a long-time and valued customer of our firm was not reporting all of his dividend earnings?"
	3. Ability to get along with people	"If the IRS overturned our judgment on a tax matter, how would you handle a frustrated customer?"
	4. Interest in accounting	"How do you think the recent SEC ruling on . . . will affect our firm?"
Public Relations Specialist	1. Ability to work independently	"How would you prepare a major term paper?"
	2. Pleasant disposition	"If another member of the PR staff was given a promotion that you wanted, how would you treat that person?"
	3. Dependability in meeting deadlines	"What are your feelings about deadlines?"
	4. Technical competence	"How would you improve the layout of this ad?"
Assistant personnel manager	1. Make decision from a variety of data	"What data would you collect to determine a promotion and how would you make your decision of the best candidate?"
	2. Write clear reports	"What improvements in your writing ability have you developed since beginning college?"
	3. Work effectively with union stewards	"How would you handle an employee's grievance?"
	4. Select effective training procedures	"How do you determine what kind of training program is most effective for a particular employee?"

FIGURE 23—continued

Job Title	Basic Differentia	Questions
Police officer	1. Problem solving	"How would you handle a situation where you are called to an apartment by a husband where his wife is threatening to kill herself with a handgun?"
	2. Highly complex psychomotor skills	"What experiences have you had with handguns?"
	3. Objectivity with all people	"How would you react to a newspaper friend of yours who wrote an article critical of your police department?"
	4. Effective public relations	"During your shift you have stopped for lunch at a crowded restaurant. Three high school students begin loudly making fun of you and your uniform. How would you handle the situation?"
High school teacher	1. Maintain discipline	"How would you handle a persistently rowdy student?"
	2. Active involvement in high school extra-curricular activities	"What are your hobbies?"
	3. Adapt learning experiences to various student learning levels	"How would you select a textbook for a freshman level course in this school?"
	4. Concern for students' development	"What would be the approach you would use in a conference with the parents of a failing student?"
Retail manager	1. Commitment to company goals	"Why do you want to work for our company?"
	2. Active involvement in community affairs	"What will you do with your spare time?"
	3. Maintain salespeople's morale	"Describe how you helped a friend with a problem."
	4. Possess relevant product knowledge	"What do you know about our line of products?"
Stock boy (part-time)	1. Carry out orders accurately	"I'm going to give you a list of orders for filling shelves. After I'm done, repeat them back to me: 'Stock one case of Del Monte 303 cans of cling peaches in Aisle 7 . . . .'"
	2. Work without supervision	"If you had a major term paper assigned, what steps would you use to complete it and when would you turn it in?"

Job Title	Basic Differentia	Questions
	3. Be courteous to customers	"What would you say to a customer who demanded to know why a favorite product was no longer being sold?"
	4. See what needs to be done and do it	"What would you do when all the shelves were filled with stock and you still had one hour left before quitting time?"
Receptionist (part-time)	1. Follow directions without being checked on	"What would you do if you had one more task assigned and your work time was up?"
	2. Pleasantly greet the public	"What would you say to a person who walked up to your reception desk?"
	3. Complete all forms accurately	"What do you do after you have completed typing a term paper?"
	4. Listen carefully to remember information	"I'm going to give you a list of four names and phone numbers. Please repeat them to me . . . ."
Fast foods employee (part-time)	1. Positive attitude conducive to a "family" image	"What would you say to a father and son (wearing a baseball uniform) who came in after a ball game?"
	2. Doesn't miss work	"What would you do if you were getting ready to drive to work on a bitterly cold winter morning and your car wouldn't start?"
	3. Perform well at a variety of work situations	"Describe three jobs you have had that you would like to do again."
	4. Work well when rushed	"I'm going to give you seven orders. After I say them repeat them back to me. (Said rapidly) "Three double burgers with everything except for one without onions, four orders of fries, and two chocolate malts and a banana shake. Also . . . Oh, make that first double burger without relish."

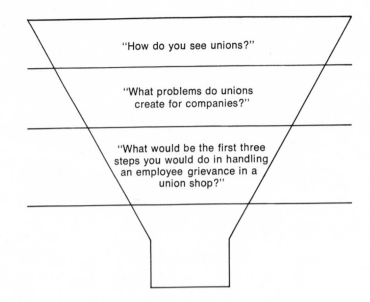

FIGURE 24

Content section of the interview. We suggested earlier that open-ended questions are especially good for getting at attitudes, values, and feelings and that closed-ended questions are especially effective at getting at specific information, descriptions of activities, and behavior. A great deal of time and preparation goes into planning to enable successful interviews. Figure 25 represents an inverted funnel sequence.

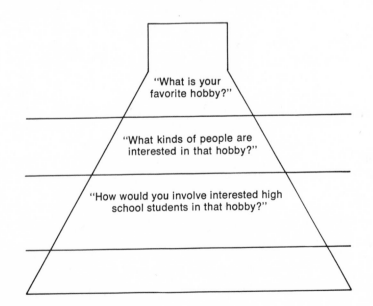

FIGURE 25

Opening the Interview

There are three subgoals which compose the opening of the hiring interview. The first important sequential step is to "Develop Rapport." *Rapport* is a French word which describes *a condition of a harmonious relationship.* Basically this is accomplished by initially sharing some perceptions, enabling the development of initial trust. Rapport involves more than "breaking the ice." It reflects the feeling of common goals, including the E feeling that "we're in this together." Rapport does much to overcome the understandable anxiety that the E feels about the unknowns of the interview situation and the strong desire to do well. Communication climates involving equality, description, provisionalism, and problem orientation may be helpful in developing rapport.

The second sequential step is to "Clarify the Situation and the Interview's Goals." Essentially, the hiring interview's goals are to be accomplished by finding the best person for a specific job. Though the interviewer doesn't state the basic differentia, he or she might clearly describe the job and the responsibilities and duties involved.

The final step for the opening of the interview is for the R to "Communicate that the E's Feedback is Important." The R does this and indicates interest in learning about the E and the E's values, attitudes, and ideas. Again, these goals are sequential and all three should be accomplished as indicated by the E's nonverbals, in order to enable the most effective exploring of content. At the end of chapter 16 there is a sample hiring interview that visualizes how these steps actually work together.

Exploring Content in the Interview

Most of the verbal communication in the hiring interview involves questions and answers. Both the R and the E have planned for this in order to enable the sharing of highly effective, detailed, and accurate communication to lead to successful job filling. Thus, the R's first goal is to "Ask Questions Related to the Interview's Goals." Helpful characteristics of questions involve planning the wording of the questions, specifically using concrete language, and choosing symbols which are at or below the knowledge and experience level of the E. *Experience indicates that the most effective way of asking a question is to carefully think out the wording and then to ask it that way.* A typical mistake of inexperienced Rs is to ask a question and then to re-ask it before the E has responded. Typically, the restatements are more closed than the original asking. If the restated question is in different words, the E might be confused.

After hearing the E's response, the R will mentally process and "Relate the Answer to the Question's Purpose." The R will relate the answer to the basic differentia. If the answer is not a full and complete one, relative to the basic differentia, the R will "Ask Follow-up Questions," probably using a planned or partially planned funnel sequence. Following up on a previous example in terms of measuring motivation, let's assume that the R asked the E, "How did you finance your college education?" and was looking for degree of personal motivation. The E's answer was, "About 40 percent of my college education was paid for by my parents, about 30 percent came from loans from my hometown bank, and about 30 percent was paid for from jobs that I had." None of these three sources of college support necessarily indicates a high level of motivation. The R, in processing this answer, might well decide to follow up on either the loans or the self-employment to get more information about the E's personal motivation. The follow-up questions of "How did you go about securing the loan?" "Why did you choose that bank?" "What previous financial dealings did you have with the bank?" or "Who recommended you take out a loan?" as follow-ups to the loan answer might provide information regarding whether the loan indicates the E's motivation or the parents'. Similarly, follow-up questions might be very helpful in providing information about the E's motivation regarding previous jobs. Follow-up questions to determine how long the E had the jobs and why he or she changed will provide significantly more information about personal motivation. If the E worked for the same company and was promoted or given raises, worked in a position that was related to the kind of work he or she is now applying for, or changed positions to a higher salary, all would indicate higher degrees of personal motivation.

The last step of the Exploring Content section of the interview is to "Support the E." As described in chapter 3, Gibb's *communication behaviors which increase supportiveness can minimize the effect of the control and evaluation that the E often perceives as a part of the interview.* If the R is making "good or bad" evaluations, the E will probably feel increased anxiety and it may be desirable for the R to redevelop rapport. This might be accomplished by the R sharing a personal experience related to one of E's comments or nonverbal behaviors, such as smiling. Even positive evaluations potentially lead to anxiety as described in chapter 8. Gibb's behaviors of description, equality, empathy, and provisionalism are probably much more effective in maintaining rapport and supporting the E. Support of the E is needed along with accurate listening, observation, and processing of E's answers to enable the R to make assessments using the basic differentia as criteria. Also, it will enable the retention of that information until a judgment is made after the interview.

Closing the Interview

The closing of the interview follows the sequential attainment of all goals. In other words, the R has determined that s/he has enough data from the E's answers, plus observations, to make a judgment about whether or not the E will be an effective member of the organization. However, as an E you may feel that you have not communicated all of your knowledge and skills of relevance to the job or that the R has misunderstood or not remembered some of what you said. Anticipating this possibility, the first step of closing the interview is for the R to "Give a Short Summary (of his or her observations and perceptions of your answers) and Allow for Clarification." We're talking here about the corrective function of feedback which enables you to double-check the accuracy of communication. If there are major clarifications made by the E, the R may choose to ask additional follow-up questions to clarify the points of confusion.

A major source of anxiety related to the interview process is the lack of knowledge of results. Employers can do a great deal in terms of enhancing positive public relations if they "Describe the Future Disposition of the Interview Data." This would entail clarifying for the E what the additional steps in processing the interview information will be and indicating when and how the E will find out the results of that processing. In this context, it may be very helpful for the R to find out times and means for future communication with the E. The E might well be considering other positions. Thus, knowing when, where, and how to call the E might be helpful for the R. The final step is to "Show Termination Behaviors to End the Interview When the Goals Are Accomplished." Here a combination of verbal and nonverbal symbols are usually used. The R might verbally refer to the completion of the interview and, at the same time as metacommunication, put her hands on her knees, turn to the side, and possibly break eye contact. These verbal and nonverbal symbols will communicate the end of the interview.

Making the Decision

After the interview, if s/he didn't have time for a full write-up, the R will probably record, using a cassette tape, shorthand, or some note-taking procedure, the key ideas to be remembered. These notes will be completed in terms of organizational forms and analyzed later in the day. This report will then be submitted to the organization and be part of your record. Fig-

ure 20 (p. 245) is an example of how one large corporation uses an evaluation form for summarizing the results of an interview. The decision is then made to select the candidates with the highest ratings in terms of the basic differentia. These people are then informed of the decision and typically another set of interviews will occur, often at the site of future employment. These follow-up interviews will essentially parallel the goals of the screening interview which we've analyzed in detail, but will involve more Rs, more specific basic differentia, and more in-depth analysis of your knowledge and skills.

Chapter 16

Taking Interviews

Objectives

Your learning should enable you to:

1. Describe the interviewee's role in a hiring interview.
2. Specify measurable goals you want from a job.
3. Identify the best sources to learn more about a job you want.
4. Determine the basic differentia for a job you desire.
5. Infer from interview questions the basic differentia being tested.
6. Develop answers to questions testing basic differentia, which positively and accurately reflect your qualifications for a job.
7. Specify nonverbal behavior to reflect interest and involvement.
8. Plan behaviors to accomplish specific interviewee goals.

Outline

I. E's role in the hiring interview: to provide information to accomplish the interview's goal
  A. Overview of E's goals in the hiring interview
    1. Before the interview
      a) Decide what you want
      b) Anticipate what basic differentia they want
      c) Plan your communication
    2. During the interview
      a) Reflect interest and involvement nonverbally
      b) Analyze the R's nonverbal symbols
      c) Analyze the questions
      d) Visualize your knowledge, skills, motivation, and relevant previous experiences
      e) Communicate complete and detailed answers
      f) Use job-relevant symbols
      g) Analyze your answers as communication
    3. After the interview
      a) Analyze your attainment of the E's goals
      b) Determine areas for future improvement
  B. E's goals are not sequential as R has responsibility and control over the interview
  C. Planning by the E is essential
  D. Main E behavior is answering questions
    1. Communication skills developed in first three skill areas are vital
      a) Accurate listening
      b) Communicating feedback
      c) Designing verbal messages to communicate meanings
      d) Sending clear nonverbal messages
      e) Adapting to R's frame of reference
      f) Monitoring R's verbal and nonverbal feedback
II. Specific E behaviors to accomplish E goals
  A. Planning to take the hiring interview
    1. Determining "What do I want?"
      a) Set specific measureable goals of what you want from a job
         Example: "I want to earn $8,000 after taxes the first year I work."
      b) Rank your goals in terms of importance
      c) Use ranked goals as criteria in selecting a position
    2. Determining "What do they want?"
      a) Talk to sources as close as possible to actual position you want
      b) List of ranked potentially valuable sources
        (1) A person who works in the position you want and in the organization you want
        (2) A person who used to have the position in the organization you want
        (3) People who work in the same position in similar organizations
        (4) Recent literature which describes the specific job
        (5) The organization's literature
        (6) Someone who works in the organization in an unrelated area
        (7) General literature on the type of job
        (8) People who work in an organization similar to where you applied
        (9) General literature on the organization
        (10) General literature on the type of organization
      c) Information to gain from source

        (1) "What are the essential skills to do this job well?"

X   (2) "What skills were missing in those people who are not doing the job well?"

        (3) Infer essential skills

3. Planning communication to accomplish goal
   a) Determine basic differentia
      (1) Use information from sources
      (2) Consult journals in that field   *updated knowledge.*
      (3) Discover information about what's unique, new, or good in the organization
      (4) "What is the in-house slang and language?"
   b) Design typical questions and answers related to basic differentia, developing best possible answers to sell yourself
      (1) Their standards are high because of high competition
      (2) Rs want to avoid hiring people who won't do the job well
4. Making an initial contact may be necessary
   a) Request by phone or mail
   b) Each should be following by resumé
      (1) Information for resumé
         (a) Name
         (b) Address
         (c) Telephone
         (d) Job objective
         (e) Education
         (f) School activities
         (g) Experience
         (h) Skills
         (i) References
      (2) Get sample from your placement service or books on interviewing
B. E behaviors during the interview
   1. Reflect interest and involvement
      a) Lean forward
      b) Avoid nervous or distracting gestures
      c) Direct eye contact
   2. Analyze the R's nonverbal symbols
      a) R's dress and personal distance
      b) Spatial relations of the room
   3. Infer the underlying philosophy of the organization and how they see people
      a) Theory X organization—assumes people don't like work and need external control and direction from people in authority
         (1) Reflective nonverbal behavior
            (a) Formal dress
            (b) Formal distance of 4 to 8 feet
            (c) Clear indications of status
         (2) Reflective verbal behavior
            (a) Referring to people as employees in positions and using full name
            (b) Pronouns such as "them" and "they"
      b) Theory Y organization—assumes that people enjoy work and are motivated by internal goals
         (1) Reflective nonverbal behavior
            (a) Informal dress
            (b) Close personal space of 2 to 3 feet
         (2) Reflective verbal behavior
            (a) Refer to people by name rather than position
            (b) Pronouns such as "we" and "us"

4. Analyze the questions asked by the R
   a) Determine the basic differentia being taped
   b) Determine how long the answer should be
      (1) Open-ended questions assume longer answers
      (2) Closed-ended questions assume shorter ones
5. Visualize your knowledge, skills, motivation, and previous experiences
   a) Relate answers directly to the basic differentia
6. Communicate complete and detailed answers
7. Use job-related symbols
8. Analyze your answers as communication; use R's feedback to determine effectiveness

C. E's behaviors after the interview
   1. Analyze your attainment of your goals
      a) Write down questions asked and your answers
      b) Check with your teacher or another applicant
   2. Determine areas for further improvement

There is a story about a book describing Ireland. It had a remarkably short chapter in it. The chapter was titled, "The Snakes in Ireland." The only sentence in the chapter was "There are no snakes in Ireland." This, too, could be a very brief chapter. A good deal more research and writing is being done regarding the R role in the interview. Unfortunately, not much is known about how to develop interviewee skills. This is remarkable and surprising in that estimates of the number of employment interviews each year run as high as 15 million.[1] As developed in chapter 17, the R, based on his or her and/or the organization's assessment of the basic differentia will develop and sequence questions which you will respond to. Whether you are applying for a part-time job or a full-time one, knowing the basis on which the R makes those decisions and the kinds of questions likely to be asked are crucial foundations for focusing on your skills as an interviewee.

Most of what is known about the E role is based on Rs' statements of likes and dislikes, which lead to what we call the "10 commandments approach." These dislikes lead to a list of things not to do and these recommendations are described in terms of "don'ts," such as "Don't shake their hand limply." A list of the R's likings lead to a recommended list of "dos," like "Do wear clean and pressed clothes." The advantage of the "10 commandments approach" is that knowing these recommendations will be beneficial for you with a wide variety of R's in a wide variety of jobs.[2] The

1. Vernon R. Taylor, "A Hard Look at the Selection Interview," *Public Personnel Review* (July 1969): 196.

2. Robert Carlson et al. "Improvements in the Selection Interview," *Personnel Journal* (April 1971): 268–75.

problems with the approach are that while they recommend what to do or not to do, you are not told *how* or *why* to do these. The "don'ts" are even less helpful. What would happen, for example, if the Golden Rule was stated as a negative proposition: "Don't Hate your Neighbor." This form of statement would tell you what not to do, but would be remarkably ineffective in telling you what to do, how to do it, or why you should do it.

Figure 26 presents a series of goals for the E. You may find some recommendations in that series to enable you to adapt your communication skills to improving your chances of success. These *goals for the E are not sequential* because, in the hiring interview, the R has primary responsibility and control for the interview.

E GOALS FOR THE HIRING INTERVIEW

BEFORE
1. Decide what you want.
2. Anticipate what basic differentia they want.
3. Plan your communication.

DURING
4. Reflect interest and involvement nonverbally.
5. Analyze the R's nonverbal symbols.
6. Analyze the questions.
7. Visualize your knowledge, skills, motivation, and relevant previous experiences.
8. Communicate complete and detailed answers.
9. Use job-relevant symbols.
10. Analyze your answers as communication.

AFTER
11. Analyze your attainment of the E's goals.
12. Determine areas for future improvement.

FIGURE 26

The most important verbal communication for the E is answering questions. Thus, the communication skills that you've developed for listening, communicating feedback, and designing messages to communicate your goals will be especially helpful. In terms of your nonverbal communication skills, those which reflect motivation and involvement and enhance a supportive climate will probably be especially helpful. As we've indicated, the better you can understand the ideas, values, and attitudes of the other communicator, the better you will be able to attain high degrees of accuracy of communication. In addition, the more effective you are at monitoring the R's verbal and nonverbal feedback, the better you will be at communicating information, ideas, feelings, and perceptions that are directly relevant to the basic differentia that the R is using.

In this chapter we'll be working with you on developing your skills in taking the hiring or employment interview by focusing on the three general steps of how to plan for the interview, what to do during the interview, and, finally, how to assess the interview after it's over. Because of the complexity and importance of the employment interview, we personally recommend that you "take one for fun." That is, that the first hiring interview you do is to enable the practicing of the complex communication skills which combine many verbal, nonverbal, and thinking skills simultaneously. Your understandable anxiety will be greatly reduced when you don't want the job.

Planning to Take the Hiring Interview

As in the R's role for the employment interview, *planning for the interview by the E is essential.* The more careful the planning, the more effective the interview will be. To guide your thinking in the planning, the following three questions may be helpful:

1. What do I want?
2. What do they want?
3. How can I get the job that I want?

Let's take a look at each of these questions in detail.

What Do I Want?

"Deciding what you want" is difficult. The "Peter Prospect states: Identify your objective."[3] And the "Peter Proposal states: Establish criteria for successful accomplishment."[4] Many people have general criteria related to the means instead of specific criteria related to the ends for objectives. For example, if a student sets a goal "to study really hard in this course" that person is focusing on the means, as opposed to another student who sets a goal of "earning an A in the course." The second goal is specific and measurable in terms of accomplishing results, where the first is not. Some people set goals for themselves that are very abstract: "I want to be happy," "I want to be successful," "I want to earn an adequate salary," or "I want to be good at what I do." The abstractness of the symbols they use to express their "ends" means that they can never really decide if they have accomplished their objectives, and so they are never attained.

Each general goal that a person wants, such as "being happy," "job success," "earning an adequate salary," and "being good at what one does" can be specified in concrete language. A procedure you might find quite helpful would be to weigh the things you want from a job and use them as specific criteria. For example, decide which is more important to you: job satisfaction or an adequate salary. In order to do that you'll probably need to clearly specify what they mean. For one person "an adequate salary" might

---

3. L. J. Peter, *The Peter Prescription* (New York: William Morrow & Co., 1972) p. 137.
4. Ibid., p. 140.

be $8,000 or more. For another, it might be $18,000 after taxes. For you, job satisfaction might denote helping other people at least one half of the time. For another it might be being respected, being complimented by your boss, or working on challenging projects for a long time by yourself.

Now that you've decided whether job satisfaction, in your terms, is more or less important than an adequate salary, we'd like you to decide how much and then use the answer to the question, "How much," to weigh them. If, for example, job satisfaction is twice as important to you as an adequate salary, you would consider this more in choosing a job.

It is important to keep in mind that your needs as well as values will continue to evolve and change over time. Using Maslow's basic needs hierarchy (figure 27), we probably move from more money-related objectives to more growth-oriented objectives. By keeping this in mind at this stage you will be less likely to lock yourself into a job where material gains are high, but future growth and personal development are not.

FIGURE 27

What Do They Want?

The second question is "What do they want?" Typically books which say they will help you as an E encourage you to do research on the prospective organization from a long list of sources of information on American business, including *Standard and Poor's Corporation Records, Fortune* (review of the largest five hundred companies), *Thomas' Register of American Manufacturers,* and the companies' literature.

Again the practical problems face you of how do you do it, what do you want to find, and why are you doing this? Some related questions that might help to identify what you are looking for in your research are, "What are they doing?" and "What is it like to work there?" You might well develop other questions to guide your research in determining "what they want" as well as whether that's the kind of job that you want. Our experience recommends that there are much more valuable sources than the above-listed materials, even if you are applying for a large business which would be discussed in those materials. Figure 28 represents potentially valuable sources of information, ranked from most through least valuable.

Basically the assumption for figure 28 is that people who are currently playing the game know what's happening more than the spectators or the

1. A person who works in the organization doing the kind of job you're applying for.
2. A person who works in the organization who recently did the kind of job you're applying for.
3. People who work in same position in a similar organization.
4. Recent literature (less than three years old) which describes the specific job.
5. The organization's literature.
6. Someone who works there in an unrelated area.
7. General literature on the type of job.
8. People who work in a place like where you applied.
9. General literature on the organization.
10. General literature on the type of organization.

FIGURE 28

critics, and that *the farther away people's data base moves from that specific, practical, and current information, the less valuable it is.* Talking to someone who's actually on the job will give you an idea of not only what the organization publicly states that they want, but will also identify unstated desires. Two helpful questions that you might use in communicating with people who are already in that position are: "What are the essential skills needed to do this job well?" and "What skills are missing in those people who are not doing the job well?" In addition, you will be able to learn the in-house slang and language to describe common occurrences from people who are actually in the position you want.

How Can I Get the Job I Want?

Assuming you have made a positive comparison between what you want and what they have to offer, your next question is what specifically do they want in terms of employee's qualifications at this time. You are essentially planning to "Anticipate What Basic Differentia They Want." The things that they're looking for most importantly, which we're calling *basic differentia, will serve as the basis for anticipating their questions and also planning your answers so that what you say will be most directly relevant to the criteria they will be using for selecting their new employees.* Each field has journals which have articles describing the most important basic differentia. For jobs in business *Personnel Journal* and *Harvard Business Review* are helpful, while for jobs in education your state's education journal may be the best. Ask your professor or a person actually doing the job for the names of helpful journals in a specific field.

Information about what's unique, new, or good in the organization that you get from your research will be known by the R, and your knowing it will be perceived positively as an indication of your strong interest in the firm and its position. For example, if you know that a business organization is about to bring out a new product line or that a school is experiencing success with a new educational innovation, this will be perceived very positively by the R.

With this information about the most specific and current basic differentia possible, you will be able to anticipate likely questions and "Plan Your Communication." In today's job market with the large number of people applying for a small number of jobs the situation is described as a "buyer's market." In figure 29 the darkened egg-shaped form represents all people applying for a job. Some of those people could do the job well and some couldn't. "False Negatives" are those people who would do well on the job but aren't hired. "False Positives" are the people who are hired but will not do the job well and eventually will be fired. As visualized in figure 29, hiring organizations can raise their cutoff criteria very high (from line B to line A) to eliminate "false positives."

ON THE JOB

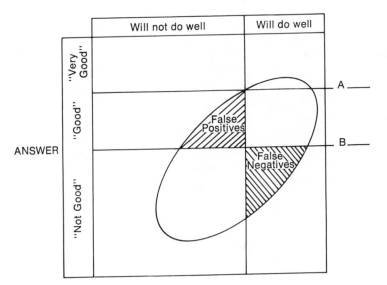

FIGURE 29

Though it is rather an inhuman perspective, essentially the R might see you as a product and that your purpose is to "sell yourself" to the organization by "very good" answers. In sales interviews, the main determinant of success is to anticipate the buyer's needs. In the hiring interview, the "buyer's needs" are the basic differentia. It might be helpful for you at this point to return to figures 21 and 23 in chapter 15 to review typical general and specific basic differentia. Of more value to you will be the specific current and position-relevant basic differentia which you've found from your research. By anticipating the basic differentia you can design typical questions and prepare answers which provide people with a clear and detailed description of your relevant background, abilities, and skills.

One final consideration may be relevant before the interview begins. Usually there won't be a need for initial contact because you will go to the employer's place of business or the employer will come to your school. If, on the other hand, it requires initiation on your part by telephone or letter, such initiation would contain an expression of your interest in the position and include, or be immediately followed by (as in a telephone call), your resumé. If you go to your local college's placement service, they will be happy to give you sample letters that could be used for initiating a contact. A wide variety of business communication books contain other samples. Figure 30 contains a sample resumé. These samples might be helpful in giving you an example of what's typically included in this material.

RESUMÉ

Name:

Address:

Telephone:

Job Objective:

Education:

College Activities:

Experience:

Skills:

References:

FIGURE 30

During the Interview

As we indicated in chapter 2, people are always communicating nonverbally. During the interview you'll be communicating nonverbally, verbally, and thinking. At least two of these will be done simultaneously. Nonverbally you will probably want to "Reflect Interest and Involvement" by the nonverbals of leaning forward, absence of nervous or distracting gestures, direct eye contact, and others described in chapters 2 and 15. Nonverbally you will be contributing to a positive communication climate and favorable connotative interpretations.

During the interview you will also be receiving information from nonverbal symbols. In addition to your planning and researching about what it would be like to work in that organization in that position, you will be collecting information during the interview. If you "Analyze the R's Nonverbal Symbols," the interviewer's dress, personal distance, the spatial relations of the interview room, as well as verbal references and pronouns it will help to indicate the underlying philosophy of the organization and how it sees people.

One way of describing philosophies of organizations is McGregor's comparison of Theory X and Theory Y organizations.[5] Essentially, Theory X organizations are much like our older stereotypes of the U.S. Army. The Theory X approach assumes people don't like to work, and so external rewards and punishments (from the lower end of Maslow's hierarchy) are necessary. External control and direction are administered by people in positions of formal authority. The Theory Y approach assumes that people enjoy work, producing and attaining goals, and are motivated by needs higher in Maslow's hierarchy. Thus, rewards are internal and participation in choosing work goals and procedures will lead to productive work guided by informal leadership.

If the recruiter's dress is informal, the spatial relations are comfortable, the personal space is close, the R's pronouns involve "we" and "us," and people are referred to by name instead of position, then you are probably dealing with a person who represents a Theory Y organization. If, on the other hand, the nonverbal signs include formal dress, more formal distance, or clear indications of status (such as the R sitting behind a desk), you're

probably dealing with a Theory X organization. If people are referred to as "employees" described in terms of Mr., Mrs., or Ms., and pronouns include "them" and "they," you have more information that this will be a Theory X organization. The kind of organization that you prefer and fit in most comfortably with goes back to your answer to the question, "What do I want?"

In terms of your thinking during the interview, you will quickly "Analyze the Question" to determine the basic differentia being measured and the

---

5. D. McGregor, *Human Side of Enterprise* (New York: McGraw-Hill, 1960).

length of answer desired. Determining the basic differentia will help you decide what you want to include in your answer. You want your answer to lead the R to call up meanings that are very favorable. The other very important question is how much does the R want you to include. This can be determined by analyzing the kind of questions the interviewer asks. If the R asks a closed-ended question, a brief answer is probably desired, possibly supplemented by a few sentences. For example, if the interviewer asks, "Do you manage your time well?" you would probably answer that you do, briefly indicate how you do it, and state an indication of its success. An answer like the following might be helpful:

"Yes, I use time management sheets daily which I prepare the night before. I've used T.M. sheets for over two years and find them especially helpful to prioritize my goals. They help me to get more work done well and enable me to get all projects done before they're due."

Verbal Communication

The main verbal communication for the E in the interview is answering questions. In this context it probably will be helpful for you to review chapter 8 on sending feedback to attain goals, Skill Area Three on sending messages to attain understanding, and chapter 15 on questions and basic differentia. By this point in the interview, your planning will have enabled you to anticipate the basic differentia which are essential and the kinds of questions they will use to measure those basic differentia. What you want to do in your answer is to "Visualize your Knowledge, Skills, Motivation, and Previous Experiences" as they relate to the basic differentia.

Figure 23, on p. 251–53, lists a variety of jobs, basic differentia, and open-ended questions to test the basic differentia. Put your hand over the basic differentia column. Read each question, infer what the basic differentia is, and briefly answer the question. Check the accuracy for each inference. Rate each of your answers from 1 percent–100 percent, based on the R's basic differentia.

Learning Experience

Sattinger's law states "It works better if you plug it in."[6] *Your answers will be optimally effective if they're directly plugged into the basic differentia.* In this context it is helpful to "Communicate Complete and Detailed Answers" to support and visualize what you're saying. The details should be relevant to the basic differentia which you've inferred from your background research. The detail can be thought through ahead of time to relate to the basic differentia. In addition, each job has a specialized language connected with it. Salespeople talk about the "Ben Franklin tie down"; people in the grocery business talk about "bruised can specials"; while people in accounting talk about LIFO and the "Big 8". If you know this language, you can "Use Job-related Symbols."

---

6. Ibid., p. 115.

Let's take a specific example of plugging your answer into the basic differentia. A very frequently asked open-ended question is "What are your future vocational plans?"[7] Let's say your research and communication with current employees indicate that it's a family-owned and run business organization which is strongly people oriented and uses a Theory Y philosophy. In addition, the employees are very satisfied and many tend to stay with the company until retirement. In addition, the work is very detailed and entails high training costs over a considerable period of time. From this data you've inferred that one of the most important basic differentia, which is not stated, is the commitment to stay with the firm for at least ten years. Knowing this and assuming that is your intent, how would you answer the question? A part of your answer would probably contain the statement that you "planned on staying with the firm for a considerable period of time." Unfortunately, other people applying for the job with qualifications much like yours are going to be saying the same thing. To enhance your chances, it would be beneficial to apply supporting detail to further consolidate and visualize the strength or likelihood of your staying with the firm. Some relevant detail you might include might lead to the following answer:

"Five years from now, if hired, I plan on continuing to work for your company. From my reading and research I find your company is the kind of small, personal, and tightly knit work group I would like to be a part of. As you probably remember from my vita, I worked at the same plant all four summers since I was 16. I greatly enjoyed working at that plant, did good work in a variety of different positions and jobs, and Mr. _____ , the personnel manager, who is one of my references, indicated that he would like to have me work for them after completing my college education, and that if I chose not to, he would be very happy to highly recommend me to any other firm."

This example from previous work experience visualizes long-term commitment to a company and is very relevant support to the basic differentia of staying with the firm for a considerable period of time. Other relevant details you might include are to indicate that you don't like traveling or moving or that you're planning on marrying someone from that town, that this kind of town is the kind you want to settle in, or that you're looking forward to joining one of the civic organizations in town. In chapter 15 there are a large number of jobs, basic differentia, and questions in figure 23. We suggest that you design answers for the four questions which are most closely connected with the kind of job you want. To make this practical and realistic, clearly specify in as much detail as possible the position and organization that you desire to work with. Then write out clear and detailed answers which reflect yourself and your abilities clearly and positively and will distinguish you from the other candidates.

Learning Experience   Figure 23 in chapter 15 lists a variety of jobs. Pick the one which sounds best to you. Write out answers to the four questions for that job including at least two specific, true details from your previous experience that directly support your possession of the basic differentia skill.

---

7. "Making the Most of Your Job Interview" (New York: New York Life Insurance).

Another goal for you as an E is to "Analyze your Answers as Communication." As you are saying the answer, think about what you are saying. After your answer is over, analyze if you said what you wanted to say and whether you provided as complete and favorable answers as possible. In addition, observe and "Analyze the R's Nonverbal Responses." From the R's nonverbal reactions, you can determine how effective your choice of answer length was. Nonverbally, was the R waiting for you to say more or had the person earlier nodded indicating that your answer was understood at that point? If the R's still leaning forward and looking at you, the person is probably anticipating and encouraging you to provide more detail or other examples. If the R asks follow-up questions, he or she is probably looking for more detail, and it probably would be helpful for you to have longer answers in the future.

After the Interview

After the interview, it probably will be helpful to go to a quiet place and "Analyze Your Attainment of the E's Goals." Your abilities to accurately measure your own skills will help to identify areas for further skill improvement. Also, assess the degree to which you accomplished your goals of describing your knowledge and skills related to the basic differentia. You'll probably find it helpful practice to write down the R's questions, what you inferred the basic differentia to be, and an outline of your answers. Then by checking with a teacher or fellow applicant, you'll be able to identify areas for improving your analysis and answers.

This careful planning and preparation, relevant and detailed communication during the interview, and follow-up assessment should enable you to "Determine Areas for Further Improvement" of your interviewing skills. Thus, you'll not only be able to cope successfully with the hiring interview, but also with the wide variety of other interview situations that you'll experience after being hired for the job you want.

Additional Learning Sources

Banaka, William H. *Training in Depth Interviewing.* New York: Harper and Row, 1971.

Brady, John. *The Craft of Interviewing.* Cincinnati: Writer's Digest, 1976.

Downs, Cal; Linkugel, Wil; and Berg, David M. *The Organizational Communicator.* New York: Harper and Row, 1977.

Fenlason, Anne F. *Essentials in Interviewing.* New York: Harper and Row, 1962.

Goldhaber, Gerald M. *Organizational Communication.* Dubuque, Iowa: Wm. C. Brown, 1974.

Kahn, Robert, and Cannell, Charles F. *The Dynamics of Interviewing.* New York: John Wiley and Sons, 1965.

Keltner, John. *Interpersonal Speech Communication.* Belmont, Calif.: Wadsworth Publishing Co., 1970.

McGregor, D. *Human Side of Enterprise.* New York: McGraw-Hill, 1960.

New York Life Insurance Company. "Making the Most of Your Job Interview." New York: New York Life Insurance Company.

Peter, Laurence J. *The Peter Prescription.* New York: William Morrow and Co., Inc., 1972.

Richetto, Gary M., and Zima, Joseph P. *Fundamentals of Interviewing.* Chicago: Science Research Associates, Inc., 1976.

Rosenblatt, S.; Bernard, T.; Cheatham, Richard; and Watt, James T. *Communication in Business.* Englewood Cliffs, N.J.: Prentice-Hall, Inc., 1977.

Schein, Edgar H. *Organizational Psychology.* Englewood Cliffs, N.J.: Prentice-Hall, Inc., 1965.

Sitzman, Marion, and Garcia, Reloy. *Successful Interviewing.* Skokie, Ill.: National Textbook Company, 1976.

Stewart, Charles J., and Cash, William B. *Interviewing: Principles and Practices.* Dubuque, Iowa: Wm. C. Brown, 1974.

U.S. Department of Labor. *Merchandising Your Job Talents.* Washington, D.C.: U.S. Printing Office, 1971.

Sample Interview for Public Accountant

R Goal   *E Goal*

Develop rapport

R: Come in, Ms. Franklin and have a chair. Would you like some coffee?

Reflect interest and involvement nonverbally

    E: *(leaning forward) Thank you, I would.*

R: I'm Bob Wilson, supervisor in the firm of Attenbury, Weston, and Schultz. I've really been looking forward to talking with you. Your department chairperson said you were one of the top graduates this year.

    E: *(smiles)*

Clarify situation and interview goals

R: As you know, we of AWS are looking for a top drawer junior accountant in public accounting. The position would begin with on-the-job training for about two years. Your work during that time would involve verifying and doing basic tax work and working with auditing teams. I began in that way and found it an excellent foundation for my career.

Communicate E's feedback is important

    In this interview we are working to understand how your skills and ability would apply to our needs. Accordingly, your answers are very important to both of us. Please feel free to express your ideas as completely as you would like (leaning forward with direct eye contact). We really want to learn about you.

Analyze the R's nonverbals

    E: *Fine, I really appreciate this opportunity.*

Ask questions: (funnel sequence)

R: To begin, why did you choose the field of public accounting?

R Goal   *E Goal*

       Analyze the
       question

E: *As far back as I can re-member, I've been good at math and intrigued by business and how it func-tioned. Based on these in-terests, I chose account-ing. Since my choice, I've taken various accounting classes which I found to be very stimulating. I rea-lized that there is a lot more to accounting than most people realize. I es-pecially like public ac-counting because of the major contribution it makes to society on the individual level.*

Relate answer
to question's
purpose

R: Why are you interested in our public accounting firm?

       Visualize
       motivation

E: *I've heard several fine things about your firm. From what I've been able to learn AWS has the size, opportunities for advance-ment, and most important the quality of reputation I'd like to be associated with.*

R: Why did you apply for the posi-tion of junior accountant?

E: *I feel that this is an excel-lent place for me to start my career. As I indicated before, my interests and skills are in public ac-counting. Further, the po-sition calls for responsi-bility. By doing my job carefully and well, I will be learning a great deal about accounting and serving the community.*

R: What three questions would you ask me if I were applying for this position?

R Goal	E Goal	
		E: *That is a very difficult question. If I were in your position, I would want to carefully plan the questions before the interview.*
	Visualize skills	*I would ascertain the three most important skills essential to job success and then ask open-ended questions to test those skills. I believe the three skills I would choose would be similar to those*
	Visualize knowledge	*in a recent* Journal of Accountancy *article: ability to work as a member of an accounting team, ability to work well with a wide variety of people, and third, careful technical competence. Three possible questions would be "What are the main ingredients for successful team work?" "How would you handle an angry client?" and "How do you handle your personal finances?"*
Support the E; ask follow-up questions		R: I really appreciate your care in preparing the questions. I also find that careful preparation leads to much more effective interviews. To follow up on your question about the frustrated client, if the IRS overturned our judgment on a tax matter, how would you handle the frustrated client?
	Communicate complete and detailed answers	E: *First, I would carefully review the IRS judgment, relevant evidence, court decisions, and the client's tax data. Next, I would meet with the person at a convenient place, possibly that person's office. In de-*

R Goal   *E Goal*

scribing the situation I would emphasize our common goals, describe our situation, and deal with any questions the person would have. To assist in handling the questions I would take the written IRS decision. Finally, to emphasize our continuing interest in the client's financial well being, I would suggest investigating other areas for the client to save tax dollars and would indicate several such areas I've discovered. Though I don't know AWS's procedures for handling this kind of situation, I believe that these procedures would help the client through this frustrating situation and emphasize our continuing service to them.

R: What would you do if you discovered that a long-time and valued customer of our firm had not reported all of his earnings?

Use job-related symbols

E: *I see PAF's as the vital link between the client and the government. As such we have obligations and responsibilities to both parties. First, I would collect all available data, including reviewing his Schedule E's for the last five years. I would presume that the person had made an oversight and would further investigate possible deductions the client could claim which could compensate for the unclaimed dividend earnings. As a junior public ac-*

R Goal   E Goal

countant, I would bring all of the data to you for your consideration and decision. The conflicts the firm faces between the interests of the client and the IRS are the most difficult to resolve.

R: What have you learned in college that will apply to this position?

Visualize
relevant previous
experience

E: *I've learned a combination of knowledge and skills related to accounting as well as interaction skills in working with others. As my resumé indicates, I was a part of several service-oriented groups that were able to accomplish significant goals on campus and within the community. For example, I helped establish free tax service for the old and the needy in conjunction with the department chairperson, the Accounting Club, and a community organization. We provided assistance for people who couldn't pay. Over the last two years I've averaged about four hours a week during the tax quarter working with these people. Through working with some of these people, I became part of a community group to restore the community railroad depot as a community center. Working together we were able to enlist the aid of the Jaycees and two local service groups. The restoration is now under-*

R Goal   *E Goal*

way. It really was exciting to see local businesspeople, the elderly, and college students working together on the restoration. I have learned a lot from my college experience, but these two examples of being able to apply the learning and interaction skills have been most meaningful to me.*

Analyze answer
as
communication

R: Those sound like two valuable and rewarding projects.

    E: *They were.*

R: What one facet of the new tax reform law will most help our clients?

    E: *I really haven't had time to study the new law in as much detail as I would like to. From my reading it seems that the tax incentives for reducing heating costs through improved insulation and the related savings of energy would be relevant to a large number of your clients. I plan to study the law in detail after the semester is over.*

Give short
summary; allow
for clarification

R: As I've understood what you've said, you understand the basic concepts of the position of junior accountant. You see the main skills involved as working as a member of the team, working with the public, and having careful technical competence. In addition, you've had the opportunity to apply your knowledge and skills through assisting the elderly with their tax work and through a community project of restoring a train station. Also, you understand the multiple responsibilities a firm

R Goal   *E Goal*

such as ours faces, and you have carefully considered how to deal with clients and their tax questions. Have I missed anything? Are there things you'd like to add?

E: *Those are the main things we talked about. My resumé provides more detail and describes other activities in addition to the tax aid and the restoration project. I do have a question. What are your in-house policies for study for the CPA exam?*

R: Because of the size of our firm, we don't have any formal study procedures. Informally, we'd be happy to work with you on your preparation. In addition, we will pay for the class of a commercially handled preparation course. Any other questions?

E: *No.*

Describe future
disposition of
interview results

R: The end of next week, I'll be getting together with my partners to make our selection of the top three candidates for the position. The top three people will then be brought back for a more in-depth series of interactions. We should be in contact with you two weeks from today. Is your home telephone number on the resumé the best place to call you?

E: *Yes.*

R: What time during the working day would be the best time?

E: *Between 2:30 and 5:00.*

R: Fine, you'll hear from us two weeks from today between 2:30 and 5:00. I've really enjoyed talking with you, and I'm sure my partners will share my enthusiasm about your skills.

R Goal   *E Goal*

E: *I appreciated the oppor-
    tunity.*

Show   R: Thank you for your time.
termination
behaviors

Skill Test

This skill test will give you the opportunity to apply your interviewing skills. You and your instructor may wish to develop additional or alternative applications of your skills. For this skill test you will work with one other person, with each of you, in turn, taking on the roles of the R and the E for a hiring interview. You will have two meetings with this person: (1) to determine the nature of the two positions being applied for and the basic characteristics of the interviews, and (2) to complete the interviews. In one interview you will be the E and in the other you will be the R. The other person will plan for and take the other role.

Prior to the first meeting, you and the other person will each individually plan the following items for the interview in which you will be the E:

1. The specific description of the job you are interviewing for. We suggest that it be a full-time or part-time job you would actually like to have. Specify the job responsibilities.
2. Describe the general characteristics of the interviewer.

At the first meeting, you will exchange these two items of information and clarify any uncertainties regarding it. You will also determine a mutually agreeable time to have your second meeting to do the actual interviews.

Prior to the second meeting, you will complete the two precommunication forms that follow: one for your role as E and one for your role as R. Share these with your instructor before the interview.

Following the second meeting and your completion of the interviews, you will each complete postcommunication forms. In these you will analyze your accomplishment of the goals as an R and as an E in a hiring interview.

"R" Precommunication Form

As the R in this interview, it will be your responsibility to maintain control of the pace of the interview and ask necessary questions and follow-up questions to determine the E's qualifications on the basic differentia. The goals for the R are accomplished sequentially, and the interview is not concluded until all have been accomplished. You will, therefore, be responsible for closing the interview at the appropriate time.

This form will be filled out individually after the first meeting with your partner. The preparation will be done individually rather than with your partner in order to more closely simulate a real hiring interview.

1. State the specific description of the job for which the person is interviewing, including the responsibilities of the person in that position.
2. List three basic differentia which you believe are important to this position. This will probably involve research with relevant professional journals and interaction with people as close as possible to the actual position. List the sources for each basic differentia following it.
3. Develop one open-ended question for each of the basic differentia which will best reveal the E's qualifications in this area.
4. Develop one specific follow-up question for each of the open-ended questions to further explore the E's qualifications.
5. Develop an outline of behaviors to sequentially accomplish each of the R's goals in a hiring interview.

"E" Precommunication Form

As the E in this interview, it will be your responsibility to provide accurate and complete information in order for the goals of the interview to be accomplished. Your behaviors should accurately and positively represent your qualifications for this job.

This form will be filled out individually after the first meeting with your partner. The preparation will be done individually in order to more closely simulate a real hiring interview where you would not know the basic differentia and questions before the interview.

1. List four basic differentia which you feel would be important to this position. This will probably involve research in professional journals and interaction with people as close to the actual position as possible. List your sources for the basic differentia after each.
2. Develop two open-ended questions which may be asked to test each of the basic differentia.
3. Write out complete answers to each of your anticipated questions to accurately and positively represent yourself for this job.
4. Make an outlined list of behaviors you will do to accomplish each of the E's goals in a hiring interview. Remember that you may not be accomplishing these goals in the order listed, as the R has control over the sequence of the interview.

"R" Postcommunication Form

A. Assess and comment on how well you felt you attained each of the R goals for the hiring interview.

Assessment: (++, +, ✔, −, −−, x = not done)

GOALS FOR OPENING THE INTERVIEW   COMMENTS:

_____ 1. Develop rapport.
_____ 2. Clarify the situation and the interview's goals.
_____ 3. Communicate that the E's feedback is important.
_____ % FOR OPENING

GOALS FOR EXPLORING CONTENT

_____ 4. Ask questions related to the goals.
_____ 5. Relate answer to the question's purpose.
_____ 6. Ask follow-up questions.
_____ 7. Support the E.
_____ % FOR EXPLORING CONTENT

GOALS FOR CLOSING THE INTERVIEW

_____ 8. Give a short summary; allow for clarification.
_____ 9. Describe the future disposition of the interview data.
_____ 10. Show termination behaviors to end the interview when goals are accomplished.

_____ % FOR CLOSING

_____ % **Total rating in percentage**

B. Make three specific suggestions for improving your skills in accomplishing R goals in the hiring interview.

"E" Postcommunication Form

A. Assess and comment on how well you felt you attained each of the E goals for the hiring interview.

   Assessment: (++, +, ✔, −, −−, x = not done)

<table>
<tr><td>BEFORE</td><td>COMMENTS:</td></tr>
</table>

_____ 1. Decide what you want.
_____ 2. Anticipate what basic differentia they want.
_____ 3. Plan your communication.

DURING

_____ 4. Reflect interest and involvement non-verbally.
_____ 5. Analyze the R's nonverbal symbols.
_____ 6. Analyze the questions.
_____ 7. Visualize your knowledge, skills, motivation, and relevant previous experiences.
_____ 8. Communicate complete and detailed answers.
_____ 9. Use job-related symbols.
_____ 10. Analyze your answers as communication.

AFTER

_____ 11. Analyze your attainment of the E's goals.
_____ 12. Determine areas for future improvement.
_____ % **Total rating in percentage**

B. Make three specific suggestions for improving your skills in accomplishing E goals in the hiring interview.

Skills in Changing Attitudes and Behavior

Overview

As you achieved the goals of previous communication areas, you have undoubtedly realized the central role of persuasion in most communicative attempts. In the broadest sense of the term, all communication is persuasive. That is, in most communication your messages have the potential to influence others' behavior, directly or indirectly.

Persuasion, as purposeful communication to lead a person to a desired behavior, serves as a basic tool for people to adjust to their environment and to adjust their environment to themselves. In societies where physical force is not the main motivator, verbal persuasion is the main facilitator for social change and/or maintenance.

Understanding the persuasive process is vital since it is so much a part of every individual's life. Every day, each of us tries to influence someone's attitudes, or we are the focus of someone else's attempt to change our attitudes. These persuasive attempts occur at the intrapersonal, interpersonal, and public levels of communication and are an important application of basic communication skills.

Each responding communicator makes a "choice" regarding his or her attitudes and behaviors. The choice to do a suggested behavior probably will be made if the perceived need for change is personally meaningful, e.g., exercising may be a good way to firm my muscles. In a real sense persuasive attempts are understandings directly related to the responding communicator's needs. If the meanings are understood, felt strongly, and fill a need for the responding communicator, s/he will likely do the behavior. We are not considering persuasion as an attempt to manipulate others.

This skill area describes materials which if adapted to specific persuasive goals should help you to be more successful in your persuasive attempts. It will also assist you in becoming more critical in making choices related to behaviors suggested in persuasive messages directed to you.

Definitions

Assertive communication
Speaking which is clear, direct, and appropriately expresses your own opinions without anxiety and with respect for others' opinions.

Attitude
A complex set of thoughts, feelings, and tendencies about people, ideas, and things which influence the likelihood of behavior. The attitude has personal meaning for the individual and is made up of three parts: the cognitive dimension, the affective dimension, and the behavior tendency dimension.

Cognitive dimension of an attitude
The thinking part of an attitude. It can be verbalized, as in an answer to the question, "What do you think or feel or believe about . . . ?" It can be represented in quotation marks.

Affective dimension of an attitude
The feeling part of the attitude. It is a description of both the intensity (e.g., strongly, moderately, slightly) and direction (favorable or unfavorable) of the majority of a person's feelings about the object of an attitude.

Behavior tendency dimension of an attitude
The cumulative effect of the cognitive and affective dimensions of an attitude is the degree of likelihood (e.g., very likely, somewhat likely) of doing a particular behavior. A particular attitude may lead to several different behaviors.

Behavior
An observable action done by a person.

Communicator credibility
The attitudes the receiver has toward the sender of a message, regarding the person's friendliness, expertness, trustworthiness, and similarity.

Effect of persuasion
A change in behavior based on changes in attitude (changes in cognition, affect, and behavior tendencies).

Chapter 17

Preparing for Behavior Change

Objectives

Your learning should enable you to:

1. Define attitude and its three parts.
2. For a given situation, describe the three parts of one of your relevant attitudes.
3. Given the description of a situation and the cognitive and affective parts of someone's attitude, infer the behavioral tendency.
4. Give examples to visualize the relationship between attitudes and behaviors.
5. Explain the magnetic field analogy of attitude structuring.
6. Using the criteria of salience and interconnectedness of attitudes, distinguish among attitudes in terms of their stability.
7. Recognize alternative means of reducing tensions associated with holding inconsistent attitudes or doing a behavior that is inconsistent with your attitudes.
8. Develop alternative means of changing a specific behavior.

I. Importance of attitudes
   A. Attitudes organize and summarize the knowledge and experiences a person has related to a given issue
   B. Attitudes are the basis for a person's interpretation of a message
   C. Attitudes are the basis of behavior
II. Nature of attitudes
   A. Definition: complex set of thoughts, feelings, and tendencies about people, ideas, and things which influence the likelihood of behavior
   B. There are three dimensions of an attitude
      1. Cognitive dimension: the thinking part of an attitude which is verbalized as a statement of the attitude
         Example: "My family's camping trips are fun."
      2. Affective dimension: the feeling part of an attitude which reflects the intensity and direction of that attitude
         Example: extremely favorable
      3. Behavior tendency: the cumulative effect of the cognitive and affective dimension
         Example: very likely to go camping with the family to the Rocky Mountains for two weeks
   C. The cognitive dimension plus the affective dimension approximately equals the behavior tendency; the relationship is modified by the influence of related attitudes
III. The relationship between attitudes and behaviors
   A. Attitudes can influence the choice of behaviors
      Example: a positive attitude toward skydiving can lead to the behavior of going skydiving
   B. Behaviors can lead to the development of attitudes
      Example: having a good experience with an individual can lead you to develop positive attitudes toward that person
IV. Attitude structure
   A. Attitude structuring is the process of each attitude becoming related to other attitudes
      1. Attitudes are structured to form a meaningful picture of an individual's world
      2. Attitude structures can be represented by a magnetic field with attitudes held and balanced around the pole magnet of the self-concept
   B. Two characteristics of attitude structuring
      1. Salience: the degree of importance of an attitude to a person for a given communication situation
         a) Values are examples of salient attitudes
         b) More salient attitudes are closer to the self-concept
         c) More salient attitudes have strongly stated cognitive dimensions and strong affective dimensions
         d) More salient attitudes are more difficult to change
      2. Interconnectedness of attitudes: the degree of association with other attitudes
         a) Connections between attitudes are based on agreement of attitudes
         b) Attitudes move around until they are in a position of close agreement with related attitudes
         c) Attitudes regarding a certain topic are called a "point of view" and filter messages about that topic
   C. Implications of magnetic-field analogy
      1. Given no motivation to change, attitudes will remain the same

2. When one attitude is changed, all others tend to change slightly to reestablish agreement

3. When an attitude is changed, those closest to that attitude are most likely to change

4. It is harder to change more salient attitudes than less salient

5. Increase the connection between two attitudes and they move closer together

6. Decrease the connection between two attitudes and they move further apart

7. When attitudes are perceived as not in agreement, there is a feeling of tension creating a need for change

V. Stability of Attitudes

  A. Attitudes remain stable because of external factors:

    1. Environment in which a person functions

    2. People interacted with

    3. Communication experiences

    4. Reference groups

    5. Behaviors

  B. Attitudes remain stable because of selective factors in receiving, decoding and thinking:

    1. Selective exposure

    2. Selective attention

    3. Selective perception

    4. Selective recall

  C. Attitudes remain stable because of internal structuring:

    1. Self-concept

    2. Salience

    3. Interconnectedness of attitudes

VI. Importance of behavior

  A. Definition: an observable action done by a person

    1. Behavior is influenced by general attitudes

    2. Behavior is influenced by the specific situation

  B. The result of persuasion is a change in behavior based on changes in attitude

  C. Various kinds of behavior change are possible

    1. A new behavior begun

    2. A new behavior continued

    3. An old behavior stopped

    4. An old behavior reduced in frequency or intensity

    5. An old behavior increased in frequency or intensity

VII. Stability of behavior

  A. A behavior tends to be repeated because external factors provide reinforcement for the behavior.

    1. Environment in which a person functions

    2. People interacted with

    3. Communication experiences

    4. Reference groups

  B. Behaviors tend to be repeated because the behavior tendencies of related attitudes tend to remain the same.

VIII. Attitude change is a difficult process

  A. Attitude change is precipitated by a feeling of tension

    1. Tension is aroused by a conflict between two or more relevant attitudes, two behaviors, or an attitude and a behavior

      a) The greater the conflict, the greater the tension

    2. Tension is reduced in a number of ways

      a) Changing some attitude or behavior

      b) Redefining the salience of one or more attitudes or behaviors

       c) Changing the relationship between attitudes

       d) Changing the external environment

IX. Behaviors are changed in many of the same ways as attitudes

    A. Positive reinforcement of desired behavior or negative reinforcement of undesired behaviors

    B. Altering the environment

    C. Heightening the awareness of a conflict or disagreement between two behaviors or a very strong attitude and a behavior

    D. Developing an attitude which has a very high behavior tendency to do the desired behavior

Reading

Importance of Attitudes

You have studied the basic elements involved in the ways people decode and think about messages. An assumption which was developed in those skill areas was that *the listener's frame of reference was the basic factor determining how a person interprets and responds to a message.* Therefore, *in terms of the outcome of a persuasive message, it is the listener's interpretation of your message, rather than the message itself, which leads to the response.* One of the purposes that attitudes serve is to organize and summarize the knowledge and experiences a person has related to a particular person, idea, situation, or thing. Having attitudes enables people to choose a reaction more quickly to a situation. Messages are interpreted through attitudes.

Attitudes are important not only because of their dominant role in decoding and thinking about messages. They also serve as an important basis for behavior and the reoccurrence of behavior. An illustrative example might be a slightly overweight friend of yours being talked into attending a Karate or exercise class. The first meeting of the class is quite rigorous and results in an extensive amount of pains, aches, stiffness, and maybe even bruises. When the second class meeting begins will your friend be there?

WILL SHE GO?

Nature of Attitudes

Attitude can be defined as *a complex set of thoughts, feelings, and tendencies about people, ideas, and things which influence the likelihood of behavior.* The attitude has personal meaning for the individual and is made up of three parts: the cognitive dimension, the affective dimension, and the behavior tendency dimension. The *cognitive dimension of an attitude* is the thinking part and can be verbalized as an answer to the question, "What do you think (or feel or believe) about . . . ?" It can be represented in quotation marks. The *affective dimension of an attitude* can be defined as the feeling part of the attitude; it is a description of both the intensity and direction of the majority of a person's feelings about a subject. The *behavior tendency dimension of an attitude* can be defined as the cumulative effect of the cognitive and affective dimensions of an attitude; it is the degree of likelihood of doing a particular behavior. A particular attitude may lead to several different behaviors.

An example of the three dimensions of an attitude might be:

Cognitive: "My family's camping trips are fun."
Affective: extremely favorable
Behavior tendency: very likely to go camping with the family to the Rocky Mountains for two weeks next summer.

In the above example, the cognitive dimension is what a person might say if someone asked, "What do you think about family camping trips?" The affective dimension is a description of the direction (favorable) and intensity (extremely) of the person's feelings about family camping trips. The behavior tendency dimension describes the likelihood of the person doing a particular action. The likelihood might be different for a different behavior. For example, if the family was going for two months, the person might be less likely to go and the behavior tendency might be described as *somewhat* likely to go camping.

WHO'S LIKELY TO MISS A PARTY TO GO FISHING?

One very important relationship to notice among the three dimensions of any attitude is that the cognitive plus the affective *approximately equals* the behavior tendency. This can be represented as: $C + A \cong BT$.

Thus, *an increase in the statement of the cognitive dimension and/or an increase in the favorableness of the affective dimension will generally lead to an increase in the likelihood of a particular, related behavior tendency.* Or, a decrease in the cognitive or affective dimension could lead to a decrease in the related behavior tendency.

Relationship between Attitudes and Behavior

There are two possible relationships between attitudes and behavior. Either the attitude influences the behavior or the behavior influences the attitude. These might be represented as:

$$A \longrightarrow B$$

or

$$B \longrightarrow A$$

An example of the first relationship might be a friend of yours trying to talk you into going skydiving. He or she might try to change your cognitive evaluations of skydiving to be more positive or change your affective dimension to be more favorable. Either or both will increase the likelihood of your going skydiving.

An example of the second relationship might be if you were watching one of the basketball players on the local varsity playing and thought: "I can play as well as that player can." At another time you then had the chance

to play against that person in one-to-one basketball and that person really beat you. That behavioral experience would most probably modify your attitude.

As people have experiences, many examples of the two relationships between attitudes and behaviors could happen. Let's imagine you went skydiving and were excited by it. The pleasurable experience would be processed and lead to increasing favorable feelings and/or stronger cognitive statements and increased behavior tendencies. The changed behavior tendency could lead to more diving, more pleasure, and maybe to buying your own parachute. Changes in attitude influenced changes in behavior and changes in behavior influenced changes in attitudes.

Attitude Structure

Each attitude an individual has usually becomes related to his or her other attitudes as knowledge and experience expands. This is called *attitude structuring.* As we indicated earlier, attitudes are extremely important to the persuader because *it is people's attitudes that lead them to behave in a certain manner.* Therefore, if we want to change their behavior, we must change the attitude related to that behavior. An understanding of attitude structuring is also vital to the persuader because this gives important information regarding the position of a particular attitude in the individual's total frame of reference. Knowing this position and related attitudes will make clear many of the barriers that must be overcome to change the attitude in that person's frame of reference.

People seek a meaningful picture of their world—one that makes sense to them. Therefore, people structure their attitudes so that they make sense to them. The structure of attitudes might be represented as a magnetic field around the pole magnet of the self-concept (see figure 31). In this representation of a person's attitude, the pole magnet is the person's self-

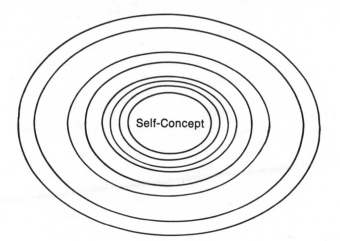

FIGURE 31

concept. Some attitudes are more important and closer to the self-concept. Some attitudes are less important and farther away from the self-concept.

The two characteristics of the structure of attitudes are *salience* and the *interconnectedness* of the attitudes. *Salience* is *the degree of importance of the attitude to a person for a given communication situation.* Values are examples of salient attitudes. The more salient attitudes would be closer to the self-concept and influenced by the "magnetic field" of the self-concept. The more salient attitudes also tend to be more strongly stated cognitively and have very strong favorable or unfavorable dimensions. The less salient attitudes would be further away from the self-concept, less influenced by its field, and, therefore, easier to change.

Learning Experience

To better understand your own attitudes, write the cognitive and affective dimensions of three of your *most salient* attitudes.

Now write three attitudes which are much less salient and would be fairly easy to change:

Why are the less salient attitudes less important to you? How likely would you be to change your very salient attitudes?

To understand attitudinal structure, the second important factor is the *interconnectedness among attitudes.* Connections among attitudes are based on the agreement of attitudes. In a magnetic field, iron filings are influenced by the field and eventually come to rest. In much the same way, *attitudes* move around until they *are in a position of close agreement with the attitudes surrounding them.* This agreement stabilizes the attitudes—especially attitudes which are more firmly held. They are stabilized both by being connected to the self-concept and by being connected to each other, especially within general topic areas.

Attitudes regarding a certain topic are typically called a point of view or frame of reference for that topic. These attitudes form a screen through which messages about that topic are filtered. Figure 32 extends figure 31 by showing the connection between attitudes and the self-concept (represented by S.C.). More salient attitudes are represented by an "A" and those less salient attitudes are represented by an "a." The broken lines represent divisions between points of view on various topics. Some of the connections among attitudes are stronger and represented by thicker lines.

This magnetic field analogy has several implications for the persuader.

1. Without motivation to change, the field of attitudes will tend to move to a position of rest and remain without changing.
2. When one attitude in the field is moved (changed), all others will have a tendency to slightly change to reestablish agreement in the field.
3. When an attitude is changed, those closest to the attitude are most likely to change.

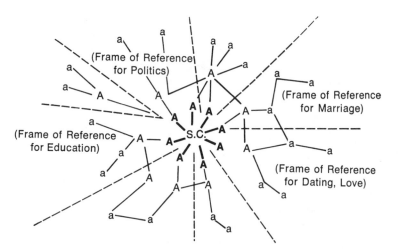

FIGURE 32

4. It is much harder to change the position of more salient attitudes than less salient attitudes.
5. By increasing the strength of the connection between two attitudes (or establishing a connection between two attitudes), the two attitudes will move together (become more closely connected).
6. By decreasing the strength of the connection between two attitudes (or showing that two attitudes are not connected), they will tend to move apart (become less closely connected).
7. When attitudes are not in agreement, tension exists, creating a need for changing attitudes.

Consider your frame of reference toward "working." (Substitute another topic if you wish.)

Two attitudes about yourself related to "working" (cognitive dimension):

1.

2.

Two most salient attitudes related to "working" (cognitive dimension):

1.

2.

Two weakly held attitudes related to "working" (cognitive dimension):

1.

2.

Consider each of the seven implications of the magnetic field analogy in terms of your attitudes toward "working."

Learning Experience

Stability of Attitudes

People do not easily change their minds. People's attitudes tend to remain stable for a variety of reasons. The first group of reasons involves *external factors* that influence attitudes to remain similar. Examples of external factors include:

1. Environment in which a person functions,
2. People interacted with,
3. Communication experiences,
4. Reference groups,
5. Behaviors.

These factors both influence the development and reinforce current attitudes. These external factors have a strong influence on most people largely because they usually are consistent with each other. Most people surround themselves with experiences and people which are like themselves.

For example, if you go away to school or a new community to work, you most likely will associate with people and experiences similar to those you've been used to. When you hear attitudes similar to your own or see behaviors of which you approve, your own attitudes will be strengthened and be less likely to change.

People decode and think about these external factors in similar ways because their frames of reference (the basic screening system) remain very much the same. These *selective factors* in *receiving, decoding,* and *thinking* function as a second group of reasons why attitudes tend to remain the same. These selective factors are:

1. Selective exposure,
2. Selective attention,
3. Selective perception,
4. Selective recall.

Together these concepts imply that people repeatedly put themselves in similar situations which reinforce their current attitudes (selective exposure) and also that people pay attention to (selective attention), decode (selective perception), and remember (selective recall) those external happenings that are similar and that reinforce their current attitudes.

The third group of factors relates to the *internal structuring* of attitudes. Attitudes tend to remain the same because the following tend to remain the same:

1. Self-concept,
2. Salience,
3. Interconnectedness of attitudes.

Attitudes also remain stable because of the way they are internally structured. Each attitude is related to so many other attitudes and to the way we see ourselves, that this structure becomes a fortress against change for most people. Because the self-concept and other salient attitudes are strong, they have a greater influence on the external factors and on the selective processes of decoding and thinking and thus are even more likely to remain the same.

Importance of Behavior

Behavior is one of the most used and least defined concepts in books on communication. When behavior is defined it often includes both observed dimensions such as actions and nonobserved dimensions such as thinking. The model of communication used in chapter 4 describes the nonobservable dimensions as decoding, thinking, and encoding. Thus, we'll use the term *behavior* to denote only observable actions. For the purposes of this course of study, *behavior* is defined as *an observable action done by a person.* Behavior can be considered to be influenced by general attitudes and also the specific situation.

The *result of persuasion* is *a change in behavior based on a change in attitude* (e.g., changes in the cognition, affective, and behavior tendencies). Figure 33 describes the relationship.

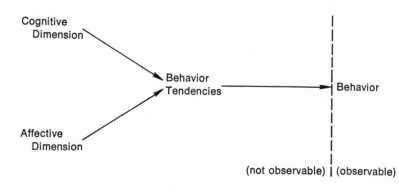

FIGURE 33

The occurrence of a change in behavior is the typical goal of persuasion and the indication of success of persuasion. For example, if you were successful in encouraging a friend to be involved in an early morning exercise program, that person would undertake and continue in the program. Or, if a cosmetics company was attempting to sell a new lanolin face cream, the intended effect of the persuasion would be for people to buy the product. The potential benefits of the exercise program or the face cream would not be realized until they were tried.

Just as an attitude can change in the cognitive, affective, and/or behavior tendency, various kinds of changes in behavior are also possible including:

1. a new behavior begun,
2. a new behavior continued,
3. an old behavior stopped,
4. an old behavior reduced in frequency or intensity,
5. an old behavior increased in frequency or intensity.

Frequently the effect of a persuasive message is considered to be either a change in attitude *or* in behavior. Both are included in our definition. The change in behavior enables the people involved to see the effect and to realize the benefits. The attitude change both leads to the behavior change *and* also continues the change. Consideration of the attitude helps the preparation of the persuasive messages, enables postmessage analysis and improvement of future messages.

Stability of Behaviors

Behaviors tend to be repeated because external factors provide reinforcement for behavior and because the behavior tendencies of the related attitudes tend to remain the same (or become stronger). As discussed in relationship to attitudes, the external factors of environment, people interacted with, communication experiences, and reference groups both influence the development of and reinforce current behaviors.

For example, if you were in a situation where a close friend was in trouble, you would most likely perform a behavior which would be helpful to your friend. This type of behavior would be probable and most likely repeated because you have attitudes (e.g., "friends help each other") with strong behavior tendencies toward helping and because such a behavior would be reinforced by your friend and others important to you.

All of the factors described above (external, selective, and internal structural factors) which result in the stability of attitudes mean that the behavior tendencies of those attitudes remain the same or become even more probable.

In summary, attitudes and behaviors are interrelated and these relationships lead to the stability of each. Attitudes are expressed in behaviors (which are reinforced by external factors and decoding and processing) leading to a strengthening of the attitude (internal structure), which leads to strong behavioral tendencies to do the behavior again, and this cycle will usually continue unless some personally meaningful persuasive force leads to a change.

Attitude Change

Many attempts to get someone to change his or her attitudes or behaviors fail because the persuasive attempts are geared only to the receiver's cognitive dimension. The classic example is the tremendous lack of success experienced by the multimillion dollar advertising campaign against smoking cigarettes by the American Cancer Society and other concerned groups. In fact some of the latest information we've seen indicates that *more* people are smoking, not fewer. The expensive lesson to be learned is that intellectual and factual appeals are less successful against habitual behaviors that are reinforced by reference groups, personal experiences of pleasure, and other related external, decoding and processing, and structural factors.

Attitude change within an individual is precipitated by a feeling of *tension* aroused by inconsistency between two or more relevant attitudes, behaviors, or an attitude and a behavior. The greater the amount of inconsistency, the greater will be the need to reduce the tension because of the interrelationship between attitudes. There are several basic ways people can reduce the tension created by conflicting attitudes, behaviors, or an attitude and a behavior. They can: (1) change some of their attitudes or behaviors; (2) redefine the salience (importance) of one or more of the attitudes or behaviors; (3) change the relationship between attitudes (or between an attitude and a behavior); or (4) change the external environment.

SHOULD HE GO TO THE PARTY?

(1) I THINK I'LL SKIP THIS PARTY

(2) THAT COURSE WASN'T IMPORTANT ANYWAY

(3) IT ISN'T PARTYING THAT'S HURTING MY GRADES

(4) I'LL GO TO THE UNION AND SEE WHAT THE KIDS THINK

"COPING WITH TENSION"

Let's consider these four options in terms of solving the following conflict: You are a devout Catholic and your fiance is an atheist. You both say (a) "I believe strongly in my own point of view toward religion and wouldn't change," and (b) "I believe that a marriage is better when both people are of the same religion." Both of you have very strong favorable feelings toward each attitude.

1. *Changing attitudes* is commonly called changing your mind. The change can be either in the cognitive or affective aspect of the attitude (either could change the behavior tendencies). In the above example of religion and marriage you might change the cognitive meaning by adding the word *probably* in the statement of your attitude: "It probably is a better marriage when both people are of the same religion." Or, you might change the strength of feeling in the affective dimension. If you didn't feel as strongly in one belief, then you wouldn't feel the tension so strongly.

2. A person can reduce the tension by *redefining the salience* of one or more of the attitudes or behaviors. In the above example, a person might move the second attitude to a less important position by thinking, "Religion is not the only factor in a good marriage when considered in light of how much we love each other and how many similar likes, interests, hobbies, friends we have."

3. An example of *changing the relationship between attitudes or behaviors* would be to minimize the tension by seeing things a different

way, by saying "atheism is not a religion," therefore, the "better marriage" attitude isn't related to us.

4. Changing the environment might mean trying to change the other's religion or making friends with people who didn't hold the "same religion" attitude.

Learning Experience

Consider a tension which you strongly felt between two attitudes, an attitude and a behavior, or two behaviors. Describe that tension.

Describe the various options for resolving a tension in terms of how you might have resolved your described tension.

Indicate the method you actually used to resolve your tension and indicate why you made that choice.

In summary, attitudes are changed through thinking about experiences or messages. Attitude change is preceded by a feeling of tension resulting from a conflict or disagreement between two attitudes, two behaviors, or a behavior and an attitude.

Behavior Change

Behaviors are changed in many of the same ways as attitudes are changed. In formation they are changed by positive *reinforcement* of the desired behavior (or a portion of the behavior) and by negative reinforcement of nondesired behavior. Second, behaviors can be changed by *altering the environment*. For example, if Ms. Rodriquez changes her reference groups or people with whom she communicates, different behaviors will be expected and reinforced. A third way is to *heighten the awareness of a conflict or disagreement between two behaviors or a very strong attitude and a behavior.* For example, if Mr. Adams strongly believes, "I never cheat" and you, as a credible source, heightened that belief and then point out that certain of his behaviors on his IRS 1040 Form could be considered cheating, he might change his behavior. The fourth way to change a behavior is to *develop an attitude which has a very high tendency to do the desired behavior.*

Learning Experience

Write down a behavior of your own that you would like to change.

For each of the four ways to change behavior, write one specific example for changing the indicated behavior.

Do the same experience with a behavior you would recommend that another person change.

Chapter 18

Communicating Effective Behavior-Change Messages

Objectives

Your learning should enable you to:

1. For a chosen behavioral change you would suggest to a friend, assess the implications of that change for the person and the implications for you in suggesting the change.
2. For a desired behavior change for two different people, infer the optimal attitude that would likely lead each of them to choose to do the desired behavior.
3. Identify a currently felt tension within yourself which occurs because of an inconsistency between two of your attitudes or between an attitude and a behavior.
4. For a specific behavior change goal, identify barriers within the listener which would limit his or her doing the desired behavior.
5. Assess your credibility for sending a given persuasive message using the four criteria for determining credibility.
6. For a desired behavior change, develop a five-step communication sequence (based on the resolution of the listener's internally felt tension) which will lead to that person choosing to do the desired behavior.

Outline

I. Setting attainable behavioral goals
  A. Attempting to accomplish too much at one time will lead to less change than desired
  B. Attainable behavioral goals are based on an analysis of a listener's frame of reference
  C. A five-step process for setting attainable goals
    1. State the specific behavior you want the other person to do
      a) A specific behavior encourages the likelihood of a real change
      b) A specific behavior provides a basis to check results
      c) The implications of your developing this behavior should be considered
        (1) The implications to you
        (2) The implications to the listener
    2. Infer the optimal attitude
      a) Definition: an attitude with cognitive, affective, and behavior dimensions that is most likely to lead to the actual doing of the desired behavior
      b) The optimal attitude would differ for each listener
      c) Sources for inferring the optimal attitude in ranked order of desirability
        (1) The listener's own statements of the attitude which led to this or a similar behavioral commitment
        (2) The stated attitudes of individuals or groups who have done the desired behavior
        (3) The attitudes people express to explain their consideration of doing the desired behavior
    3. Discover the current state of the optimal attitude for the listener
      a) Is it different in cognitive expression?
      b) Is it different in affective response of direction and strength?
      c) Is it different in behavior tendency?
    4. Identify a relevant tension which would lead to a need for a change to the optimal attitude
      a) The need for change is related to a feeling of tension
        (1) Such tension is created by inconsistencies within people
          (a) A difference between two attitudes
            Example: "I want to earn high grades," and "I don't want to study."
          (b) A difference between two behaviors
            Example: A person making a contribution to the humane society and kicking defenseless dogs
          (c) A difference between an attitude and a behavior
            Example: Having the attitude "energy conservation is crucial" and doing the behavior of wasting gasoline by poor driving habits
        (2) Tension is removed by rebalancing the attitude structure or removing the difference between an attitude and a behavior
      b) Most needs that are effective motivators for change,
        (1) Already exist in people
        (2) Are based on an inconsistency in people's attitude structure or between their attitudes and behavior
    5. Discover specific barriers
      a) If the cognitive and affective parts of the optimal attitude are already somewhat developed within the person, specific barriers may have stopped them from doing the behavior
        (1) Lack of time
        (2) Lack of money

   (3) Lack of self-confidence to do behavior
   (4) Negative reinforcement by friends or reference groups for doing the behavior
   (5) Related interfering attitudes
   (6) Habits which interfere with doing the behavior
   (7) Former negative experience with the behavior
   (8) The publicness of the behavior
   (9) The time lag between messages about the behavior and doing the behavior
  b) Potential barriers related to the sender
   (1) Time available for developing and sending the message
   (2) Potential number of messages possible
    (a) Attitude change occurs gradually
    (b) One message will have limited results
   (3) The credibility of the sender
   (4) The communication skills of the sender
   (5) The resources available to the sender, such as money or assistance
    (a) Especially important in a long-term effort

II. A five-step sequence for achieving attitude and behavior change
 A. Overview of communication sequence
  1. Raise the awareness of the receiver: "I do have a problem"
  2. Develop the tension created by an inconsistency they have which is not now resolved: "I see why I have the problem and want to solve it"
  3. Show how the suggested change in behavior will resolve the tension: "I believe the behavior will solve the problem"
  4. Reinforce the future success of the suggested change: "I see that the behavior will work for me"
  5. Recommend specifically how the behavior can be done: "I will do it"
 B. The choice of doing the behavior is that of the responding communicator(s)
  1. Use supportive communication behaviors
  2. Use assertive communication behaviors
 C. Accomplishment of each step
  1. Awareness Step
   a) Goal: to have the listeners realize their personal problems
   b) Accomplished by visualizing the symptoms of the problem
    (1) Use several examples
    (2) Provide evidence regarding the seriousness of the symptoms
   c) Nonverbal signs of accomplishment
    (1) Facial expressions of interest, concern, surprise, tension
    (2) Body tension
    (3) Leaning forward
  2. Inconsistency Step
   a) Goal: to develop and make vivid the listener's inconsistency within attitude structures or between an attitude and a behavior so a solution is strongly desired
   b) Based on an internal need of removing the inconsistency to reduce the tension
   c) Accomplished by
    (1) Reviewing vividly a very strong attitude or behavior that a person believes in
    (2) Visualizing the attitude or behavior that is inconsistent with (1)
    (3) Verbalize the consequences of that inconsistency for the person
     (a) Fear appeals can be helpful if concrete and solvable
   b) Nonverbal signs of accomplishment include
    (1) Grimacing
    (2) Smiling ironically
    (3) General body tension
    (4) Nodding

   3. Resolution Step
     a) Goal: to show how the suggested change in behavior will resolve the tension by re-moving the inconsistency (The behavior should directly follow from the optimal atti-tude and clearly resolve the tension)
     b) Substeps in bringing resolution
       (1) Introduce the optimal attitude by relating it to the listener's self-concept and other strongly held attitudes
       (2) Identify the desired behavior change as the best way to remove the tension
       (3) Provide support to show that the behavior will solve the problem
       (4) Overcome potential barriers within the listeners as related to you as sender
     c) Two basic approaches to resolution
       (1) Presenting both sides of an issue when the other side will likely be known or heard
       (2) Drawing definite conclusions for the receiver
     d) Nonverbal signs of accomplishment include:
       (1) Confident smile
       (2) Nodding
   4. Reinforcement
     a) Goal: to further motivate the listener to try the behavior by picturing the success of the behavior in removing the inconsistency and, therefore, the tension
     b) Accomplished by projecting the listener into the future and picturing the satisfac-tion he or she will experience after doing the behavior
     c) Nonverbal signs of accomplishment include
       (1) Enthusiastic head nodding
       (2) Smiling
   5. Behavior Step
     a) Goal: to encourage that the behavior be tried
       (1) The sooner it's tried, the more likely the change will actually be made
     b) Accomplished by a short appeal to action that specifies how the behavior can be done.
       (1) "After sell," by reviewing the positive reasons for doing the behavior, is helpful
       (2) "Providing a handle," by relating the behavior to something within the person's everyday life, is helpful (Example: "Everytime you open the refrigerator door, ...")
     c) Nonverbal signs of accomplishment include
       (1) Emphatic agreement
       (2) Actual signs of doing the behavior
     d) Verbal commitment is a positive step
III. Feedforward for persuasive messages
  A. Feedforward should be planned for each of the five steps in the communication sequence
    1. Review feedforward in chapter 11
    2. The time spent on each step is determined by the feedback received during the mes-sage
    3. Continue with each step until the desired feedback is received
IV. Determining an appropriate communication situation
  A. The situation affects the impact of persuasion by influencing the listener's attention, com-prehension, and acceptance of the behavior
  B. Choose a place for sending the message
    1. Talking in a place that is familiar to the receiver will make him or her more comfortable
    2. Informal situations are more effective
  C. Choose a time for sending the message
    1. Consider when the listener's important needs are strongest
    2. Consider the time between the message and when the behavior can be tried is shortest

     D. Acceptance of the behavior change is more likely when the listener actually participated in the change process
        1. Verbally involve the listener
        2. Encourage the listener to commit to do the behavior
V. Determine goal attainment
     A. Intermediate goal: to get the desired reaction to each of the five steps of the communication sequence
     B. Ultimate goal: help the person decide to do the desired behavior
     C. Determined by observing the behaviors of the listener

Reading

Because most attitudes and behaviors are very stable, setting attainable behavioral goals is a crucial consideration in changing attitudes and behavior. Beginning students of attitude change usually tend to make their goals too comprehensive for a given setting. An example would be trying to persuade people with contrary attitudes that abortion should be legalized and that they should work in an abortion clinic. This goal would probably involve reversing the cognitive and affective dimensions and drastically changing the behavior tendencies of a rather salient and interconnected attitude. The attainability of such a behavioral goal is extremely unlikely in such a short time.

The following five-step process will help you in setting attainable goals for specific individuals. In Skill Area Three you developed skills in adapting messages to specific listeners. It will be helpful to review that area as well as the discussion of frame of reference in chapter 3. As you know from your skill development, in any given situation you may have a common behavior that you wish one or more people to do. However, each one of them may have a different strongly felt tension that would most optimally motivate that person to make the change. Therefore, the five-step process which follows assumes a prior analysis of your listener(s) frame of reference for this behavioral change.

Goal-Setting Process

1. State The Behavior You Want The Responding Communicator To Do

It is vital to plan in terms of a specific behavior change both to encourage the likelihood of a real change and also to provide a basis for you to check your results. Thus, if you believe a friend would benefit from buying a smaller car, you would know your persuasion had been successful when she bought one. *It is desirable for the behavior change to be beneficial to the listener.* An important consideration at this point in your goal setting is that of the implications of your developing this behavior. By developing this behavior change, what are the implications for you and your listener(s)?

Learning Experience

Write specific behaviors which you would recommend the following people do, which they do not now do.

A close friend (Specify who)

A close relative (Specify who)

A group to which you belong (Specify group)

2. Infer The Optimal Attitude

The optimal attitude would be an attitude with cognitive, affective, and behavior dimensions most likely to lead to the actual doing of the desired behavior.

For example, if the desired behavior was for a particular person to buy a smaller car, the optimal attitude *for this person* could have the following dimensions:

Cognitive: "A smaller car would save money on gas and repairs."
Affective: Very strongly favorable.
Behavior tendency: Very likely to buy a new car.

The phrase "for that person" is stressed because an attitude that would be motivational for one person might not be an optimal attitude for another.

There are several possible *sources for inferring the optimal attitude.* If the person has previously made the behavioral commitment, then the attitude which led to the behavior previously could be the optimal attitude. Thus, if the person held the above attitude before buying a smaller car previously, the attitude would work again. The better you know the person, the more you will be likely to accurately infer the attitude.

A second possible source for inferring the optimal attitude would be to examine the stated attitudes of individuals or groups who have done the desired behavior. The most accurate inferences would be based on the attitudes of opinion leaders or members of the person's reference group. Less accurate inferences would be likely from people dissimilar to your friend. Examples of using the second source for inferring the optimal attitude are salespeople asking former customers what made them decide to buy or teachers asking students at the end of a course what motivated their learning. You might investigate articles or books in the library that describe individual or group attitudes related to the behavior change you are working for.

Third, if you cannot discover individuals or reference group members who have done the desired behavior, attempt to discover the attitudes people express to explain their consideration of doing the desired behavior.

Learning Experience

In the following two behaviors, specify a person (for each) to whom you might recommend the behavior. Then infer the optimal attitude for that person which would lead to the behavior. Indicate which of the three methods for inferring attitudes you used.

Behavior	Person	Optimal Attitude	Method
A. Repair his or her car			
B. Take a mile hike every day			

3. Discover The Current State Of Optimal Attitude

As developed in chapter 17, it is important to consider the specific components of the inferred optimal attitude. It may be that the listener does not hold the attitude in the cognitive dimension; has developed the cognitive dimension of the attitude but not a strongly developed affective dimension; or that the first two components are established but specific barriers restrain that person from actually doing the behavior. Therefore, an important step is considering the current development of the optimal attitude (see figure 34).

A persuader will have already made an *assessment of the current status of the receiver's attitudes* related to the optimal attitude. Before beginning plans for a persuasive attempt, it is helpful to specifically state the three dimensions of the attitude you are attempting to change and specify how they differ from the optimal attitude:

What is the *current status* of the *specific optimal attitude* you want your receiver to hold after your message (that is, how does this person think and feel about the attitude *before* the message)?

(1) Cognitive dimension (before the message). The responding communicator says " _____ ."

(2) Affective dimension: (before the message). The responding communicator feels _____ .

(3) Behavior tendency dimension: (before the message) the responding communicator is _____ likely (unlikely) to do the desired behavior.

How is the *attitude* the receiver holds *before the message different* from that which would lead him to the desired behavior?

  a. Is it different in cognitive expression?
  b. Is it different in affective response (direction and strength)?
  c. Is it different in behavior tendency?
  d. Is it so different that it would be more efficient to develop a more attainable goal?

The goal of the message(s) will be to reduce the differences between the current state of the optimal attitude and optimal attitude to zero difference.

Consider a friend who smokes. Write the optimal attitude for this person which would likely lead that person to quit smoking.	**Learning Experience**
Based on this person's frame of reference, write the current state of that optimal attitude.	
Compare and determine which dimensions would be most difficult to change.	

4. Identify A Relevant Tension

It is essential to determine, through analysis of that person's frame of reference, an existing tension related to the desired behavior. As developed in chapter 17, *attitude change is preceded by the existence of a need* for change within the receiver. Without a personal need for change an individual (or group) will most likely continue holding current attitudes and doing current behaviors. Simply giving facts and/or opinions (yours and other people's) is only slightly persuasive—often not at all persuasive. Unless the facts and/or opinions are related to a felt need which will lead to a change in the receiver's attitudinal structure, the opinions and facts will soon be forgotten—many of them before the end of the message.

This *need for change is related to a tension* created by the difference between two attitudes, two behaviors, or an attitude and a behavior currently

FIGURE 34

done by the receiver, that are relevant to the desired behavior. Needs are effective motivators in persuasion because people want to reduce the tension associated with needs. When their normally balanced attitude structure is upset, a tension is created until the structure and behaviors are rebalanced.

Most people deal with certain amounts of tension due to differences among their attitudes and/or their attitudes and behaviors. They reduce the tension by one or more of the methods discussed in chapter 17. It often takes a meaningful personal experience or a persuasive message to direct the tension reduction to a desired behavioral outcome.

Consider the example of studying for courses in school. Let's say Paul had the attitude "Consistent study is necessary for me to accomplish my goals for this course," or "It is important to study before tests." Paul had a mildly favorable affective dimension toward consistent study and was, therefore, somewhat likely to do consistent study. This attitude was very salient and connected to attitudes Paul held about himself, his parents, and his future uses of the course-developed skills (e.g., he was going to be a salesperson). As with many students, however, other things took the place of consistent study. Therefore, Paul felt a tension because of the difference between a salient, interconnected, and fairly strong attitude and his behavior. Paul had been able to handle the tension by minimizing the importance of the attitude because of the absence of any tests or assignments which would reveal his lack of consistent study. A test, experience, or message from his instructor could increase the tension to a level where the need for change would be strong enough to lead to a change in attitude and/or behavior. Given the attitude structure described for Paul, he would be very likely to reduce the tension by more study. When the immediate need had passed, he would be most likely to return to former behavior. This example might be visualized as in figure 35.

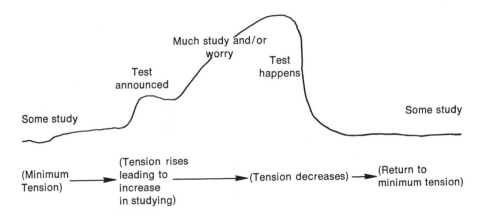

FIGURE 35

Most of the needs that a persuader can effectively use in persuasion both (1) already exist in people and (2) are based on an inconsistency in people's attitudinal structure or between their attitudes and their behavior. Therefore, once you have discovered the specific tension which this person is experiencing, you are ready to relate the optimal attitude and the resolution of that tension by doing the desired behavior. See figure 36.

Desired Behavior	Existing Tension	Need	Optimal Attitude
To lose ten pounds	"I'm too heavy for my current clothes." "New clothes are too expensive."	clothes that fit	"Losing ten pounds will definitely lead to my clothes fitting again." A: very favorable BT: very likely to lose 10 pounds

FIGURE 36

By such a process you are able to discover an attitude which will be personally meaningful to that person. For other people an optimal attitude might be "becoming more attractive" or "being healthy," in terms of their current needs and tensions.

5. Discover Specific Barriers

A consideration of barriers should first include limitations of developing the attitude or doing the behavior. You might review those potential limitations, which follow. If you have discovered that the optimal attitude is already held in the cognitive dimension and has a strongly developed affective component, then it is likely that the person perceives that there are barriers which limit him or her doing the behavior. Because of the strongly reciprocal effect of behaviors on the strengthening and development of attitudes (as well as the reverse), the turning point in helping a person change might be to remove perceived barriers. Thus, by doing the behavior the person can experience the reinforcement and relief of tension that will further strengthen the attitude and lead to continued doing of the behavior. Potential listener-related barriers include:

1. lack of time
2. lack of money
3. lack of self-confidence to do the behavior
4. negative reinforcement by friends or reference groups for doing the behavior
5. related interfering attitudes
6. habits which interfere with doing the behavior
7. former negative experience with the behavior
8. the publicness of the behavior
9. the time lag between messages about the behavior and actually doing it.

To visualize these potential barriers, let's imagine that you are a runner and have talked unsuccessfully to a friend, Sally, about her starting to run.

The following statements, which she might make, could indicate the existence of such barriers:

1. Time: "My schedule is too busy to include running."
2. Money: "I couldn't afford a warm-up suit like you have."
3. Self-confidence: "I'll probably just quit after a few days like everything else I try."
4. Negative reinforcement: "My parents said they heard it could be dangerous."
5. Interfering attitudes: "I think it's unladylike."
6. Habits: "But I don't like to get up early when it's coolest for running."

"How will my friends react?"

7. Former negative experience: "I tried it once, and I pulled a muscle."
8. Publicness: "Are you kidding, let people see me running!"
9. Time lag: "I couldn't start for awhile because I have a sore foot."

What other potential barriers related to the listener would you add to our list? You might consider reasons you or others have used to explain why you didn't do something you had planned or agreed to do.

There are also potential barriers or limitations associated with you as the sender of a message to gaining attitude or behavior change. Several of these potential barriers include:

1. The time available to you to develop and send your message. The time available becomes more important as the difficulty of the change increases. For example, if you have been called on short notice and given five minutes of a student senate meeting to try to change the senators' minds on a decision which took them several weeks to make, your chances of success will be limited.
2. The number of messages you will be able to send. Attitude change, especially on important issues, usually happens gradually because of the salience and interconnectedness of attitudes discussed in chapter 17. Therefore, sending only one message designed to bring change (called "one-shot persuasion") usually has only limited results in terms of actual change and retention of change. As people

return to the other influences in their lives, any change begins to decrease.

3. Your credibility as a communicator will influence your ability to change another person's attitudes and behavior. As you remember from chapter 9, credibility includes how the listener sees your friendliness, expertness, trustworthiness, and similarity. If any one of these is not perceived positively in terms of the particular issue you're dealing with, your chances for success will be limited. It is especially important to remember that your credibility will change depending on the issue you're dealing with.

4. Your communication skills will directly influence your success in changing attitudes and behaviors. The skills you have developed in the first three skill areas will be extremely valuable. Your skills in reading feedback and adapting to specific listeners will be especially important.

5. The resources available to you in the form of money or assistance may be important, especially if the change will occur over a period of time.

Your careful consideration of barriers both related to the listener and related to yourself may lead to your revising your original behavioral goal to one that is more attainable. This consideration will also let you know what barriers need to be overcome in your message in order for the person to do the behavior.

Fill in the following statement in terms of your own experiences.
"I would like to have the person I live with,_____,
have the following attitude:"
Cognitive:
Affective:
Behavior Tendency:

Assess the attainability of that attitude by considering each of the following elements:
Time available
Number of messages
Your credibility
Your communication skills
Resources available

Write the desired behavior for the person you live with.

Assess the circumstances which influence the attainability of the behavior.

Time lag between message and behavior:

Publicness of behavior:

Learning Experience

Differences between this and previous behaviors:

Strength of current habits and behaviors:

Rewards or punishments likely to be received:

Developing Persuasive Messages

After an attainable goal for the specific listener(s) has been set and the optimal attitude for that person determined, you are ready to plan a message (or series of messages) which will lead to behavioral change. Each message should have a specific attainable behavioral goal. The following communication sequence is a basic format which can be adapted to all persuasive attempts. If your persuasive goal and related circumstances indicate the need for a series of messages over a period of time, develop an overall communication sequence to represent the overall plan for change within the receiver(s). Then develop sufficient individual messages to accomplish your overall specific goal.

The goal of this five-step communication sequence is to move the listener to choose to, and actually do, the desired behavior. The five steps of the communication sequence are (1) Awareness, (2) Inconsistency, (3) Resolution, (4) Reinforcement, and (5) Behavior. The steps raise the awareness of the receiver, develop the tension created by an inconsistency they have which is not now resolved, show how the suggested change in behavior will resolve the person's tension, reinforce the future success of the suggested change, and recommend specifically how the behavior can be done. In the listener's words this process of change could be stated in this way: (1) "I do have a problem"; (2) "I see why I have a problem and want to solve it"; (3) "I believe the behavior will solve the problem"; (4) "I see that the behavior will work for me"; and (5) "I will do it." The goals of the five steps are sequential—one should be fully accomplished before going on to the next.

As discussed in the Overview to this skill area, we do not view attitude and behavior change attempts as manipulation of another person. By using Gibb's communication climate of problem orientation and assertive communication behaviors, you open up an option for behavioral change to the person. The process highlights the change in terms of the needs and goals of the person. The decision as to whether the change will actually be made is his/hers.

Awareness Step

The first step in helping someone decide on a behavior change is having him or her realize that there is a problem. Organizations, such as Alcoholics Anonymous, say this is often the most difficult step. The receiver must have a vivid personal awareness of the tension created by this problem. This step is most often accomplished by visualizing the symptoms of the problem that the person is experiencing. Often, several examples are necessary. Offering evidence regarding the seriousness of the symptoms may be helpful in having the person realize the significance of the tension s/he feels. It is important that this step is vivid and concrete. For example, advertisements often accomplish this step of persuasion by picturing a person with no friends or a housekeeper with a floor to be cleaned—thus implying a tension which is currently unresolved. If the person is quite aware of the tension, then the Awareness step may be quite short.

Do not mention the desired behavior you are encouraging in the Awareness step so that the focus is on raising the tension.

The specific goal of the Awareness step is for the listener to say intrapersonally or to you, "I really do have a problem!" Nonverbal signs which might indicate that you have achieved this goal are facial expressions of interest, concern, surprise, tension; leaning forward; or general body tension.

For the behavioral goal of having a person eat more healthful foods the awareness step might go like this:

> "Joe, I know you've talked about being tired most of the time. Just walking across campus does you in. I can tell it's affected your success on the basketball court, and your grades have taken a real dive. I'm concerned because you don't seem to feel any better and I've been reading some articles that suggest that continued tiredness is usually a symptom of a serious problem."

Inconsistency Step

The second step helps the person understand the reason for the tension and leads the person to really want to reduce the tension. You may have been in situations where you realized you were tense but weren't ready to take action to reduce the tension. The goal of the Inconsistency step is to develop and make vivid the listener's inconsistency within his or her attitude structure or between an attitude and a behavior. Thus, the person decides that the problem should be solved.

THE CARROT AND THE STICK

An old story is told about a farmer with a mule who couldn't be moved. The farmer pulled, pushed, threatened, and finally hit the mule with a stick, all without success. Another person bought the mule. The new owner tied a carrot to a stick, climbed on the mule's back, and held the carrot in front of the mule. The mule walked toward the hanging carrot. The carrot symbolized internal motivation and the stick, external motivation.

"IS THE MOTIVATION EXTERNAL OR INTERNAL?"

To apply this to attitude and behavior change, we are suggesting that instead of telling a person that s/he "needs to" do something (the stick approach), you call up a need s/he already has (the carrot approach) in terms of removing a personal inconsistency which is leading to a feeling of tension. It is the clear realization of a personal inconsistency that explains "why" a person would want to change his or her behavior.

It is not enough for the person to recognize the personal inconsistency. The consequences of that inconsistency must be felt vividly enough to want to make a change.

The following three steps may be helpful in developing the tension related to the inconsistency.

1. Vividly review the very strong attitude or behavior that the person is strongly committed to.
2. Visualize the person's attitude or behavior that is inconsistent with the very strong attitude, value, or consequence.
3. Verbalize the consequences of that inconsistency for the person.

Each of the steps could be developed through the seven means for increasing understanding described in chapter 10. For example, the Inconsistency step might be developed by a detailed visualization of a situation (for example, tension felt when you don't know what to say during a pause on a blind date).

Fear appeals are often used to develop or increase awareness of an inconsistency; however, they must be used with care. Research findings generally show a positive relationship between the intensity of fear arousal and amount of attitude change, *if* recommendations for action are explicit and possible for the receiver.

The specific goal of the Inconsistency step is to have the listener say intrapersonally or to you, "I understand the reason for my problem and want to solve it!" Physical signs which might indicate a felt need are grimacing, smiling ironically, revealing general body tension, and so forth, as you describe the need situation. Do not suggest the specific behavior you want the person to do at this time, so that the focus can be on the development of tension to the point that change is likely.

Continuing on with our example of moving someone to do the behavior of eating more healthful foods, the Inconsistency step might be handled in this way:

"Joe, I've heard you often express your strong feelings about maintaining good health. You spoke of your two uncles, John and Bill, both the same age; John enjoying middle age as an active, healthy person and Bill tired, overweight, and constantly sick. You even said once you'd rather die early than be like Bill. You quoted detailed reports of the growing number of unhealthy Americans. It seems you really feel strongly about good health, Joe. And yet, I see you every day eating food that is difficult for your body to use. You skip at least two meals a day and fill up on candy and soft drinks you have in your room. That seems like a strong contradiction for an athlete and someone committed to good health. We were talking about some of the consequences you're experiencing now, that are directly related to the unhealthy food you eat. And your uncle Bill is a good example of what is further down the road for you."

Consider a person you know who is overweight. Write the name of that person. What is one strongly felt personal inconsistency of this person which would likely motivate him or her? Describe the inconsistency in terms of agreement or disagreement of attitudes (or an attitude and a behavior).

Write at least five sentences describing how you would develop or heighten the tension produced by the nonresolution of that need within the person in order to develop readiness to change, using the three-step approach.

Learning Experience

Resolution Step

After the listener becomes aware of the personal inconsistency that has negative consequences for him or her, the person will want to reduce the resulting tension. As reviewed in chapter 17, there are many ways that a person could reduce this tension. Among the possibilities for Joe are to decide that: (1) good health is not so important; (2) moderately good health is good enough for him; or (3) he should change his behavior to eating more healthy foods. The goal of the Resolution step is to clearly show the person how your suggested behavior will best resolve the inconsistency. During this step you develop the attitude which will most likely lead him to the suggested behavior. This attitude is developed by showing its agreement with other positive attitudes and/or reference groups already held by the receiver; or by showing its disagreement with negative attitudes and/or reference groups held by the receiver (see the illustration on page 324).

Diagrammatic Visualization of the Establishment of a New Attitude in Persuasive Communication
(Hypothetical example of how to persuade a mother to subscribe to Playboy)

"Before" Attitude	"After" Attitude	"How to"	Behavior
1. Cognitive: "I don't have time to read it" (inferred from actual statement)	1. Cognitive: "I'll buy it for the good articles it contains."	1. Review attitude in value of reading "good" articles.	1. buy a subscription to *Playboy*
2. Affective: moderately favorable (inferred from some of her friends reading and enjoying it)	2. Affective: quite favorable	2. Develop internal motivation for reading more good articles to more closely agree with the above-stated attitude.	
3. Behavior tendency: not very likely to subscribe	3. Behavior tendency: very likely to subscribe.	3. Associate *Playboy* with the attitude toward reading good article (in terms of her meaning of good).	
		4. Use after-sell that the only place to get them is *Playboy*.	

Visualized "Before" Attitude	Visualized "After" Attitude	Visualized "How to"	Visualized Behavior
α^+	A^{++} (Attracted to by Agreement of Attitudes)	$\alpha^+ \diagdown A^{++}$ (Attracted to by agreement with already-held attitude	 for *Playboy*

Your suggested behavior should directly follow from the optimal attitude and clearly resolve the tension created by the identified inconsistency. The substeps in developing the optimal attitude and encouraging the listener to believe that doing the behavior will solve the problem are: (1) Introduce the optimal attitude by relating it to the listener's self-concept and other strongly held attitudes; (2) Identify the desired behavior change as the best way to remove the inconsistency and the resulting tension; (3) Provide support to show that the behavior will actually solve the problem; and (4) Overcome any potential barriers within the listener and related to you as the sender.

The following are research results and suggestions concerning two basic approaches most often used in developing overall resolution in a receiver.

Presenting both sides of an appeal. There is often a question in the mind of a persuader as to whether he or she should present the drawbacks or limitations of the behavior or product during the message. In terms of research findings, the following suggestions have been made:

1. Present one side when the receiver is generally friendly, or when your position is the only one that will be presented, or when you want immediate, though temporary, attitude change.
2. Present both sides when the receiver starts out disagreeing with you, or when it is probable that the receiver will hear the other side from someone else.
3. When opposite views are presented one after another, the one presented last will probably be more effective. Tell your side last.

Also, better educated individuals are affected more favorably by the presentation of both sides, while less educated individuals are more affected by the communication which uses only favorable arguments (an interesting point to consider when hearing politicians speak).

Generally, the receiver for whom presenting both sides of a message is *least* effective is the poorly educated individual who is already convinced of the point of view you advocate.

Drawing definite conclusions for the receiver. A problem often faced in developing a persuasive message is whether to make explicit recommendations for the satisfaction of the inconsistency developed or to allow the receiver to draw her own conclusions.

Generally, research suggests that there will be more opinion change in the direction you want if you explicitly state your recommendations (behavior to be done) to the receiver, rather than let the person draw personal conclusions. An exception to this suggestion may be made in terms of a highly intelligent receiver—where implicit recommendations are often better.

The specific goal of the Resolution step is to have the receiver say intrapersonally, "I can see what causes my tension and I'm satisfied that by doing what the communicator suggests, I'll remove the inconsistency!" Physical signs suggesting accomplishment of this goal would be confident smiles, nodding, and so forth.

Continuing with the eating-better-foods example, let's say that the sender inferred that the optimal attitude which would lead Joe to do the behavior was, "Eating better foods will increase my chances of becoming the captain of the basketball team"; that the main barrier within Joe was the influence of his friends who weren't on the team; and the significant barrier related to the sender was low credibility in terms of expertness. If these were the result of the listener analysis, the following might be a brief idea of what the Resolution step might look like:

> "I know how much you're hoping to be captain of the team and, with the playing you did at the beginning of practice, the team really thinks you will be. I've been doing a lot of reading on what gives athletes energy because of my problem last year with wrestling. Research shows that eating a balanced diet significantly improves a person's energy. Bill Walton is a good example. By eating a balanced diet you could maintain good health, which is important to you, and relieve the tension you've been feeling lately by your lowered performance. Look at the evidence I've found on the results of eating a balanced diet. . . . That doesn't mean that you can't go out with the guys and enjoy snacks occasionally. . . ."

Learning Experience

Consider the same friend (identified earlier) who is overweight. You have now identified a strongly felt internal tension which will motivate this person to reduce the tension by changing an attitude and/or behavior. You are recommending that the person begin a program of jogging to get back in shape. List four barriers (physical or psychological) which would limit the likelihood of the person doing the behavior. Then indicate how you would assist the person in removing each barrier. Be specific.

Reinforcement Step

The goal of the Reinforcement step is to further motivate the listener to try the suggested behavior by picturing the success of the behavior in removing the inconsistency and therefore removing the tension situation. This step projects the listener into the future and pictures the satisfaction he will experience after doing the desired behavior. Advertisements often accomplish this step by picturing a person with many dates after doing the suggested behavior or a housekeeper with a beautiful floor after doing the suggested behavior.

The specific goal of the Reinforcement step is to have the listener indicate to you or intrapersonally, "I can see it will work—how satisfied I'll be after doing the suggested behavior!" Physical signs which indicate accomplishment of this step might be enthusiastic nonverbal agreement, smiling, and so forth.

For our basketball player, Joe, the Reinforcement step might be:

> "Joe, can you imagine how great it will be to really feel full of energy again. I really think you have the best chance of anyone on the team for captain if you regain your old hustle."

Behavior

The Behavior step is vital to persuasion. The goal of this step is to encourage the behavior to be tried. Research suggests that the sooner the receiver begins to put the suggested behavior into action, the more likely it will be that the change in attitude developed will become a stable part of his attitude structure.

This step is usually a short, concise appeal to do the specific behavior. You should encourage the receiver to do the behavior *as soon as possible* or at least to *openly* express a strong commitment to the behavior. For example, "So tomorrow when you find yourself thinking about how you would choose among many outfits, read the label first. This will insure that you stretch your clothing dollar." It is helpful to provide a "handle" (related event, place, thing within the receiver's daily life) by which the receiver can repeatedly connect the optimal attitude with the new behavior. For example, if Ann were trying to reduce speed while driving, suggest that each time she sees a speed limit sign she should check her speedometer and make sure she is right at the limit.

If the previous steps have been successful, the receiver will be motivated to try the behavior. "After-sell" techniques (a follow-up review on the positive reasons for taking the action) usually maximize the probability that the person will follow through with your suggestion. Implementing the behavior would be discussed here—for example, how, when, and where to do the behavior.

The specific goal of the behavior step is to have the listener commit—"I will do the suggested behavior at the earliest possible time!" Physical signs which might indicate accomplishment of this step are nonverbal signs of emphatic agreement or actual signs of doing the behavior.

For Joe, the behavior step might be:

"Joe, the season starts only three weeks from now. Why not start this week to eat three balanced meals a day. I'll work on it with you. Just try it for three weeks and see what a difference it makes in your hustle!"

Feedforward for Persuasive Messages

Feedforward, as developed in Skill Area Three, should be planned for each step and contingency messages used until that step is fully accomplished before moving on to the next step. The amount of time spent developing each step during the communication will be determined by your receiver analysis and the feedback received when sending the message. For example, if the receiver is fully aware of a personal inconsistency and already feels tension, then less time will be necessary to develop it than if he or she were only partially aware of the inconsistency.

The phrase—*accomplish each step*—should not be misinterpreted to imply manipulation of the responding communicator. This person is an active participant in the development of personal motivation to change and will ultimately make a choice regarding the suggested behavior. The choices regarding the meaningfulness of the inconsistency and the connection between the suggested behavior and resolving the inconsistency are an internal process done through personal thinking. If the inconsistency and tension are personally meaningful, the connection between the behavior and resolving the inconsistency is perceived as strong, and the related barriers are overcome, there is a strong likelihood that the behavior will be done. Your use of a supportive communicative climate (see chapter 3) and development of your personal credibility (see chapter 11) will enhance an open atmosphere conducive to consideration of change.

Determining an Appropriate Situation

In developing a persuasive plan, it is essential to choose an appropriate situation for sending the persuasive message(s). You might review chapter 4 on the relationship of situation to communication. Communication situation refers to the total circumstances surrounding the communication event. The situation for communication affects the impact of a message by contributing to or detracting from the *attention* receivers give it, their *comprehension* of it, and their *acceptance* of recommendations contained in it.[1]

Consider specifically the overall communication climate within which you send your message. Persuasive attempts are often perceived negatively by receivers unless handled in an open supportive communication climate. Review Gibb's suggestions for establishing a supportive climate and nonverbals which indicate such a climate in chapter 3. In general, informal situations are more effective.

Factors of time and place may enhance the effectiveness of a communication.[2] For example, a message of using a new method of studying may be more readily accepted just before final exams. It is also usually the case that a receiver will feel more comfortable and therefore more receptive to a persuasive message if that message is received "on home ground"; that is, in a place that is familiar to the receiver. Consider the difference between a boss stopping to talk to an employee in the employee's office versus calling the employee in to the boss's office. Review the concepts of physical space and the influence of environment on communication from chapter 2.

Opportunities for verbal interaction between the sender and receiver also tend to increase the satisfaction both draw from the experience of communicating and potentially increase the effectiveness of communication by permitting immediate adaptation by the sender. Research also suggests that attitude change is more persistent over time if the receiver actively participated in, rather than passively received, the communication.[3]

1. Howard Martin and Kenneth Anderson, *Speech Communication: Analysis and Readings* (Boston: Allyn and Bacon, Inc., 1968), p. 120.
2. Ibid., p. 121.
3. Philip Zimbardo and Ebbe Ebbesen, *Influencing Attitudes and Changing Behavior* (Reading, Mass.: Addison-Wesley, 1969), p. 23.

In a one-to-one persuasive setting, this concept is usually applied by asking the receiver for direct replies to questions. The persuader then builds directly on those feedback statements so that the satisfaction for the tension developed is a "cooperative" effort.

In a one-to-many persuasion situation, the communicator can simulate the direct interchange atmosphere by effective use of "rhetorical questions," sensitive adaptation to the specific receivers, and use of pauses. Actual participation can often be elicited by asking for hand raising, looking directly at someone, or acknowledging some obvious response. For example, you might ask the receivers how many have ever been involved in an accident—wait for hand raising or not—and react to that response, such as "Then you would most likely agree with me that. . . ."

Additional support for such listener involvement (actual or psychological) is that acceptance and behavior change are more likely when a person is asked to verbalize an idea to others—to commit himself publicly.

Determining Goal Attainment

As in all communicative interactions, the attitude behavior change can be assessed in terms of the degree to which your communication goals were accomplished. In attitude change you have both intermediate goals and an ultimate goal. Your intermediate goals are to get the desired reaction to each of the five steps in the persuasive sequence. Your feedforward preparation enables you to cope with the listener's reactions. Your ultimate goal is to help the listener do the desired behavior. The success of your behavioral goal can be determined by observing the behaviors of the receiver following the persuasive message.

Additional Learning Sources

Bettinghaus, Erwin P. *Persuasive Communication,* 2d ed. New York: Holt, Rinehart and Winston, 1973.

Clevenger, Theodore, Jr. *Audience Analysis.* Indianapolis: Bobbs-Merrill Co., Inc., 1966.

————. *The Speech-Communication Process.* Glenview, Ill.: Scott, Foresman and Co., 1971.

Ehninger, Douglas. *Influence, Belief, and Argument.* Glenview, Ill.: Scott, Foresman and Co., 1974.

Holtzman, Paul. *The Psychology of Speaker's Audiences.* Glenview, Ill.: Scott, Foresman and Co., 1970.

Karlins, Marvin, and Abelson, Herbert I. *Persuasion,* 2d ed. New York: Springer Publishing Co., 1970.

Larson, Charles. *Persuasion: Reception and Responsibility.* Belmont, Calif.: Wadsworth Publishing Co., 1973.

Lerbinger, Otto. *Designs for Persuasive Communication.* Englewood Cliffs, N.J.: Prentice-Hall, Inc., 1972.

Monroe, Alan H., and Ehninger, Douglas. *Principles and Types of Speech,* 7th ed. Glenview, Ill.: Scott, Foresman and Co., 1974.

Simons, Herbert. *Persuasion: Understanding, Practice, and Analysis.* Reading, Mass.: Addison-Wesley, 1976.

Zimbardo, Philip, and Ebbesen, Ebbe E. *Influencing Attitudes and Changing Behavior.* Reading, Mass.: Addison-Wesley, 1969.

Skill Test

This skill test is designed to provide an opportunity for you to accomplish a change of behavior in a personally meaningful situation. With your instructor you might determine a format in which you will apply this skill test. You may also want to develop additional skill tests to apply your skills in encouraging a behavior change.

Forms for your message preparation and postcommunication analysis follow. Share your preparation with your instructor before you actually send your message(s).

Precommunication Form

On separate sheets of paper, complete your preparation for your message by completing the following substeps involved in Goal Setting, Message Preparation, Feedforward Planning, and Determination of an Appropriate Situation. When you have completed your preparation, share it with your instructor before sending your message.

Goal Setting for Your Specific Listener(s)

1. Describe your self-chosen persuasive situation, including a description of your specific listener.
2. State the specific behavior you want your listener to do. The doing of this behavior by your listener will constitute successful accomplishment of this Skill Test.
3. State the optimal attitude for this person that will most likely result in his or her choosing to do the desired behavior. State the cognitive, affective, and behavioral tendency of the optimal attitude.
4. State the current state of the optimal attitude within the listener, indicating its cognitive, affective, and behavior tendency.
5. State a tension which your listener is experiencing that would be resolved by doing the desired behavior. Describe the internal inconsistency which led to the tension.
6. List the barriers within the listener that will limit the person from doing the desired behavior.
7. Estimate your credibility with this listener for this goal regarding your trustworthiness, similarity, expertness, and friendliness.
8. List any other barriers related to you as the sender of the behavior change message.
9. Describe the implications of this behavior change for your listener and for you in making the suggestion.

Message Preparation

10. Develop a Communication Sequence to attain your behavioral goal by using the five steps of Awareness, Inconsistency, Resolution, Reinforcement, and Behavior. A phrase outline is usually a helpful format to use. Put in your outline what you will say in your message. Do not be concerned with the actual wording but use the type and level of symbols that will best communicate with your listener. Use your skills in applying the seven principles for effective understanding as you develop your message.

    In the left margin of your outline, indicate where you are accomplishing each of the following:

Development of tension
Showing why the tension exists because of inconsistency
Development of optimal attitude
Connection of optimal attitude and desired behavior
Evidence and/or reasoning to support recommendations
Overcoming of barriers
Improving credibility

Feedforward Planning

11. For each main part of your message (the Awareness, Inconsistency, Resolution, Reinforcement, and Behavior steps), plan for at least three potential reactions of your chosen listener(s). Again, as in the skill test for Skill Area Three, you might put a sheet with the following headings alongside your developed outline and then develop your feedforward parallel to your development of each step. Use the following format and plan for at least three expectancies for each step:

Expectancies	Likely feedback indicating expectancies	My contingency messages
1	1	1
2	2	2
3	3	3

Communication Situation

12. Describe the situation in which you will communicate your message, indicating the basis for your choice. If you do not have control over the situation, state any adaptations of the situation you could make to maximize goal attainment.
13. Indicate the channel(s) you will use to send your message.

Postcommunication Form

On separate sheets of paper, complete this form and share it with your instructor.

1. Assess the sequential accomplishment of each step of the Communication Sequence. List the actual feedback you received at each step and compare and assess that with the desired feedback from your feedforward planning.
2. Provide evidence for the change in behavior and assess your overall success in accomplishing your behavioral goal.
3. Make two suggestions for improvements in your message or handling of feedback based on your listener's responses.

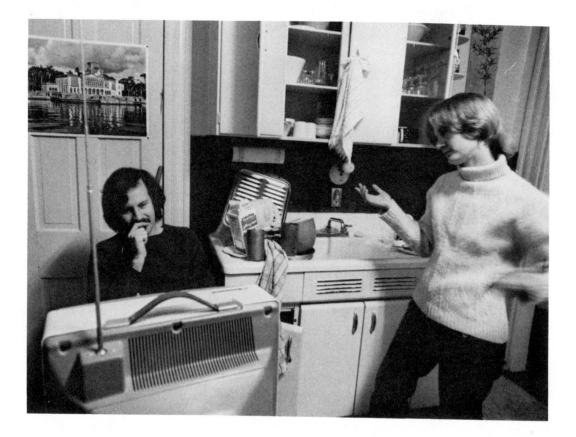

Skills in Adapting Communication to Personal Goals (Appendix)

This project is designed to enable you to specify and further develop communication skills relevant to your personal or professional lives. The skills you work on may be different than ones you've already developed in this course or may be applications of skills.

Following are brief descriptions of specific goals and projects which previous students have chosen. You are encouraged to choose a project goal which will be meaningful to your personal and professional uses of communication skills. The following are only intended as examples.

GOAL	PROJECT
Assess personal communication skills	Keep a log of your verbal and nonverbal communication in two personal, academic, and social situations. Determine a way to keep notes and develop criteria and a method for analyzing the effectiveness of communication in terms of accomplishing personal goals. Analyze the data and write a paper describing the data and your assessments.
Determine how to solve job-related problems	Prepare open-ended questions to interview three high school basketball coaches. Determine what problems they have with team members, the school administration, and parents; what communication procedures they use to solve the problems; and how they choose which communication procedures to use. In a paper describe the problems, the solutions, and how you will develop the communication skills needed to solve the problems.
Improve marriage-related meaningful communication	Determine areas of interpersonal relations in marriage where changes will improve the meaningfulness of interaction. Read *Peoplemaking,* by Virginia Satir, and select five activities which would improve meaningful interaction for the selected areas. Plan how to use the activities and measure their effects. Share each activity with a good friend. Describe in a paper the improvements experienced in meaningful communication.

The following steps should be completed and shared with your instructor before going ahead with your project:

1. State a specific personal and/or professional communication goal.
2. Identify specific communication skills which will be needed to accomplish your goal.
3. Assess your currently developed levels of these skills.
4. Describe a specific project which will lead to the attainment of your goal.

5. List specific steps you will take to complete your project. Include:
   a. The communication skills you will need to accomplish the steps of your project, and
   b. The background research prior to doing your project.
6. Specify how you will communicate the accomplishment of your project to your instructor.

It may be helpful to check with your instructor after completing the first four steps. After contracting for a specific self-chosen project, complete the project as planned and communicate the results to your instructor.

Index